CW01163524

Nauticus In Scotland: A Tricycle Tour Of 2,462 Miles, Including Skye And The West Coast

Nauticus

In the interest of creating a more extensive selection of rare historical book reprints, we have chosen to reproduce this title even though it may possibly have occasional imperfections such as missing and blurred pages, missing text, poor pictures, markings, dark backgrounds and other reproduction issues beyond our control. Because this work is culturally important, we have made it available as a part of our commitment to protecting, preserving and promoting the world's literature. Thank you for your understanding.

NAUTICUS IN SCOTLAND.

A

TRICYCLE TOUR OF 2,462 MILES.

INCLUDING SKYE & THE WEST COAST.

LONDON:
SIMPKIN, MARSHALL & CO., 4, STATIONERS' HALL COURT, E.C.

COVENTRY:
ILIFFE AND SON, 12, SMITHFORD STREET AND VICAR LANE.

PREFACE.

I WRITE in the hope that the record of my experiences will induce wheelmen and others to explore the less frequented parts of Scotland.

I am indebted to "Scottish Gazetteer" for the historical notes; the others are duly acknowledged. These have been inserted with the idea of making the story a sufficient guide to the ordinary tourist. Minor details about the various places may be obtained from the local guide books, which are to be found at most of the hotels.

I have to thank the Editor of "Boys' Own Paper" for permission to publish my story before the usual time.

1882.   NAUTICUS.

INDEX.

PLACES VISITED.

	PAGE		PAGE
Abbey Crag	39	Belford	4
Abbotsford	8	Ben Arthur	25
Aberdeen	175	Ben Ledi	43
Aberfeldy	46	Ben Cruachan	28
Aboyne	176	Ben Blaven (Skye)	79
Achrisgill River	128	Ben Coulbeg	119
Alexandria	23	Ben. Lawyers	45
Allan, Bridge of	39	Ben Lomond (ascent of)	24
Alloway Kirk	15	Ben Eay	98
Alnwick	3	Ben Muich-dhui	178
Almond Glen	81	Ben Glamich	79
Altnaharra	137	Ben More Assynt	122
Allness	158	Ben Hope	138
Amulree	63	Ben Spionnadh	129
Arbroath	54	Ben Nevis	24
Ardoch, Roman Camp	38	Ben Wyvis	116
Ardrech Castle	123	Betty Hill	149
Arrochar	25	Berwick	4
Assynt Loch	120	Berridale	154
Auchnasheen	98	Birkhill	10
Auchterarder	182	Blair Atholl	64
Aultgraat burn	158	Blairgowrie	180
Awe Lochs	28	Blasted Heath (Shakespeare)	169
Ayr	14	Blantyre Priory	20
		Bothwell Bridge	20
Badcaul	125	Bothwell Castle	20
Ballater	176	Bonar Bridge	157
Balmacarra	91	Braemar	178
Balmoral	177	Braemore	116
Balquhidder	43	Bracadale	86
Banchory	176	Brechin	50
Banff	130	Bridge of Allan	59
Bannockburn	40	Bridge of Earn	60
Beauly	160	Bridge of Tilt	65

INDEX.

	PAGE		PAGE
Bridge of Turk	43	Doune	41
Broadford (Skye)	75	Drumclog (Battle)	16
Brora	156	Drumlanrig	12
Broom Loch	104	Drummond Castle	35
Bruan Falls	65	Drumnadrochet	165
Buller of Buchan	174	Dryburgh Abbey	7
Burns' Cottage	14	Duirness	126
Burns' Mausoleum	15	Dunbeath	154
		Dumbarton	22
Cairndow	32	Dumfries	11
Carlisle	195	Dunbar	185
Caledonian Canal	160	Dunblane	38
Callander	34	Duncansby Head	152
Cambuskenneth	40	Dundee	54
Cape Wrath	131	Dundonald Hills	116
Cartland Crags	18	Dunfermline	58
Cawdor Castle	168	Dunkeld	46
Chasm (remarkable)	158	Dunnottar Castle	51
Comrie	85	Dunolly Castle	30
Connel Ferry	29	Dunrobin Castle	156
Corra Linn Falls	18	Dunse	187
Craigforth	40	Dunstaffnage Castle	29
Crieff	34	Dunvegan (Skye)	85
Cullen	171		
Cumnock, Old	14	Edinburgh	184
Cumnock, New	13	Elgin	171
Clyde, Falls of	19		
Culloden Moor	167	Falkland Palace	56
Coupar Fife	56	Fillan's St., Pool	27
Coupar Angus	48	Foyers, Falls of	162
		Falloch, Glen	27
		Ferntower	36
Dalkeith	188	Findhorn River	170
Dalmally	28	Fleurs Castle	6
Dalnacardoch	66	Fishery, Herring	155
Dalwhinnie	66	Fochabers	171
Dee River	177	Forth River	40
Devil's Elbow	179	Forfar	48
Devil's Cauldron	35	Forres	168
Devil's Beeftub	193	Fort Augustus	164
Dingwall	159	Fort William	69
Dirie More	116		
Dochart Water	44	Galston	18
Dornoch	157	Gairloch	103

INDEX.

	PAGE			PAGE
Garry, Falls of	70	Kilmorack Falls		160
Garve	111	Kilt Rock (Skye)		83
Glammis Castle	48	Kincardine O'Neil		176
Glasgow	21	Kineff		53
Glen Farg	59	Kinlochewe		101
Glen Shiel	72	Kircaldy		57
Glen Roy, parallel roads of	68	Kinross		59
Golspie	156	Kyle-Akin		90
Glencroe, Pass of	32	Kyle-Rhea		91
Great Glen	70	Kyle-Skou		123
Glengarry	70			
Gualin	129	Lanark		17
Gaelic service, a	122	Lauder		187
Gretna Green	194	Laxford River		127
Grey Mare's Tail	10	Langholm		205
Glen Sligachan (Skye)	89	Ledmore		119
		Leny, Pass of		43
Haddington	185	Linlithgow		183
Hamilton	19	Loch Achray		42
Handa Island	125	,, Alsh		91
Hawick	205	,, Assynt		120
Helmsdale	154	,, Awe		28
Huntingtower	60	,, Bracadale		86
Huntley	205	,, Broom		104
Hope, Loch	141	,, Carron		92
Houna Inn	151	,, Coruisk		78
		,, Etive		29
Insch	205	,, Ewe		104
Inverary	32	,, Fyne		32
Inverlochy Castle	70	,, Katrine		24
Invermoriston	165	,, Laggan		67
Inverness	161	,, Lochy		70
Inversnaid	33	,, Lomond		23
Inveruglas	24	,, Long		24
Inchnadamph	120	,, Lubnaig		43
		,, Inchard		128
Jedburgh	6	,, Maree		98
John-o'-Groat's	151	,, Naver		137
Jean Town	97	,, Ness		161
		,, Oich		70
Kenmore	46	,, Scavaig		89
Kelso	6	,, Sligachan		78
Kilchurn Castle	28	,, Snizort		84
Killiecrankie	63	,, Skene		10
Killin	45			

INDEX.

	PAGE		PAGE
Loch Tay	44	Perth	180
„ Torridon	99	Pass of Awe	28
„ Voil	44	Peterhead	172
Loudon Castle	16	Philiphaugh	8
Luss	23	Pitlochrie	63
		Poolewe	104
Macdonald, Flora's Tomb	83	Portree (Skye)	79
Martyr's Monument (Stirling)	39	Portsoy	172
MacLeods. Maidens (Skye)	86	Prince Charlie's Cave	79
MacLeods. Tables	86	Pulpit Rock	26
Mary, Queen's escape	59		
Mary's, St. Loch	9	Quiraing Mount (Skye), ascent of	81
Melrose	8		
Melvich	150	Rob Roy's Cave	26
Moffat	11	Rob Roy's Death and Grave	43
Moncrieff Hill	60	Roslin	190
Montrose	54	Rowardennan	24
Moy	67	Roxburgh Castle	6
Musselburgh	185	Rumbling Bridge	77
Meikle Ferry	157	Rhiconich	128
Merkland, Loch	133	Roads, Scotch	197
Moin, The	141	Roman Camp, Ardoch	38
Moness Falls	46	Regalia, adventures of the	51
More, Strath	142		
Muthill	38	St. Andrews	54
		St. Mary's Loch	9
Nairn	168	Sanquhar	13
Nidpath Castle	192	Scourie	125
Newcastle-on-Tyne	2	Scour-na-Gillean Mount	78
Newark Castle	8	Shiel, Glen	72
New Lanark	18	Seal Oil and Skins	173
Naver, Strath	145	Sheriffmuir	38
Necropolis, Glasgow	22	Skye	74
Nith, Valley of	12	Sligachan, Glen	76
		Smoo Cave	126
Oban	30	Spean Bridge	69
Ord of Caithness	154	Spittal of Glenshee	179
Ochtertyre	35	Stack Mount	127
Ossian's Grave	63	Staffin Bay	83
		Stirling	39
Pass of Caithness	154	Strath Earn	181
Peebles	191	Strath Sleet	157
Penicuick	191	Strathmore	50
Parallel Roads (Glenroy)	68	Strath Naver	138

INDEX.

	PAGE		PAGE
Strath Peffer..	159	Torridon, Loch	99
Strome Ferry	92	Turrit, Glen and Falls of	35
Struan	85	Tweed, rise of	193
Suil Veinn, Mount	121	Tayinlone (Skye)	85
Sweno's Stone	170	Twisel Castle and Bridge	5
Stonebyres, Falls of	17	Tyndrum	27
Stonehaven	50		
Subterranean Stream..	122	Unapool	123
		Ullapool	117
Tain	158	Urquhart Castle	165
Tarbet	26	Uig (Skye)	84
Taymouth Castle	46		
Taynuilt	29	Wick	153
Thornhill	12	William, Fort	69
Thurso	138	Wrath, Cape..	130
Tongue	138	Wallace's Cave	18
Trossachs	42		
Tomdoun	71	Yarrow, River	9

ADVERTISEMENTS.

THE ROYAL HOTEL, INVERNESS.

This well-known Hotel is one of the largest, best furnished, and most comfortable in the North of Scotland, and though immediately *opposite* the principal entrance to the Railway Station, is entirely removed from the bustle, noise, and other disturbing influences which usually affect the comfort of hotels in close proximity to the railway. Table d'Hôte daily. Dinner *a la Carte* The Porters of the Hotel await the arrival of all trains, and the Hotel Omnibus attends all the Canal Steamers. The tariff of charges is strictly moderate.

JOHN S. CHRISTIE, Proprietor.

SLIGACHAN HOTEL, SKYE.

Picturesquely situated at the foot of the Cuchullin Hills. Nearest Point for Loch Coruisk, Loch Scavaig, &c., &c.

Posting.   Fishing.   Letters and Telegrams by Porter.

J. A. BUTTERS, Proprietor.

Patronised by H.R.H. Prince Leopold.

ROYAL ✢ HOTEL,
CUPAR FIFE.
J. ✢ MACQUEEN, ✢ PROPRIETOR.

N.B.—THIS IS THE LARGEST HOTEL & POSTING ESTABLISHMENT IN THE COUNTY

QUEEN'S HOTEL, MONTROSE

FAMILY and COMMERCIAL.

Splendid Stock Rooms. Baths. hot or cold and Billiards.

'BUS ATTENDS ALL TRAINS.

J. HECKFORD, Proprietor.

READ

THE

WHEEL WORLD,

3D. MONTHLY.

ADVERTISEMENTS.

THE COVENTRY MACHINISTS' Co.,
LIMITED,
Makers of the Celebrated

CLUB BICYCLES,
AND
CHEYLESMORE & IMPERIAL TRICYCLES.

The "CHEYLESMORE."

As supplied to H.R.H. THE PRINCE OF WALES, and ridden by "NAUTICUS" on his tour in Scotland.

The "IMPERIAL."

The lightest, most rigid, and easiest running front-steering Machine in the market. Ball Bearings Driving Wheels and Cranks.

The "SPECIAL"    The "CLUB."

With non-vibrating rubber Suspension Springs.

Head Office and Works: CHEYLESMORE, COVENTRY.

BRANCHES:

MANCHESTER ..	9, Victoria Buildings.	DUBLIN ..	21, Bachelor's Walk.
BIRMINGHAM ..	77, Colmore Row.	NEW YORK ..	189, Broadway.
LONDON	.. .. ..	.. ..	15, Holborn Viaduct.

NAUTICUS IN SCOTLAND.

PART I.

INTRODUCTORY.

MY tricycle outing this year was to have been a trip to Crieff and back. Finding, however, that the Scotch roads were almost unknown to the English cyclist, I became fired with a desire to explore them, and to give my experiences to my brother wheelmen. I forthwith proceeded to draw out a programme for an extensive tour in the " Land of the mountain and of the flood ;" and, the theoretical part being settled, I turned my attention to the practical side of the matter. What machine was I to ride? My " R.A." wanted a complete refit; should that be done, or one of a new kind procured ? The importance of the occasion decided me to go in for what I considered the best tricycle extant—viz., the " Cheylesmore "—so poor " chummy " was reluctantly given up in its favour.

Now for a companion, a good fellow, who would enter keenly into my scheme, and assist me to carry it out in its entirety. I wrote to my old friend P. " He had engagements." He did not like to promise. How unfortunate! A comrade, it seemed to me, was absolutely necessary in that rugged country, if only to come to the fore in case of accident.

Happy thought! Advertise. Having heard of a companion for life being obtained by this means, I thought that at least I could get suited with a fellow traveller for a month or two. Through the columns of that widely-circulated journal, *The Cyclist*, I became acquainted with Mr. T. He entered warmly into the whole business, ordered a new machine for the occasion, and agreed to meet me at Perth on July 15th.

This being too late in the year to commence a long tour, I had another shy at P., who, to my great delight, said he would accompany me until relieved by T. Everything was now cut and dried, fine weather only was required to make the whole affair a success. I met P. at King's Cross Station on June 3rd. He popped his bicycle ("Club") into the train; I had sent my "Cheylesmore" on by "goods." During the railway journey I unfolded my plan to P., who expressed his approval, and we passed the time agreeably in discussing the *pro's* and *con's* of the same. I found my tricycle at Newcastle-on-Tyne, and rode it down to the Royal Turf Hotel (B.T.C.).

In the evening we sallied forth to see the town, where preparations were being made to celebrate the Stephenson centenary. Even the statues were being cleaned for the occasion, and our sense of the ridiculous was tickled by seeing this operation performed on the great man himself. There he sat, in a calm and dignified position, while a workman, placing one arm affectionately round his neck, with the other "wired" into his nose, eyes, and other sensitive parts of the face with the utmost energy. Surely, thought I, he will kick out presently or remonstrate in some way, so life-like was the marble. But no; he took all these delicate attentions without moving a muscle.

Passing on to the high level bridge we observed a vessel coming up the river, and, wishing to see the working of the floating bridge, we hurried down just in time to see it swing back into its place, so easily had this ponderous mass been raised and turned. Mr. Welford, editor of "Cycling," called during the evening, gave us some hints about our route, and kindly promised to escort us for a few miles.

FIRST DAY.
Newcastle, Alnwick.

9.15 A.M. Left Newcastle, and trundled along a road deep in dust, an evil there certainly was no occasion to complain of again. Mr. Welford left us at Morpeth, and from thence the road was firmer, but loose stones impeded the running. After having gone some distance, my tricycle, which had been working rather heavily, suddenly flew round to the right, nearly throwing me. On examination

WE INSPECT ALNWICK CASTLE.

I found that the adjusting screw of the right wheel had been set too tightly, and that the friction had caused the metal to swell, thus jamming the wheel. I slackened the screw a little, and it gave me no further trouble.

When about five miles beyond Morpeth, we came to a long rise, and at the summit were agreeably surprised to find a tribute to Nelson, in the shape of a monument. The situation is a good one, as it overlooks a considerable tract of country, with Coquet Id. Lighthouse and the sea in the distance.

3.30 p.m. Passed a lofty column surmounted by a lion; this, we were informed, had been erected to the memory of the late Duke of Northumberland, by his tenants. A few minutes' run down the hill brought us to the bar gate of Alnwick, and we soon found our way to the "Star," one of the good old-fashioned coaching inns, and, as it now commenced to rain, we decided to remain for the night.

Our first day's experience was a good illustration of the fact that it is easy enough to determine upon anything before-hand, but to carry it out is quite another matter. For instance, to-day's programme was to visit Otterburn and Flodden, but a strong gale had caused us to slant off for Berwick, and here we were stopping thirty miles short of that. Under any circumstances I could not have gone much further, for what with the extra weight of my tricycle and gear,* the want of training, and the effects of a sleepless night, I was completely done up, and only too glad to take a short rest.

An hour or two later we inspected the exterior of the Castle, remarkable for the curious stone figures on the walls, representing warriors in various attitudes of attack and defence. These, I understand, were originally placed there to delude the enemy into believing that the garrison was prepared to give them a warm reception. On our return to the hotel, P. assisted me to take my machine to pieces, to see if there was anything wrong with it: we found nothing in particular amiss, the new bearings were rather tight, and three of the spring washers for the saddle had split; these I replaced with some punched out from a sheet of india-rubber, which, although lacking elasticity, stood the tour very well.

The brogue was stronger here than we expected. A gentleman in the smoking room gave us a long story about the intelligence

*My Cheylesmore had been specially strengthened for the tour, and I had several heavy guide books in my bag.

of his sheep dog. We kept him going by an occasional "yes," "quite so," "exactly," &c.; but on comparing notes afterwards we found that neither of us had taken in one-tenth of what he had said, so broad was his accent.

DISTANCE.

Newcastle to Morpeth ..	.. 14 miles.	Good.
Morpeth to Alnwick ..	.. 20 „	Undulating; loose stones.
Total	.. 34 „	

Strong side wind; fine.

SECOND DAY.

ALNWICK, BELFORD, BERWICK-ON-TWEED.

LOOKED round the town. The best view of the Castle is from the private grounds on the other side of the river.

12.45 p.m. Left Alnwick, and travelled on a capital undulating road to Belford, where we arrived at 3 p.m., and lunched at the "Blue Bells." Beyond Belford the road was not so good.

The view of Berwick, before descending into the vale, was very striking. The declining rays of the setting sun tipped the church steeples with gold, and brought into bold relief the ramparts and tiled roofs of the historic little town: the old bridge and airy modern viaduct stood out clearly, and the river on one side, and the sea on the other, formed a silvery frame for the picture.

After stowing away our steeds at the "Red Lion" we had some tea, then strolled round the walls, which are kept in excellent condition. While following an orderly crowd of well dressed people round the cliffs, we noticed a clearly defined shale stratum underlying the red sandstone; in several places the action of the waves had split the shale into square blocks, so that one might almost imagine them to have been prepared for the builder's use.

While taking our way homewards we came across a genuine pair of stocks, showing signs of age and use—a real curiosity in these degenerate days. They were just outside the town hall, and while there P. told me of his bewilderment at Alnwick the day before, when, in answer to his question, "What's the name of that building?" a man replied, "Hey, mon, that's the toon harl." "What?" "The toon harl," bawled his informant, as though he were deaf. P. was nonplussed, but while having his third pipe it suddenly dawned upon him that it must have been the town hall.

DISTANCE.

Alnwick to Berwick* .. .. 30 miles. Undulating and good.
Strong wind against; fine day.

THIRD DAY.

BERWICK, COLDSTREAM, KELSO, MELROSE.

9 A.M. Recrossed the Tweed, and took the Coldstream road—in excellent condition, and nearly level. The bridge across the Till is the very same over which the English troops marched on their way to Flodden Field.† This is a lovely spot; above the bridge romantic Twisel Castle towers up on the brink of a picturesque cliff, which bends the river nearly to a right angle; below, a mansion peeps through the trees, and the stream, overhung by the weeping ash and other feathery foliage, winds its way placidly onwards between the grass-grown banks. It was some time before I could drag P. away, and he often alludes to this as being one of the most charming views that we have seen.

Noon. Crossed the Tweed by a splendid bridge, and entered Scotland at Coldstream. We pulled up at a cottage to celebrate the event in a bumper of milk, and were struck by the extreme neatness of the interior. There were all kinds of knick-knack ornaments—one of them being a ship under full sail, in a narrow-necked bottle; how it got inside puzzled both the good dame and ourselves. We asked her about Kelso, and drew forth the vernacular reply, "Aye! Kelso is a bonnie place."

* Berwick is one of the few walled towns remaining in Great Britain, and, from being the key of the two countries, it has frequently changed hands. The names of Wallace, Bruce, Northumberland, and Douglas are conspicuous in its history. In 1551 Berwick was made a free town, which it still remains, with many privileges peculiar to itself and its citizens. Halidon Hill, where the Scots were defeated by the English in 1333, is two miles N.W. of the town.

† "On the morning of the 9th September, 1513, Surrey crossed the Till with his van and artillery at Twisel Bridge, his rear guard column passing about a mile higher by a ford. This movement had the double effect of placing his army between King James and his supplies from Scotland, and of striking the Scottish monarch with surprise."

On leaving Coldstream, the splendid condition of the road and the scenery through which we were passing put us into the highest spirits, and caused us to form golden opinions of the country through which we were about to travel so many miles. Kelso was reached at one o'clock, and, after some refreshment, we had a look round. Cricket appears to be a fashionable game on the borders, for a gathering of the *élite* were witnessing an animated match which was taking place on a capital bit of ground in the suburbs.

After visiting the ruins of the Abbey* in the centre of the town, which were not nearly so extensive as we had been led to expect, we at 2 p.m. started for Roxburgh and Jedburgh, cordially endorsing the old lady's statement that Kelso was a "bonnie place."

About two miles out we quitted the highway, and went down by a rough track to the river, close to the viaduct: here we found a footbridge with a stile at each end, over which the machines had to be lifted. We now reached the village of Roxburgh. Where was the Castle? "Two and a-half miles up there," was the answer to our query. Having gone a mile " up there," we came to a road which ran at right angles in each direction, taking the left, we presently met a country man, who did his best to explain the way to us. At first his brogue was so broad that we could only just make out that he was directing us to the new instead of the old Castle; then, in his anxiety to please us, he became so excited that we failed to understand a single word he said. Thanking him for his well meant efforts, we returned and tried the other way, eventually reaching the ruin, which is really only a mile and a-half from Kelso, whereas we had gone about nine. I was responsible for this blundering; on the map I had seen that Roxburgh lay near the high road to Jedburgh, and concluding that the Castle was in the village, I had decided to take it on the way. It proved to be on the Maxton road, in another direction altogether.

Leaving our machines by the road side, we ascended the knoll; very little of the ruin† remains, but we were rewarded for our trouble by a delightful view of the Tweed and Teviot meandering through a rich and varied landscape, in which Fleurs Palace forms a conspicuous object. Having lost so much time, we abandoned our intention of visiting Jedburgh, and made for Melrose.

* Kelso Abbey, a good specimen of pure Saxon architecture, was built in 1128, and demolished in 1569. James III. was crowned there in 1460.

† Was an important fortress. A large holly tree on the North side of the Tweed marks the spot where James II. was killed, by the bursting of a cannon during the siege.

WE TAKE THE WRONG ROAD.

The scenery along the banks of the river was charming, but our machines worked heavily on the stiff clayey road. When three and a-half miles from Melrose we turned off to the river, and crossed it by a foot-bridge (1d.). Leaving our vehicles, we walked half a mile further to Dryburgh Abbey,* which stands on a wooded peninsula almost surrounded by the Tweed; the rugged grey outlines of the ruin being finely relieved by the soft green of encircling orchards. Having paid sixpence to a guide, we were shown the last resting-place of Sir Walter Scott, and everything of interest.

Leaving Dryburgh, P. went ahead to hunt up a suitable hotel in Melrose. and being on a high road, with the railway on one side and the river on the other, we did not think of asking the way, but hastened onwards. I had just laboured up a long slope, and was looking forward to an easy run down into the village, when P. appeared with the news that we were going to Dalkeith as fast as we could paddle, so we had to return and take a bye-road under the railway viaduct. One mistake leads to another, thought I, but if we go on in this way it will take us six months to carry out the tour; the map must be studied more carefully in future.

7.30 p.m. Reached the King's Arms just in time to escape a heavy downpour. I, as usual, exposed my lamentable ignorance by asking the name of the curious M shaped hills which had been in sight most of the day, it not having occurred to me that they were the celebrated Eildon Hills.

DISTANCE.

Berwick to Coldstream	14 miles.	Level; good.
Coldstream to Kelso	9 „	Splendid.
Kelso to Melrose	14 „	Heavy in places when wet.
Our way to Roxburgh and Dryburgh	13 „	
Total	50 „	

Fine day; fresh wind against; wet night.

* Founded in 1150; destroyed by the English in 1844. The principal remains of the building are the Western gable of the nave, the ends of the transept, and part of the choir, all beautifully overgrown with ivy.

FOURTH DAY.

Melrose, Abbotsford, St. Mary's Loch, Moffat.

After breakfast visited the Abbey.* To dilate upon such a work of art would be somewhat akin to painting the lily, so I will pass on to Abbotsford, which we reached in time to join the first party at 10.30 (admission 1s.). We were shown Sir Walter's chair, and the desk at which most of the MSS. of his books were written; a chair made from the wood of the house in which Wallace was betrayed; Napoleon's desk and pistol taken at Waterloo, also a lock of his hair; a lock of Prince Charlie's hair, and his spurs; Rob Roy's gun and purse; Claverhouse's pistol; a 6ft. 5in. sword, and many other interesting relics. After seeing the garden screen and the grounds, we started at noon for Selkirk.

Skirting that town we crossed the bridge, and followed the north bank of the Ettrick to the cairn which marks the site of the battle of Philiphaugh.† Two miles beyond this we paused to scan the ruins of Newark Castle,‡ a roofless tower, which we should have pronounced unsightly, had not Sir Walter Scott immortalised it in verse. From here the scenery underwent a change; the trees gradually thinned, until there was not even a shrub to relieve the monotonous expanse of green on every side; the hills grew higher and higher, until they seemed to toss their rounded heads in all directions; habitations became few and far between, the road rough and stony, and the valley narrowed to a glen. In short, we had entered upon the Southern Uplands, of which we had heard so much, and were so anxious to see.

A cairn, far away on a mountain top, excited our curiosity, and a chance passer-by informed us that it had been erected in honour of the eldest son of the house of Dalkeith, the foundation was laid at his birth, and a foot added to it every year until he came of age, and there it remains.

The road gradually ascended through the glen, its newly metalled surface causing me a frequent dismount, but P. on his bicycle man-

* A splendid specimen of gothic architecture, 258ft. by 137ft. Founded in 1136, destroyed and rebuilt several times, was bombarded by Cromwell. The heart of Robert Bruce was deposited there.
† In 1645 General Leslie defeated the Marquis of Montrose.
‡ The scene of the Lay of the Last Minstrel.

UNCOMFORTABLE QUARTERS.

aged to pick his way along the edge, and soon ran me out of sight. A squall gathering ahead, I thought to dodge it by slipping into a cottage hard by. While there I beguiled the time by inducing a pretty girl to talk Scotch to me, and looked forward to chaffing P., who I expected was getting a ducking. Supposing the shower to be over I went on, and after all came in for the heaviest part of it: this rather took the weather-wise conceit out of me, because, as it happened, had I gone straight on I should have escaped with a few drops.

The rain having chilled my bones and damped my spirits, I was only too glad to sight the Gordon Arms—a dreary looking place outside, certainly, thought I, but sure to be well stored with creature comforts for the weary traveller. P., who had got in dry, had ordered luncheon, and my mouth watered in anticipation of something hot and savoury. Imagine how my lower jaw fell, when, on being shown into a cheerless room, I beheld a scraggy piece of cold beef placed on a bare deal table. Well, instead of grumbling we ordered two glasses of whiskey, to see if that would brighten us up a little, but no, the wind whistling in every crevice of the wretched tenement searched us through and through; so bolting our dismal meal, we called for our bill.

"Seven shillings, if you please, Sir."

The dormant volcano nearly burst forth, but smothering our indignation, we firmly and politely requested written details; as these were not forthcoming, we put down five shillings and departed, with a resolution to give the "Gordon Arms" a wide berth another time.

We were not in the best of humours, and the soft state of the road and the monotonous scenery did not tend to improve matters. I tried hard to rake up some enthusiasm concerning the celebrities of the neighbourhood, without success. For instance, I shouted to P., "That building was the last residence of Hogg, the poet."

"Humph, what a muff he was not to live in a more civilised place."

The glen opened out at St. Mary's Loch, and knowing P. to be a great ladies' man, I pointed out Dryhope Tower, the birth-place of the "Flower of Yarrow." Alas! it did not interest him at all. When in full view of the loch, I commenced to recite—

"The swan on sweet St. Mary's Lake
Floats double, swan and shadow."

On looking round, in the expectation of seeing P. entranced, I was just in time to catch sight of that gentleman going at full speed round the corner. To tell the truth, in spite of some pretty bits here and there, I was rather disappointed with the loch myself. Tibby Shiel's Town is on the peninsula between the lochs; passing that by, we went in for four miles' collar work to Birkhill. I found P. at the solitary cottage, who greeted me with, " Do come in here, I have never seen anything like it in my life." Following him inside, I saw a cupboard-bed, a novelty to us, and our questions about it much amused the inmates.

Although tired, we felt bound to see either the Mare's Tail, or " Dark Loch Skene,"* and on hearing that the water was too low for us to see the fall to advantage, we set off for the lake on foot. P. and the guide outstripped me, and after wading up the boggy hill side for a mile and a-half, I saw them seated in full view, but on my approach, P., instead of bursting forth into raptures, maintained an ominous silence. And, gentle reader, I tell you in the strictest confidence that we felt rather angry with poor Sir Walter for having caused us this fatigue and delay by his description of grandeur, which we failed to discover. The fact is that the peculiarities of the lake are only to be seen when the sky is dark and obscured, whereas on the present occasion the evening was bright and clear.

Returning to the cottage we solaced ourselves with a jug or two of milk, then commenced the descent into Moffat dale; this had to be executed with caution, as the road was bad and crossed by several open burns. The whole of this district is one extensive sheep walk, and I witnessed this evening an instance of the intelligence of the collie dog. He was at his master's heel: the shepherd pointed, off went the dog and took up a position about a quarter of a mile away, where he stood awaiting further instructions. On a peculiar shout being given, he scoured round, driving the sheep in the desired direction until another cry sent him up higher, and so on.

A rather steep run down of three miles and a-half brought us to the foot of the gorge,† and we emerged into a pastoral vale, while the trickling stream, which had been our companion from Birkhill, swelled into Moffat Water. The road remained soft and undulating

---
* " The character of the scenery is uncommonly savage."
   " Some ruder and more savage scene
    Like that which frowns round dark Loch Skene."—*Marmion.*

† The Grey Mare's Tail (400 ft.) is only about 300 yards off the road.

RELICS OF THE POET BURNS.

until near Moffat, when it improved, and the town, embosomed in hills, looked very pretty as we approached. Right glad were we to find comfortable quarters at the "Star," at 9 p.m.

DISTANCE.

Melrose to Selkirk ..	.. 7 miles.	Level; good.
Selkirk to Gordon Arms ..	.. 13 ,,	Steady incline; loose and stony in places.
Gordon Arms to Birkhill	.. 10 ,,	Rather loose.
Birkhill to Moffat ..	.. 11 ,,	Rather loose; ups and downs; fair surface.
Total	.. 41 ,,	

One shower only.

FIFTH DAY.

MOFFAT, DUMFRIES, SANQUHAR.

MOFFAT consists of one broad street, and a splendid hydropathic establishment. The fame of its mineral waters attracts great crowds in the season, but when we were there the tide of fashionables had not set in.

10.45. a.m. Left Moffat, and, after following the Carlisle road for a mile, we turned off to the right and ascended steadily, through a country somewhat like the best part of Kent, to Kirk Michael, where it was more open. From the brow of a hill we had an extensive view of picturesque Dumfries, and the plain on which it is situated. After a smart run down of a mile, we came to heavy level ground, which continued for the remaining five. The first sixteen miles from Moffat had been simply perfection, firm and smooth, without a loose stone or a speck of dust.

1.15 p.m. Drew up at the "Commercial" hotel just in time for the market dinner, a great treat after yesterday's experience. The farmers were a jovial set of fellows, and evinced great interest in our trip.

Burns had now to be "done." At the "Globe" hotel I saw the lines which had been scratched by the poet on the window pane of his chamber; in a room below, his punch bowl and chair are still kept in his old corner. After seeing the mausoleum got an old inhabitant to shew me the spot where Bruce killed the Red Comyn.* It is not in Grey Friars Church as I imagined, but in Comyn Court, about three hundred yards S.W. of it.

On rejoining P. we discussed our route to Ayr. I wanted to go by Dalry,† to see the place where Bruce encountered a score of Englishmen single handed, but as we could not be sure of finding the exact spot, and it was rather a round-about way, we decided in favour of the Nith valley.

3.30 p.m. Left Dumfries, having quite enjoyed the bustle of the town after our late lonely rides. Wheeling through a flat agricultural country we passed Ellisland, and came to Thornhill; from thence the scenery became more varied, and we presently caught sight of Drumlanrig Castle, a heavy structure standing in splendid grounds. Our road led us down to the Nith, and we had a delightful drive by its side for two or three miles. At nearly every bend of the river P. stopped and went into raptures; and well he might, for the rocky banks were exceedingly romantic and diversified. At one place we stepped carefully to the edge, and peering over the vertical cliff saw the inky stream gliding silently by. A little further on a torrent, white with foam, brawled over its rugged bed, and the rocks, no longer perpendicular, presented a moss-covered surface relieved by patches of lichen and brushwood. The beautiful woods on both sides abounded with flowers and ferns; the scented air, the notes of the thrush, and the cooing of the dove, lent enchantment to the scene.

Alas! this Elysium did not extend very far; the variegated foliage gradually came to an end, the ravine opened out, and smooth verdant hills once more presented themselves to our vision.

This kind of rapid travelling resembles a panorama, for no sooner is one kind of view off than the next is on. Plains, castles, waterfalls, villages, go by in such quick succession that to give a comprehensive account of what one sees is well nigh impossible. I am quite aware that Scotland is pretty well known to most travellers, and that details can be obtained from guide books. My object is to give a cyclist's experience for those who may care to follow in my track, hoping that it may also be of some use to the

---

* This violent action induced Bruce to raise his standard, and the struggle with England terminated by the victory of Bannockburn, and the possession of the throne by Bruce.

† A mistake. The fight took place near Tyndrum. The road by Dalry is reported to be a good one, with fine scenery.

general tourist. For example, most of the Nith Dale scenery which I have just endeavoured to describe is lost to the railway traveller owing to the numerous tunnels through which he has to pass. Were he to take the road from Thornhill to Sanquhar, he would be amply repaid for his trouble.

Reached Sanquhar at 7.30, and although this was the middle of June, we longed for a fire. There had been a hard frost the night before, and we found great difficulty in keeping ourselves warm.

DISTANCE.

Moffat to Dumfries	.. .. 21 miles.	Splendid.
Dumfries to Sanquhar ..	.. 26 ,,	Very good road; lovely scenery.
Total ..	.. 47 ,,	

Lovely day.

SIXTH DAY.

SANQUHAR, AYR, GALSTON.

SANQUHAR is a small town resting in an amphitheatre of hills, with verdant haughs sloping down to the river. It took a prominent part in the days of the Covenanters, for here the two famous declarations were made. A stone marks the spot, and the inscription terminates as follows:—

"If you would know the nature of their crime,
Read the story of the killing time."

Crichton Peel, or the Castle of Sanquhar, which has made its mark in history, is now in a dilapidated condition.

While preparing for a start, to our surprise we were shown a "Coventry Rotary" tricycle. Its history is that it ran away with its possessor, the doctor, and pitched him off, the poor man's leg was broken, and his fiery steed has been rusting in the stable ever since.

9.15 a.m. Started for Ayr; on reaching the lip of the basin, we saw before us a glen and a fertile plain beyond it, in which we distinguished the spires and steeples of New Cumnoch. Our road ran along the side of the glen, and consisted of a series of nasty ups and downs, which should be ridden with care.

At New Cumnoch we were surprised to see the shops closed, and the women going to kirk; I enquired the reason from a knot of idlers. "It's a fast day," was the reply. "A fast day!" exclaimed I; "is it a vigil?" Evidently thinking that I was poking fun at them, they gave me an evasive answer, but determined to satisfy my curiosity, I accosted a respectable looking man, who told me what I ought to have known before, viz., that it is the custom of their church to set apart a day of preparation before Sacrament Sunday.

The surface improved towards Old Cumnoch, a town built on both sides of a steep ravine. Before descending we stopped at the "Dumfries Arms" for refreshment. Presently, feeling anxious about my tricycle, which I had been obliged to leave in a rather precarious position, I went outside; to my dismay I found one man on it, another testing the strength of the spokes, a third trying to pull the tyre out, to see how it was stuck on, and a fourth turning the different handles; in another moment it would probably have been over the brow of the hill. Of course one must be prepared for a certain amount of curiosity, and by all accounts the Scotch are not lacking in that speciality, but really this was too much of a good thing, and I could not help asking them rather angrily, "How would you like me to go to your houses and pitch your furniture about to see how it is fitted together?" They apologised, and we parted on good terms, but in future we found it necessary for one of us to stand "sentry go" on these occasions, and I advise cyclists in Scotland to be on their guard against the meddlesome habits of the people, and carefully to examine their vehicles before making a start, as I frequently found nuts loose and gear displaced.

Beyond Old Cumnoch, trees once more threw their grateful shade over us, the hills toned down, the prospect became more animated and the running excellent. About eight miles from Ayr, the eye roamed over a well cultivated country to the blue sea in the distance, and an easy decline brought us to

"Auld Ayr, whom ne'er a town surpasses
For honest men and bonnie lasses."

After a capital luncheon at the "King's Arms," P. pottered about while I went off to Burns' Cottage (two miles, entrance 2d.) and saw the recess bedstead on which he was born, and the wall which had been partly blown in on that memorable night. Much of the original furniture of the cottage remains, and the old clock is still ticking away, They were preparing for the annually increasing rush of visitors by putting up a turnstile entrance to the old house (no longer a public), romance having to give place to necessity. Nothing remains of Alloway Kirk but the four walls, which are in a very shaky state. A new stone has just been erected over the grave of Burns' father, the old one having been gradually pocketted by the relic-loving public.

I next crossed the road to the Monument* where are preserved a lock of Burns' hair, the bible he gave to Highland Mary, and many other interesting things. After surveying the "Banks and Braes of bonnie Doon" from the top of the building, I came down to the gardens, looked at the grotesque statues of Tam O'Shanter and Souter Johnny, and walked on to the "Auld Brig," but had a prettier view from the New Bridge.

On my return to the hotel, P. and I questioned the ostlers concerning the best way to Galston. As their opinions differed, we selected the shorter of the two, and passed over the newest of the "Twa Brigs," which, according to Burns' prophecy, has not stood well, and is to be replaced.

The road was good for the first four miles, then it struck across the hills and became rough and steep; we were compensated for this by obtaining two splendid views. One embraced the Carse of Ayr, the other overlooked Galston with its massive Kirk, and Loudon Castle nestling in the woods behind. Southward we could see far away to the Isle of Arran, while to the N.W. mountains and valleys alternated, until lost in the hazy distance.

Having duly admired the beauties of the scene, I cautiously commenced the abrupt descent, and my vehicle was just beginning to get speed on, when the pin of the brake smashed, and had I not been uncommonly smart in jumping off and stopping the machine, there would have been either an undertaker's or a blacksmith's bill to pay. As the village is out of the line of tourists, we found a lack of accommodation, and had to put up at separate inns. I handed over my tricycle to the blacksmith, who promised to do what he could for it. In the course of conversation that evening I was much amused by being asked if we were Southrons. On replying in the affirmative, my companion remarked, "Ah! when I saw your friend riding into the town I was sure that he was a *foreigner*."

I was told that we should have done better if we had avoided the hills and come round by Kilmarnock, as the road is good all the way, and it is only two and a-half miles longer.

* The guide informed me that last year he had registered as many as 1,700 visitors in one day.

DISTANCE.

Sanquhar to New Cumnoch	..	13 miles.	Loose, with two or three miles of tiresome ups and downs.
New Cumnoch to Old Cumnoch.		5 ,,	Good.
Old Cumnoch to Ayr ..	..	16 ,,	Very good.
Ayr to Galston	..	15 ,,	Ten miles of hill, with roughish road.
About Ayr	..	6 ,,	Very good.
Total	..	55 ,,	

Beautiful day.

SEVENTH DAY.

GALSTON, STRATHAVON, LANARK.

I FOUND my tricycle ready for me. There was not sufficient metal to square the brake handle as I wished, but the blacksmith had made a very good job of it by inserting a larger pin of a more pliable metal, which would give me warning before it broke.

9.10 a.m. Left Galston for Lanark. Yesternight we had heard great things of Loudon Castle: " It was the Windsor of Scotland ;" under a gigantic yew tree in the grounds an important treaty had been signed, &c., &c. Be that as it may. when it came to the point we contented ourselves with a peep from the roadside, and imagined the rest. After paddling most of the way up a long slope through a wooded ravine, we walked the latter part of it on to the table land above. Loudon Hill, to which we soon came. is a remarkable crag, and from its isolated position looks as if it had dropped from the clouds. Having scanned the scene of the battle[*] which took place there, we left our wheels, and struck across the fields to Drumclog Cairn,[†] having been told that it was half a mile away. After trudging more than a mile, we saw it on a slope far ahead, and not thinking it worth while to waste any more time, we returned and proceeded.

The road was heavy enough before, now it became stony and rutty as well. To make matters worse we found ourselves on a dismal moor, and our solitude was made the more apparent by a

[*] Robert the Bruce defeated Pembroke, in 1307.
[†] Here the Covenanters defeated Claverhouse, in 1679.

curlew and a plover, who circled round and round, uttering most piteous cries, as though to say, "What strange beings are you? Have you come here to rob us of the early worm?" Keeping to the broader track of the two, we came down to a place where four roads met, about fourteen miles from Galston. Here a blacksmith had established himself. He pointed out the most direct route to Lanark, but finding that it was unrideable, we went *via* Strathavon.

There were two roads from Strathavon to Lanark, of fourteen and seventeen miles respectively; we were recommended to take the latter. I now see by my notes that we passed through Stonehouse, which, according to my map (Black's 4/6), we ought not to have done. I certainly have a distinct recollection that the seventeen miles appeared extra long ones, also that the road was very rough and bumpy. Cyclists following on our track would do well to make frequent enquiries hereabouts. I afterwards found it a good plan to note the principal villages on the route, and to ask the way from one to another.

Soon after crossing the highway between Glasgow and Douglas the whole Vale of the Clyde opened out before us. Having lately read "Scottish Chiefs," my mind was full of the traditions and beauties of the neighbourhood. Imagine my disappointment at seeing the air thick with smoke, while far and near tall chimneys vomited flames and steam. What would chivalrous Wallace say to all this? thought I. Coal, coal, everywhere! Roads, houses, people's faces were alike begrimed with it.

We had a long run down to the river, where we escaped from the smoke, and hoped to have a pleasant spin along the banks, but a series of clayey ups and downs bothered me greatly. P., on his bicycle, could ride over these without much difficulty, and as it had commenced to rain, I told him not to wait for me. I stopped to see the Stonebyres Falls, which are now open to the public on the payment of threepence. The surroundings are pretty enough, but the Falls did not come up to my expectations.

After four more miles of ploughing through a sticky surface, I had still harder work in pushing my three-wheeler up the abrupt conical hill upon which Lanark is situated, and I was very glad to get into dry clothes, and have something to eat at the "Victoria" Hotel.

By and by we walked out, and saw a colossal statue of Wallace in front of the Town Hall, but as no one could tell us where he had stabbed Hesselrigge, we trudged off through the rain to Cartland

Crags.* I had pictured in my mind a wild place extending for miles, whereas the ravine is of no great dimensions. We crossed the new bridge, and scrambled down to Wallace's Cave—a mere crevice in the rock—in which he could easily have been seen from the opposite bank. We were incredulous about its identity, but were told that generation after generation had believed in it, so we felt bound to follow suit. Apart from Wallace associations, it is a delightfully picturesque spot, which everyone should visit.

DISTANCE.

Galston to Strathavon ..	.. 18 miles.	Hilly; not a good road.
Strathavon to Lanark ..	.. 17 „	Ups and downs by Clyde; clay soil.
Total	.. 35 „	

Moist afternoon.

EIGHTH DAY.

LANARK, BOTHWELL, GLASGOW.

AFTER breakfast we procured tickets from the landlord, and set off for the river, which was hidden by the irregular ground until we came upon it at New Lanark. Having been disappointed with Stonebyres, I was quite prepared to pooh! pooh! the Upper Falls. The first few yards after entering the lodge gates (6d.) dispelled that notion, and frequent exclamations of delight burst from us, as one lovely bit after another came in sight.

Corra Linn† plunges into a basin—a magnificent amphitheatre of rock—overhung by noble trees, the foliage of which was dripping from the mist arising from the cataract. After lingering for some time, and taking views from different points, we wandered along the banks of the river for half a mile to the Boniton Fall, where the walk terminates.

*" Each rugged rock proclaims great Wallace' fame;
Each cavern wild is honoured with his name.
Here in repose was stretched his mighty form,
And there he sheltered from the night and storm."

† Has obtained its name from a tradition that the daughter of one of the ancient kings of Scotland, named Corra, was there drowned, in consequence of her horse having taken fright and leaping with her into the gulf below.

Halting on the iron foot-bridge, we glanced up stream. The banks were low, and a man was fly-fishing in water broken by the uneven bottom into a number of little cascades. A few steps brought us immediately over the main Fall; here we spun out the enjoyment as long as possible by taking the scenical plums one at a time. Beneath our feet rushed a mighty volume of water, at first gliding smoothly like spun glass over the well-worn ledge, then breaking into a broad mass, white as wool, it leapt into the abyss below, the glittering spray exhibiting a rainbow brilliant in all its colours. Close on our right we had a profile view of part of the Fall, separated from the rest by the rock on which we were standing. The river, which had been turned at right angles, flowed rapidly between the picturesque cliffs, now broad and with a placid surface, then narrowed and ruffled by a projecting point. Bright sunshine, with alternate light and shade, completed the charming picture.

P. had been silently taking it all in for some time, when, observing him about to speak, I eagerly listened for some poetic remark to record in these pages. Slowly and thoughtfully he muttered, "There are thousands of good men at this present moment on a strict allowance of half a gallon of water a day, *washing included*, and look at all this doing nothing. It's wrong, decidedly wrong!"

On our way back we took repeated views from different points, and had another good look at Corra Linn, but both agreed that we admired Boniton more. Let me tell those who, like myself, have seen Niagara and other noted waterfalls, that it will be well worth their while to take some trouble to visit the Falls of the Clyde.

Glasgow being our next halting place, we made enquiries as to the best way, but, as usual, could get no trustworthy information. P. stayed behind to write a letter, and I went on by the Hamilton road. I re-traversed the Clyde side, which had been such irksome travelling the day before, but having now a dry surface, and the slopes more in my favour, I got on very well. I also enjoyed the views of the different magnificent country seats, and for the first time met excursion parties on the road. After ten miles, trees ceased, the vale opened out, the track turned away from the river, and rose by an easy gradient until it joined the highway to Hamilton.

Skirting that town by the Palace* grounds I came to Bothwell Bridge†, which, to my disappointment, has been so modernized and built about, as to rob it of the halo of romance with which "Old Mortality" had invested it in my mind.

Two miles further I rang at the lodge gates, which are about a mile from the Castle. A comely lass appeared, and informed me that it was not an open day, but on telling her that I was an Englishman travelling to see all the great sights of Scotland, she, with the courtesy which I have always experienced in this country, readily agreed to make an exception in my favour. While walking through the park I had a glimpse of the old Castle just beyond the modern mansion, and presently found myself on the edge of a steep brow, immediately overlooking the now placid waters of the Clyde. The exceeding loveliness of this tranquil spot took me quite by surprise, for, to tell the honest truth, I thought that I had left the river for good.

"How about your guide book?" the reader may say. "Why did you not read it up the night before."

Well, what with arriving late, cleaning up the machine, changing clothes, consulting one's creature comforts, and writing up notes, it may be imagined that I felt more inclined for a gossip in the smoke-room than for reading about "ornate environs" and other dry guide book details. This part of our duty was therefore generally scrambled through in the morning. But as I have already taken the reader into my confidence, I may as well tell him that I skimmed through every imaginable book on Scotland before leaving home, and considered myself a perfect guide book on wheels. Nevertheless, it often happened that, after giving P. a graphic description of some place, we found on arriving there that it did not tally in the least—the fact being that I had been descanting on something a hundred miles away.

To return to our story—we were talking about Bothwell Castle.‡ The Clyde, still, broad and deep, here makes a fine sweep round this truly noble ruin, and through the stately trees on the opposite bank can be seen the picturesque remains of Blantyre Priory.

* Not open to the public.
† Bothwell Bridge is famous for the engagement between the Covenanters and the Royal Troops, under the Duke of Monmouth, in 1679, when the former were completely defeated. The bridge was rebuilt in 1826.
‡ Anciently possessed by the Moray family, afterwards conferred on Aymer de Valence, Archibald the Grim, Lord Crichton, Lord Ramsay, Patrick Hepburn, Francis Stewart, Marquis of Hamilton, Lord Douglas.

"O Bothwell bank, thou bloomest fair."

The exterior of the castle is draped with ivy, which forms a pleasing contrast to the red stone of the building; of the interior little remains but the bare massive walls and turrets, tenanted only by rooks. While rambling about the grass grown court, I mused upon the strange vicissitudes of fortune which had caused the castle so often to change hands, and in imagination I contrasted its present condition with that of by-gone times, when its floors had re-echoed with the tramp of armed men, and its walls had rung with choruses from the war songs of the day.

Having bestowed some of my pocket money on the lady keeper, I wheeled off towards Glasgow, the signs of its proximity being manifested by the houses and people, which increased and multiplied continuously during my seven miles ride.

The East end of Glasgow, like that of many other cities, is not the most select, and the unusual sight of a tricycle set the children screaming, the boys running, and the people shouting, which brought me into public notice in anything but an agreeable manner. It was bad enough in England, but I was nearly overwhelmed by these excitable citizens, and I had to undergo two miles of unenviable notoriety before I could hide my diminished head in the "St. Enoch's" Railway Hotel, where I expected to find P., for we had agreed to meet at the "Station" Hotel. He was not there, however, and, finding that there were two other stations with hotels attached to them, I tried them, but without success. As time went on I felt more and more uneasy at his non-appearance, and was much relieved to spy him working his way through the crowd in St. George's Square, and to hear that only a trifling accident had caused the delay. P. exclaimed at the grand appearance of "St. Enoch's" Hotel, which he thought far too good for humble cyclists, but although everything was conducted in first-rate style, we had not to dip into our purses so far as we expected. In the evening we walked down to the docks, and through the principal streets. The trains, trams, and 'busses rushing about, and the busy crowds of people rendered the scene full of life and excitement.

DISTANCE.

Lanark to Glasgow .. .. 25 miles. Very good on the whole.
Lovely day.

The road from Hamilton dips to Bothwell Bridge, otherwise it is level and good.

NINTH DAY.
Glasgow, Dumbarton.

Our first visit was to the cathedral, which was founded in 1123. At the Reformation it narrowly escaped destruction, and is now, I understand, the only Gothic cathedral in Scotland remaining entire. The choir has been screened off, and is used for a parish church, which spoils the interior.

On leaving the cathedral the striking appearance of the Necropolis attracted our attention, and crossing the intervening ravine by the "Bridge of Sighs," we wended our way among the massive tombs of some of Scotland's greatest men, to the summit, which is crowned by a colossal monument to John Knox. From that point we could see the great city, with its countless factory chimneys, extending for miles over a flat country. Returning to the hotel by St. George's Square we noticed the fine buildings and statues for which the city is justly celebrated.

3 p.m. Left Glasgow, passing the University, which presents an imposing appearance. The road led us westward along the Clyde, through a pleasant vale, with some pretty villas and pleasure grounds. Rounding the hill Dunbirch, we had our first view of the celebrated Dumbarton Rock, which rises abruptly from the low bank of the river, and were rather disappointed with its height and size.

5 p.m. Arrived at Dumbarton, and by way of experiment located ourselves at the Temperance Hotel. When putting my tricycle away I found part of the tyre loose on the left wheel; to secure this, I melted the remaining composition by applying a candle flame to the hub, and pressed the tyre into its place, binding string tightly round it to keep it there until the composition had hardened. Our first temperance meal was not encouraging; washy tea, half-boiled eggs, a meagre allowance of bread and scrape, with a melancholy looking chap for a messmate.

After our frugal meal we walked down to the rock. Its outline resembles a camel's back, and there are forts on both peaks. We scanned the "beak"* with great interest, and pictured the gallant Crawford at work with his ladders. Formerly the stronghold was almost surrounded by the river Leven, and the entrance was effected

---

* Surprised and taken by Captain Crawford in 1571. Considered one of the most gallant exploits in Scotch history.

by a slope up to the North Gate. At the present time the ascent is made by a flight of steps on the South side. A coast-battery man showed us Wallace's prison, his 5ft. 6in. sword (supposed to have been left behind when he started for England), some ancient Highland weapons, and the Earl of Mar's dungeon. He then took us up to Wallace's seat, the highest point of the rock, commanding an extensive view. Northward is the high land about Loch Lomond, and across the Estuary we could just discern Greenoch, backed by the Argyle Hills. Dumbarton Rock,* which looked so insignificant in the distance, is in reality a mile in circumference, and 560 feet high. They say that it is strongly magnetic, and experiments have been made on parts of it. We were surprised to see so great a curiosity as Napier's first marine engine lying on the green, exposed to the weather, and at once went through the gate to examine it. While doing so, a man came up and demanded entrance money, which was paid with reluctance, there being no notice of such a charge. Dumbarton still keeps up its reputation for shipbuilding, and we saw a fine steamer which had just been launched.

DISTANCE.

Glasgow to Dumbarton ..　　.. 14 miles. Level and good.
Fine.

TENTH DAY.

DUMBARTON, LUSS, BEN LOMOND, ARROCHAR.

9.30 A.M. Got under way. Passing by Smollett's birth-place and monument, we came to Alexandria, and a mile further we enjoyed a good view of almost the entire length of Loch Lomond.† A charming ride of three miles brought us to Balloch Ferry, and afterwards, while bowling along the side of the lake, its many pretty little bays brought to my recollection Sydney Harbour, and the happy days I had spent there. The avenue of trees through which we were passing, and the beautifully wooded island close to the shore, rendered the approach to Luss more lovely than anything we had yet seen.

* The Monkish tradition is, that when St. Patrick, who was a native of the adjacent parish of West Kilpatrick, sailed from the Clyde to convert Ireland, the Devil, in a rage, tore this huge rock from the neighbouring hill, and threw it after him.
† Loch Lomond is about 23 miles in length, greatest breadth 5 miles.

We stopped at the village for a view from the pier, then P. went on while I interrogated an artist. He advised me to avoid Rowardennan Hotel, and to sleep either at Inveruglas or at Arrochar. On arriving at Inveruglas I found P. in rather an excited state, and he told me that the woman was a regular " Meg Dods ;" she did not care to give us either food or lodging, evidently looking upon a cyclist as a doubtful character. This being so, we took the ferry, and lunched at the Rowardennan Hotel, where, as we had been warned, the charges were high.

At three o'clock we commenced the ascent of Ben Lomond* from the back of the hotel. The track is very easy to follow the whole way, and the higher parts are marked with cairns to assist the traveller in thick weather. We made two halts for scenery. From the first point we had a glorious view of the lake, islands, and the park lands on the borders; from the second, Dumbarton Castle and the Firth of the Clyde could be distinguished. At the top we joined two tourists, whom we had seen ahead of us all the way, and got their guide to tell us the names of the different places.

Northward a chaos of mountain tops extended to Ben Nevis, the perpendicular cliff of which could be clearly distinguished. Eastward Lochs Katrine and others could be clearly seen, but Edinburgh and Stirling were obscured by a slight haze. Southward we could just see Greenock and the Isle of Arran; westward the head of Loch Long gleamed in front of the Argyleshire Hills.

From our stand point it was interesting to trace the course of the Forth, which started from the base of the mountain as a mere brook; but being constantly fed by rivulets which ran to meet it, the infant stream widened continually as it wound through the valley, destined, we knew, to become a mighty river, carrying trade to all parts of the world.

The guide led us down by a short cut over the ramps, a proceeding I did not at all approve of, for I was so shaken up that my legs almost refused to carry me, and I should advise the tourist to stick to the beaten path. When about half way down, the wind shifted to N.E., and blew hard, a cloud capping the mountain. The whole business took us 4¼ hours, including half an hour at the top; but as it gave us a clearer idea of the country through which we were about to pass, we considered that our time and labour had not been thrown away.

* Height of Ben Lomond above the sea is 3,242 feet, and the lake 32 feet.

Preferring "Meg Dods" and the chance of a cheap cup of tea to another heavy bill at Rowardennan, we looked about for a ferry boat. As it was blowing a gale, we had doubts about getting one, but by paying double fare (five shillings) we induced two men to take us over, and the wind being fair, we flew over in no time. On entering the Inn at Inveruglas we were, to our great surprise, greeted with smiles, and found that the hostess was ready to give us tea, beds, and everything that she had refused before. "Too late, my lady!" We had made up our minds to push on to Arrochar, and, therefore, only condescended to discuss a meal.

8.40 p.m. Got on wheels. The wind had subsided as quickly as it had risen, and the five mile ride, in the cool of the day, by the side of the lake, was very delightful; but that from Tarbet to Arrochar, across the Isthmus, was positively romantic. Below our feet playful rabbits darted in and out among the ever deepening shadows of the trees, and towering above our heads the bold outline of the mountains showed distinctly against the evening sky. Just before arriving at Arrochar, we had a capital view of Ben Arthur. The irregular peak is very remarkable; but to my eye it was as much like a cobbler as the top of the hill near Grasmere is like a woman playing an organ, *i.e.*, there is no resemblance whatever. When it came to ordering the evening meal, P. said that it was high time to go in for the staple food of the country, and forthwith ordered a basin of porridge, so I was fain to do likewise. He polished his off, and slept like a top; I stuck half way, and saw all kinds of strange things during the night.

DISTANCE.

Dumbarton to Arrochar.. .. 23 miles. Delightful ride.
One hour's hard blow; rest of the day very fine.

ELEVENTH DAY.

*Arrochar, Tyndrum, Dalmally, Taynuilt.

Before breakfast I strolled on to the pier. Looking seaward Loch Long seems rather tame and monotonous, but the sequestered village at the head is prettily situated, and in the calm bright morning all seemed to speak of peace and contentment.

* I understand that the road from Dumbarton to Arrochar by Helensburgh and Gareloch, is a good one, and the scenery lovely.

Our account really was a " little " one, which proved the wisdom of coming two miles out of our way to escape the charges of the more fashionable hotel at Tarbet; and I have much pleasure in recommending the Arrochar Inn to all tourists who desire comfort, good attendance, and economy. Unfortunately for the average tourist, the present coaching arrangements render it rather difficult to get at, here cyclists have the advantage, four miles, more or less, being immaterial to them.

9.30 a.m. Ran across to Tarbet, then headed North by the side of Loch Lomond. Near the 24th milestone was a very lovely little glen, crossed by a bridge and watered by a dashing splashing brook—a kind of spot which brings all the poetry of one's soul to the surface.

From a point jutting into the lake not far from this, we took a survey. How different from the view near Luss ! The scene might now be described as grand, and Ben Lomond, (which we had thought a shapeless mass,) by displaying his Northern face—a double peak, with precipices of 2,000 feet or more—showed what a fine fellow he really was.

A pedestrian pointed out Rob Roy's Cave* on the opposite shore, and told us that the said practical gentleman used to sling his prisoners over the rock in front of it, and duck them until they agreed to pay a certain ransom. I have no doubt they did not take long in making up their minds on the subject.

Close to the 27th milestone, I saw P. (who generally led the way) dismount, and walk across the green to an upright isolated rock. I followed suit, and assisted to examine this curiosity.

In its face we discovered a recess containing the remains of a fire. This puzzled us, because it was too shallow to afford shelter, yet it had evidently been hewn out by dint of considerable labour.† A short time after we had resumed our journey we came to a hamlet, and while approaching the school I heard the girls singing with gusto:

"If a body kiss a body, need a body cry?"

" Decidedly not, my little dears," cried I, aloud, and taking this as a sort of invitation I felt very much disposed to avail myself of it, but knowing that P. would highly disapprove, I curbed my inclination and looked the other way.

* Bruce took refuge here after Dalry.
† Later on we learned that it was the Pulpit Rock. This at one time was used for public worship by the Minister of Arrochar.

A HARD RIDE.

Passing by Ardlin at the apex of the Loch, we soon came to Inverarnan, where we rested awhile, and sought advice about our future route, which had not yet been definitely settled. All hands agreed that Glencoe was quite impassable for our vehicles, and they were equally sure that we should find the road to Oban a good one. This settled the matter, and off we trundled again.

The road now began to rise steadily through Glen Falloch. About a mile from Inverarnan we paused to admire the mountain burn (Falloch Water) rushing between and falling over variegated rocks, and cooled our heated brows for a few minutes, under the shade of umbrageous foliage. From hence a steeper gradient and bad surface compelled us to walk for some distance, and a blazing sun, reflected by the now barren sides of the Pass, beat fiercely on our heads, but as I had taken the precaution of putting some leaves in my hat I did not fear sunstroke.

We had a capital L.O.H. run from the watershed of the Pass down to Crianlarich, where we intended to have luncheon; but hearing that the charge for a cold meat repast was 2/6, we preferred hunger to extortion, and mounting again, made for Tyndrum. This being only four miles, we expected to reel it off very quickly, and revelled in the idea that we had shown the Crianlarich landlord that only moderate terms would satisfy the independent wheelman.

We soon began to sing a different tune, for we found out that "four miles more or less" is on some occasions very material, even to the cyclist. What with the heat, a road consisting of a series of tiresome undulations and a loose, sandy surface, we had reason to regret our impetuosity, and wished we had resigned ourselves to the tender mercy of the napkin-flapping, white-chokered waiter.*

I am afraid we did not pay much attention to St. Fillan's Church, and the miraculous Pool,† but ploughed and growled all the way to Tyndrum. The sight of the village surrounded by barren hills had a further depressing effect, and I had hardly sufficient strength to propel my "Cheylesmore" to the hotel door.

Alas the day! We had jumped from the frying pan into the fire. Instead of the comfortable quarters at Crianlarich, we found the

* When at Alnwick we asked our messmate to recommend us an hotel at Berwick, he said, "I always go to the 'Red Lion,' where you get waited upon by a comely maid. I hate these white-chokered individuals, they're always fussing about and looking for tips."

† In this pool lunatics were annually immersed, then bound hand and foot, and placed in St. Fillan's, in the expectation of effecting a cure. The last instance known was in 1844.

utmost disorder (owing to the hotel having just changed hands), and, in exchange for the juicy sirloin we had so scornfully left behind us, we were offered the remains of a scraggy rib. To crown all, the chief object of our toil had not been gained, for the charge was the same. P. stuck to his principles like a brick, and contented himself with a biscuit, while I, poor weak mortal, was compelled to fortify the inner man—to disgorge my coin, and pocket my pride instead.

At 3 o'clock started again. The King's Field* had no attraction for us, our sole idea being to get clear of this wretched neighbourhood. We had been warned that the road to Dalmally was very " coarse "—" like the bed of a torrent " would have been nearer the mark, for it had evidently been neglected since the opening of the railway. The grim sides of the Pass were deeply furrowed by spates, which crossed the road at intervals and scattered its surface with loose stones, and in many places huge boulders of rock.

What a time we had of it to be sure! P. declared that he had never had so much practice in mounting and dismounting. At last we gave it up, and resigned ourselves to walking.

When about five miles from Dalmally our eyes were refreshed and our hearts gladdened by a glorious view of Glen Orchy. We thought Ben Cruachan† (3,390ft.) more Alpine than any other mountain we had seen during the tour; and a glimpse of Loch Awe, with the river winding among the hills, greatly enhanced the effect. The descent into the valley was long, and in some parts precipitous, but the condition of the road improved. It was 7.15 before we arrived at Dalmally, and gladly would we have remained at this charming village, but its popularity had already filled the inn with fashionable folk, so after some light refreshment we journeyed onwards.

After leaving Dalmally the road took a long detour round the head of the Loch, then inclined up to the new hotel, from whence is a lovely look out on Kilchurn Castle‡ and the islands. Where

* At Dalry, or King's Field, King Robert Bruce was encountered and repulsed by the Lord of Lorne. "Bruce's personal strength and courage," says Sir Walter Scott, "were never displayed to greater advantage than in this conflict. He was forced to abandon his mantle, with the brooch attached to it."—See "*Lord of the Isles.*"

† " To geologists Ben Cruachan is very interesting. It is composed of reddish granite or porphyry, and near the bottom is found argillaceous schistus, intersected with veins of quartz and lapis ollaris. On the top the sea pink grows luxuriantly, and sea shells have been found on the very summit. Bunawe is the best starting point for the ascent; it takes 8 or 9 hours."—*Scottish Tourist.*

‡ " Child of loud-throated War! the mountain stream
Roars in thy hearing: but thy hour of rest
Is come, and thou are silent in thy age."—*Wordsworth.*

all is "ever charming ever new," one's powers of description are apt to fail, so I will only state that the Pass of Brander was literally awe inspiring, and the mountain and river scenery at the Bridge of Awe* exceedingly romantic.

9.40 p.m. Arrived at Taynuilt less tired than we had been in the middle of the day at Tyndrum; so wonderfully had the beauties of nature nerved and supported us during this eventful day.

DISTANCE.

Arrochar to Inverarnan ..	.. 11 miles.	Level and good.
Inverarnan to Crianlarich	.. 6 „	A hog's back; rough in places.
Crianlarich to Tyndrum ..	.. 5 „	Loose sand; tiresome ups and downs.
Tyndrum to Dalmally ..	.. 12 „	Most of the way unrideable.
Dalmally to Taynuilt ..	.. 14 „	Delightful scenery; bad road.
Total	.. 48 „	

Very fine; hot sun.

TWELFTH DAY.

TAYNUILT, OBAN, DALMALLY, INVERARY.

9.15 A.M. Left Taynuilt (a few houses, rather bleakly situated). Four miles of rough road—mostly down hill—conducted us to Loch Etive, which is fringed with wood, and guarded by imposing mountains. At Connel Ferry the Loch contracts and is almost bridged by a reef of rocks; it was half ebb, and the tide rushing and roaring over the ledge formed a salt water cataract, a phenomenon which neither P. nor I had ever seen before.

Two miles beyond this we left our machines inside a gate, and walked half a mile to Dunstaffnage Castle,† on a promontory jutting into the lake. The door was locked, and as opening it meant loss of time and money, we contented ourselves with a view of the interior through a crack in the ancient doorway, and found it

* The scene of Sir Walter Scott's story of the "Highland Widow."
† The seat of the Pictish as well as the Scottish Princes. In Dunstaffnage was long kept the famous stone now in Westminster Abbey. It was considered the Palladium of Scotland and is fabled to have been "Jacob's pillow." Between the castle and the chapel is a rock having a remarkable echo. If a person speaks aloud at this rock the sound is heard at the chapel as if it proceeded from that spot.

difficult to realise that the rough uncemented pile before us had once been a celebrated stronghold, although it was founded on a rock.

After looking round the chapel we regained our steeds, and rode over a hill and down rather a steep slope into Oban. P. took his bicycle to the blacksmith to have a spoke tightened, and I employed myself in sticking on the tyre of my small wheel, and repairing other minor damages brought about by the rough treatment of the previous day.

Oban! Oban! Oban! had been dinned into my ears ever since I first gave out that I was going to Scotland, and what did I find after all? A village of hotels in an ordinary land-locked bay, and the stories I heard of the discomforts which the majority of tourists have to put up with in this place caused me to rejoice that I had taken it in the early part of my tour. There is one thing, however, which should be seen by everyone, viz., Dunolly Castle,* which is on a high cliff overlooking the bay. The keep and a few fragments of the walls only remain; they are beautifully overgrown by ivy, and stand well out from the green sward and park-like surroundings. To our taste this, with the addition of Clack-a-Koin, was more picturesque than other celebrated ruins.

Just before taking my seat at the commercial dinner-table at the "King's Arms," I sent my boots to be mended, and before I had risen they were returned to me strongly soled. This is not related as an illustration of the length of the meal (although I had two helpings of the best bread-and-butter pudding that I have ever tasted), but to show how smart and obliging is the Scotch workman.

P. and I now put our heads together, and taking into consideration the unsettled appearance of the weather, the chances of having a trip to the islands and back without being able to land, and the length of our purse strings, we decided to reserve Staffa and Iona for another occasion, and to make for Inverary.

We saved the wear and tear of our vehicles and boots by taking the train to Dalmally, and I particularly noticed that the best bits of scenery are either entirely lost, or imperfectly seen from the railway carriage.

7.40 p.m. Left the train at Dalmally, and asked a bystander to explain the way to Inverary; whereupon he pointed out a dip in the mountain range high up in the sky. Our eyes did not meet, and neither P. nor I had the moral courage to suggest it, but I am sure that we

* Mentioned by Sir Walter Scott and Wordsworth.

should both have been only too glad of an excuse to postpone this formidable journey until the morning.

We first had four miles of dangerous ups and downs, next a heavy plough through a wood skirting the shore of Loch Awe, then (at Cladich), by way of variety, the road struck straight up over the mountain range. Up, up we toiled, steeper and steeper became the way. "Scenery!" cried P., and those who desire to get the finest view of the loveliest lake in Scotland* should take this road, bad as it is. On we strove. Near the village of Lechnahan one bit of the road was almost too much for me; before coming to it I put on a tremendous spurt (pushing); it was no use, my vehicle stuck fast in the gravelly soil; however, strength and perseverance won the day.

Three and a-half miles of this pleasure trip (?) in the mountains brought us to a bleak pass, where the gradient was less severe, and beyond the watershed the character of the road changed entirely. It became hard and smooth, and zig-zagged down at a pleasant angle, so that we were able to cock up our legs and run down nearly the whole of the remaining seven miles, without putting foot to pedal. We *did* enjoy it, and while careering through the Duke of Argyll's magnificent woods—which boast some of the finest timber in North Britain—with the music of a murmuring stream on our left, all our fatigues were forgotten, and we only regretted that many of the surrounding beauties were partially obscured by the deepening twilight. It was 11 p.m. before we sat down to our evening meal at the Argyll Arms.

DISTANCE.

Taynuilt to Oban	12 miles.	Rough road.
Dalmally to Inverary	16 „	Mountainous, with eight miles of bad surface; scenery glorious.
Total	28 „	

Very fine.

---

* There are 24 islets on Loch Awe, about which are many fabulous tales. On Elan Fraoch are the ruins of an ancient Castle of the chief of the Mac Naughtons. The whole district abounds with memorials of distant ages.

THIRTEENTH DAY.

Inverary, Pass of Glencroe, Arrochar.

I walked out before breakfast, prepared to find Inverary* quite a large town, instead of which it consists of a few houses on a low point projecting into the lake. The high land comes close down to the water's edge, leaving no room for the village to extend, and there is very little level ground about the Castle. I examined the celebrated cross, which is much smaller than I had been led to expect.

In the forenoon we strolled through the park, and walked by a winding path to the top of Duniquoich (700 ft.), a singular wedge-shaped hill, and much enjoyed the view of the Castle, with its charming environs, Loch Fine, dotted with sailing boats, and the mountains beyond. We felt inclined to remain in this neighbourhood to see the waterfalls and other attractions, but, as the saying goes, "the Crieff girls had hold of the tow rope;" so we packed up our traps, and at one o'clock bade farewell to Inverary. We followed the windings of the road round the arms of the loch, thereby obtaining a variety of views. One shower compelled us to take shelter under some trees near the ruins of Dundarrow Castle, and another drove us into Cairndow Inn, where, having fortified ourselves with oatcake, washed down by whiskey and water, we decided to face the weather.

Just beyond the inn our road turned to the left, and became very steep for nearly a mile, then we managed to ride, but it was heavy work; this, together with the rain and the dreary glen (Kinglass), formed a striking contrast to our pleasant morning at Inverary.

Two miles from Cairndow our way led across the river Kinglass, and up into Glencroe, the gradient again compelling a dismount. I had been told that this pass should be seen in a storm; in this respect we were in luck, at any rate. Heavy masses of clouds were driving across the glen and enveloping its highest peaks, while every now and then the sun broke through, making the rocks glisten again; grand—no doubt, but pass or no pass, give me a fine day when travelling, and I will promise to be satisfied.

We certainly were glad to reach " Rest and be thankful,"† and to see a long stretch of more cheerful looking country before us. We

---
* The old tower and castle as described in the Legend of Montrose, have been removed.
† The rest was erected by General Wade's soldiers when making this road.

could trace our road for miles winding through the vale, and fondly hoped to have a spin similar to that of yesterday into Inverary. I tried it on, and nearly went a cropper over the precipice; P. also had a narrow escape, so we curbed our impatience until the steepest bit had been passed. The road was rough and bad down to the lake side, and very soft the rest of the way to Arrochar, where we arrived just in time to escape a heavy downpour.

DISTANCE.

Inverary to Cairndow Inn	..	9 miles.	Level and good.
Cairndow Inn to Arrochar	..	14 ,,	Mountainous; loose surface.
Total ..	..	23 ,,	

Showery afternoon; wet night.

FOURTEENTH DAY.

Arrochar, Loch Katrine, Crieff.

A WILD morning, with heavy rain. P., having a cold, did not care to venture out, but being anxious about my letters I determined to brave the elements.

9.50 a.m. Cycled to Tarbet, and took the ferry to Inversnaid (fare 16d., including piers). A pretty cascade falls into the lake close to the landing place. After pushing my vehicle up a long steep hill, I was riding along the level, when, hearing a shout, I dismounted, and had just time to draw my frail vehicle on one side to save it from being crushed by the coach; the driver, when passing, bawled something which sounded like a rebuke for having presumed to occupy the king's highway on the same day as himself.

My attention was now drawn to what appeared to be a bicycle track—a closer inspection convinced me that this was the case— and I can only compare my astonishment to that of Robinson Crusoe, when he saw the footprint of a savage in the sand. The mystery was soon solved, for the first person I saw at Stronachlachan was H., a gentleman who had answered my advertisement, but with whom I had not closed, as our respective plans did not fit in. He had intended to spend the day at the hotel, but good naturedly consented to accompany me to Callender.

12.40 p.m. Started in the steamer for the trip down Loch Katrine (2/6). The scenery for some miles was bleak and uninteresting. On nearing the East end, the lake became more closely hemmed in by ruin-strewn hills, while craggy pyramids, clothed with natural wood, cropped up promiscuously on both shores. After passing Ellen's Isle and the "silver strand," the vessel appeared to be running straight on to the bank; just at the very moment when a terrific crash seemed inevitable, a turn of the helm, like the wave of a wizard's wand, displayed a narrow channel of deep blue water, guarded by chaotic rocks artistically ornamented by birch and fir, with the peak of Ben Venu in the background. At the same instant a gleam of sunshine lighted up this sylvan scene, which was viewed by all in silent rapture. Everyone seemed, as it were, spell bound, until the touch of the vessel against the rustic pier brought us back to the material world once more.

We mounted our steeds, but the greasy and irregular state of the road through the Trossachs claimed our closest attention, and, sad to relate, the ground rendered classic by Scott was got over as quickly as possibly, all the poetry of the scenery being buried in slime and slush. The wind was strong against us, and H. on his bicycle fared very little better than I did. Glad were we to sight Callender, and still more so was I to find a train nearly due. Wishing H. "*bon voyage*," and stepping into the carriage, wet and muddy as I was, I soon found myself under the hospitable roof of my friend at Crieff.

DISTANCE.

Arrochar to Tarbet	2 miles.	Capital.
Inversnaid to Stronachlachan ..	5 ,,	Good.
Trossachs to Callender	10 ,,	Ups and downs; clay surface.
Total ..	17 ,,	

Raining most of the day.

CRIEFF

lies on a slope near the head of lower Strath Erne, commanding an extensive view of that fertile vale. In the town a curious old Cross and a pair of iron stocks can be seen, but all traces of the Kind Gallows have long since been swept away.

Crieff is very healthy, it is a capital touring centre, and there is

SEEING THE SIGHTS.

plenty to see in the immediate neighbourhood. During a visit of eight days we* saw

DRUMMOND CASTLE (4 miles)

on the opposite side of the Strath. The keep is the only ancient part remaining, Cromwell battered down the rest.

The Castle has sheltered crowned heads, but its celebrity is principally due to the display of flower gardens, which we had the bad taste to think too prim and formal.

BAVICK FALLS (2 miles).

This lively mountain burn commences with a fall of 30 feet, and after forcing its way through a narrow water-worn passage, it falls again, and so on, thus working through a lovely little glen on to more level ground, where it settles down into a sedate stream.

TURRET FALL (1 mile East of Bavick).

A flight of steps takes the visitor down to a seat, from which he can at leisure watch the Turret leaping from the rocks above into a cauldron near him, from whence it escapes by a subterranean passage. The current of air produced by the Fall diffuses the spray around, thus continually moistening the mossy rocks and ferns, which spring from every crevice. Although on a small scale, both of these Falls are exceedingly pretty.

LORD MELVILLE'S MONUMENT AND THE DEVIL'S CAULDRON.

Cycled through Ochtertyre. All Scotch proprietors appear to be very liberal in throwing open their domains to the public, but Sir Peter Murray goes further and lends boats to those who care to row on his lake. This serpentine piece of water, the splendid show of rhododendrons, and the natural way in which the grounds are laid out produce a very pleasing effect.

Leaving our steeds at Comrie, we walked by an easy winding path to the monument on the summit of Dunmore, and the day being clear, the country about Perth was very distinct. The trees rather interfered with our view of the Upper Strath, but we had delightful peeps of a smiling verdant vale, encompassed by gloomy frowning mountains.

On our way back we turned aside to see the Devil's Cauldron. Here the Lednoch, for the space of about 100 feet, rushes madly

* P. joined on the second day.

between walls of smooth rock, upwards of 20 feet in height, and only 4 or 5 feet apart, then makes a plunge into a dark basin.

These basins, or cauldrons, are evidently formed by the friction of stones whirled round and round by the mass of water struggling to find an exit.

We roamed along the banks, and amused ourselves with watching the adventures of pieces of wood in the water. When thrown into a particular corner above the Fall, the stick was slowly but surely drawn to a certain point, when it was suddenly sucked down to the bottom. We could clearly see it being hurried along the bed of the stream, until it rose to the surface only to be carried over the Fall. This brought to my mind a sad accident which occurred some years ago in India, owing to this fatal undertow. The ship to which I then belonged was lying at anchor in a tidal river. A party of us were returning from shore, and our boat was just ranging alongside, when the bowman, in reaching out with his boat hook, over-balanced himself and fell overboard. We were all ready to seize him directly he rose to the surface. Poor fellow! he was seen no more.

Comrie has the reputation of being one of the prettiest villages in Scotland. Frequent shocks of earthquake are felt there. After some refreshment at a very clean little Temperance Inn, we strolled on to the bridge. It is an axiom that water always finds its own level, but here we noticed a distinct ridge in the middle of the river. The confluence of the Lednoch and Earne takes place just above the bridge, and this phenomenon may be due to the reluctance of these rapid streams, being of different densities, to unite, or perhaps to a bank of sand.

Not having time to see the remains of the Roman Camp, we cycled back to Crieff by a level and good road.

Distance.

Crieff to Comrie and back .. 13 miles. Level and good.

One day my hostess drove me to Loch Turret, a wild place in the hills, and through the park lands of Abercairney, Ferntower, and Dollary, all pretty and within an easy walk of the town.

At a lawn-tennis party my "Cheylesmore," was trotted out for inspection, and, against my friend's advice, I foolishly allowed a youngster to play about with it, thinking that it could come to no harm on soft grass. He ran it backwards and forwards, making the left wheel the pivot in turning it, and when I came to examine the machine I found the whole of the tyre on the left wheel loose. This damage was irreparable, because nearly all the composition had been wrenched out, and none could be procured in Crieff. My sole object in mentioning this is to warn the cyclist that to the saying "Don't lend your wife or your gun," he must add, " or your tricycle."

PART II.

FIFTEENTH DAY.

CRIEFF, ARDOCH CAMP, DUNBLANE, STIRLING.

RAINED until noon. 3 p.m. P. and I started on a circular tour. Trees lined the road to Muthill, which made it very muddy; from thence we struck across the hills to Ardoch, the country being open and monotonous. Just above the village is the Roman Camp,* which we stopped to examine. This interesting ruin measures 140 yards by 125, the Prœtorium being 20 yards; it is well defended with ditches, and traces of a wall are also noticeable. I understand that this is the best preserved camp in Britain. There are others somewhere near, but our investigations were brought to a premature conclusion by a heavy shower of rain, and when it ceased we thought it advisable to make the best of our way onwards.

We paddled by the site of the battle of Sheriffmuir,† and soon afterwards ran down to Dunblane. Passing the palatial Hydropathic Establishment on the outskirts of the town, we took shelter from another shower, and occupied the time by inspecting the ruins of the Cathedral.‡ They are very fine, but the effect is spoiled by the nave being roofed in, and used as a Kirk.

Observing some pretty girls about, I asked if there was still a "Flower of Dunblane" to be seen and saluted, but unfortunately this, like many other good old customs, has died out.

After leaving Dunblane the road led us over the river Allan, past the railway station, and up a slope through fields and hedgerows. Having gone about two miles, we were carelessly riding through a wood at the top of a hill, when—*Tableau!*—the Carse of Stirling in all its glory lay mapped out before us. I declare, it was exactly like the rising of a curtain in a theatre. We simultaneously dismounted,

---

* Supposed to have been the work of Agricola during his fourth campaign. It was capable of containing 26,000 men.

† Fought in 1715, between the Royal troop under the Duke of Argyll, and that of the Pretender under the Earl of Mar.

‡ Founded in 1142.

and gave vent to our feelings of wonder and delight. In front and beneath lay the pretty village Bridge of Allan, backed by the perpendicular face of Abbey Crag,* the huge monument to Wallace on its summit seeming, as it were, to dispute our passage. On the other hand the enchanting vale, bathed in the golden tints of the setting sun, smilingly attracted us towards its far-famed capital, which rested picturesquely on a wedge-shaped rock in the middle of the plain.

The road had been excellent from Muthill, but directly we came to the tram which runs from Bridge of Allan to Stirling, the surface became rough and pitty; moreover, to my dismay, the tyre of my left wheel worked loose. P. assisted me to secure it with string, and I managed to get into Stirling all right. Directly I had stabled my steed at the "Queen's" hotel, at 7.30 p.m., I hunted about for some composition. There being none of the proper description, I made shift with india-rubber solution, lashing the tyre with leather bootlaces as an additional security.

DISTANCE.

Crieff to Muthill	8 miles.	Level and good.
Muthill to Ardock	7 „	Hog's back; easy gradient.
Ardock to Dunblane	7 „	Very good.
Dunblane to Stirling	5 „	Excellent.
Total	22 „	

Showery; fine evening.

SIXTEENTH DAY.

STIRLING, DOUNE, CALLENDER, TROSSACHS.

STIRLING is a curious town, having a mixture of ancient and quite modern buildings. After breakfast we found our way up to Greyfriars' Church (now East and West Kirk). Between that and the Castle is a hollow called the Valley, where tournaments used to take place; it is now a cemetery, tastefully laid out and ornamented with monuments of more graceful designs than those usually found in Scotland. One of these, encased in glass, is very

* The Scottish army, under Wallace, was stationed on Abbey Crag, to oppose the passage of the English under Warenne, in 1297.

remarkable. It represents two females reading the Bible under the protection of an angel, and the inscription runs as follows:—

> "Margaret, Virgin Martyr of the Ocean Wave, and her like-minded sister, Agnes; bound to a stake within the flood mark of the Solway tide. They died a martyr's death, the 11th May, 1685."

There is a small craggy pyramid, called the Lady's Hill, on the South side of the cemetery, where the ladies used to sit and smile on their favourite knights. A flight of steps conducted us to the Castle, and we were fortunate in having an intelligent Highland corporal to show us Douglas' room,* and whatever there was of interest in this renowned fortress: from the battlements he pointed out the notable places in the neighbourhood.

I am sure that the prospect from Stirling Castle will not disappoint even the most *blasé* of travellers. Eastward is a richly cultivated plain interspersed with hamlets, the spires and buildings of Allan showing in the distance. Southward are the Campsie Fells, and the field of Bannockburn. By looking carefully we could just make out the "Bore Stone" flagstaff. Westward, in the foreground, the house of Craigforth nestles among trees on a knoll, and the fair vale of Monteith stretches away to the Ben Lomond range. Northward lie the Abbey Crag, Bridge of Allan, and the park land of the Ochil hills; nearer the walls the curious terraced mound called the King's Knot, the Heading Hill, the Old Bridge (formerly called the Gate to the Highlands), and the tower of Cambuskenneth Abbey. I must not omit to notice the river Forth, which looks like a gigantic snake wriggling its way through the valley, its convolutions are so tortuous that the channel from Stirling to Allan, a distance of six miles as the crow flies, extends to nearly twenty-one by the river.

I made enquiries about the supposed subterranean passage from the Castle to Cambuskenneth Abbey. Our guide said that it had been traced to the river, and two old men told me that they had struck it beyond that when digging the foundation of a house.

Satisfied that everything had been seen to advantage from the Castle, we abandoned the idea of taking another view from Wallace's Monument; and, after a mouthful of bread and cheese, started at 3.30 for Callender, intending to take it easy and spend a quiet evening there.

---

* "Ye towers! within whose circuit dread
A Douglas, by his sovereign, bled."—*Lady of the Lake.*

MISTAKES. 41

Thinking that the old bridge was the scene of Wallace's great triumph, we stopped at it on our way out of the town, and asked a man if it were so. He replied, "Oh, yes, that is the very bridge, and I will show you where it was blown up." He pointed out the centre arch, which we could see was of more recent construction than the remainder, and did not doubt but what his tale was true.*

Remounting, we proceeded along a level road by Craigforth and Blair Drummond. As the afternoon was particularly fine, I proposed, and P. agreed, that in order to make sure of a bright calm evening at the Trossachs, we should push on there at once. We took into consideration that this would entail our staying the night at an expensive hotel, but the importance of the occasion decided us to throw economy to the winds.

Seven miles from Stirling we turned to the right, and while careering down a hill, we had a "glance and go" view of bonnie Doune Castle,† and regretted that we had not time to see more of it.

Just before coming to the bridge over the Teith, I saw two broad roads branching off, this surprised me, as I only remembered noticing one on the map. To make sure I asked the way to Callender, and was directed to take a road that made an acute angle with the one we were on. This puzzled me greatly, but every fresh informant said that it was the main road, and the only way, so on we went. It, however, became narrower and rougher as we proceeded. After passing a Castle (Clan Gregor), we emerged on to a bleak moor, and the road was almost unrideable. Now came the news, "You have come quite wrong, this is the old road, you should have gone through Doune." Although we ought to have determined our route quite positively before starting, still it was very vexatious to have been thus misdirected by people who should have known better. It was too late to return now, so we blundered along on a track which is not marked in Black's map at all. The latter part of the way ran close along the right bank of the Teith, and, although fatigued and irritated, I could not help admiring the beauties of the river scenery, and envying a loving couple who were billing and cooing in a quiet nook, unseen as they thought—ha! ha!

* This bridge was built in 1208. In 1745 the Southmost arch was broken down by order of General Blakeney, to prevent the approach of the rebels, but was afterwards rebuilt as it now remains. The new bridge stands below this, and the old wooden bridge which Wallace destroyed in the great battle of Stirling, 1267, spanned the river half a mile further up stream.

† Queen Mary resorted to Doune Castle as a hunting seat. "Glen Dhu" held it all the time Prince Charlie was absent with the Highlanders in England, as related in "Horne's History of the Rebellion."

Instead of going through Callender we turned to the left, and passed by the new "Hydropathic," joining the main road about two miles from the town. When I last came this way I could hardly force my machine through the mud; this had now dried into hard ridges, which rendered cycling positively dangerous. P. on his bicycle nearly came to grief several times, which rather rubbed him up the wrong way. At the foot of Loch Achray I tried to cheer him up, by remarking that we were coming to the pretty part. He replied, "High time, too, the game isn't worth the candle; I haven't seen anything yet to *make a song about.*

7.30. p.m. Drove our jaded steeds to the door of the Trossachs hotel. Even then (June 27th) it was nearly full, but as all the arrangements were excellent we did not experience any inconvenience. The folly of doing so much hard work on an empty stomach was now apparent, for I could only take a little toast soaked in tea.

8.30. p.m. We walked quietly down through the Trossachs* and by the lake to a point beyond the "silver strand." There was not a breath of wind; the trees and rocks were reflected in the glassy surface of the lake, while overhead the sky was flushed with the different sunset tints. All was silent, calm, and beautiful. The most enchanting part of all was the passage leading up to the pier, which I have before described, and the yacht-like steamer lying alongside completed the picture.

P. was satisfied, so I was happy.

DISTANCE.

Stirling to Doune..	8 miles.	Level and good.
Doune to Callender	8 ,,	We took the wrong road.
Callender to Trossachs ..	8½ ,,	Ups and downs; clay soil.
Total	24½ ,,	

Beautiful day.

SEVENTEENTH DAY.

Trossachs, Balquhidder, Lochearnhead, Killin.

Heavy rain all night. When it cleared up at 10 a.m., P. and I followed the stream up to the dam at the S.E. end of Lock Katrine, then struck over the brae to the pier. There is no track, and it is a

* Signifies rocky territory.

good climb, but the following is P.'s opinion, given at the highest point :—

"Now I can see and understand what the Trossachs really are. I was all in the dark before ; everyone should take a view from an elevated position like this."

The spot which had enchanted us so much twelve hours before was not like the same place this morning. A gale howled through the trees, and lashed the surface of the lake into wavelets. Noisy people were about ; in short, the charm was gone, and anxious to retain last evening's impressions, we hastened back to our quarters. After luncheon we packed up our traps and demanded our bill. It was comparatively heavy, but this was counterbalanced by the beautiful situation of the hotel and its many comforts; moreover, by staying there, we had been enabled to see the Trossachs under exceptionally favourable circumstances, so we both agreed that our money had been well laid out.

3.15 p.m. Got under way; the road was dreadful, but soft mud was preferable to hard ridges. The two prettiest bits on our way back to Callender, in our estimation, were the head of Loch Achray, and the prospect from the "Brig of Turk."

Headed North after crossing the bridge near Callender, feeling thankful to find ourselves once more on a firm, smooth highway. We worked up through the Pass of Leny, by the side of a copious mountain stream, which bustled along in fine style. Our machines rattled merrily round Loch Lubnaig,* copse-fringed, and overshadowed by stern Ben Ledi. At "King's House" inn I was directed to take a bye-road on the left for Balquhidder; P. being out of sight ahead, I went there alone.

Leaving my tricycle by the way side, I walked up a knoll to the old Kirk, looked in, and saw a single grave in the middle of the ground, enclosed by the walls of the ruin. This I took to be the one I sought for—I was wrong, it was a Saint's resting place. Rob Roy's†

---

* Crooked Lake.

† "His death was in conformity to the romantic peculiarities of his life. He was confined to bed, when a gentleman, who had done him an injury, paid him a visit. Being informed that the stranger asked admission to his chamber, he exclaimed that 'An enemy must not behold Rob Roy MacGregor in the posture of defeat.' He made his family raise him up, put on his clothes and warlike accoutrements, and then he received the stranger with dignified civility. When he was gone, the dying man desired again to be laid in bed, and ordered the piper to be called in, and instructed him to play 'I shall never return,' and not to cease sounding the pipes while breath remained in the breast of Rob Roy. He was punctually obeyed, and expired with the 'Voice of battle' pealing around him."—*Waverley Anecdotes.*

is marked by a slab (bearing the faint traces of a sword) on the left of a raised tombstone near the East gate of the old Kirk. Loch Voil is hemmed in by steep hills, the East end being softened by a rich covering of wood, and by a placid stream running through verdant meadows. Altogether it forms a pleasing landscape, and I regretted that P. had missed it.

On regaining the highway, I made a short stay at the inn, then proceeded on a mile of level ground to the verge of a hill overlooking Loch Earn, and a considerable stretch of country. The declivity to Lochearnhead is considerable, and should be ridden with care. P. having waited an hour for me had gone on, so I followed, and the road being in splendid condition, I tried to paddle up through Glen Ogle, but after going a mile and a-half I gave in, and walked the remaining two and a-half to the summit.

A train, puffing and panting on the opposite side of the glen, seemed quite out of place in these solitudes. The road down into Glen Dochart was very precipitous for a mile, then nearly level, but the deep ruts and the soft surface made it difficult to get on at all, and I was too much occupied in taking care of my neck to enjoy my first view of Loch Tay, and the wild mountain scenery in this region.

The Dochart rushing madly over its boulder strewn bed, and by romantic islands at Killin Bridge, is a sight to be seen and remembered; I thought it wildly picturesque.

8.30 p.m. Found P. at the " Bridge of Lochy " inn.

DISTANCE.

Trossachs to Callender..	8½ miles.	Ups and downs; clay soil.
Callender to Lochearnhead	13½ ,,	Rideable hills; good surface.
Lochearnhead to Killin	8 ,,	Four miles' rise (good); remainder miry.
To and from Balquhidder	4 ,,	A very fair bye-road.
Total	34 ,,	

Very fine.

EIGHTEENTH DAY.

KILLIN, TAYMOUTH, ABERFELDY, DUNKELD.

At Killin, stern Glen Dochart and pretty Glen Lochy unite on a level plain, which extends for a mile to the head of Loch Tay, thus affording an extraordinary contrast of scenery in a small area. The following is what we observed in a short walk before breakfast: High above against the sky stood out a bare rugged mountain top (Ben Lawyers).* A little way down its side a sprinkling of the dark hardy Scotch fir caught the eye, 'lower still the land was clothed with dense foliage, and partially cultivated, and so on down to the rich haugh and cornfields. Again, how different the scene from the two bridges. At Killin it was quite exciting to watch the Dochart tumultuously roaring past. From Lochy Bridge the stately river, overhung by weeping willows, seemed motionless; while the elegant villas dotted about, and the cattle calmly browsing, rendered it like a meadow scene in Hampshire.

But, gentle reader, there is another and yet a greater attraction to this wonderful place. "Can it be a waterfall?" say you.—No. "Fingal's grave?"—No. You give it up? Well, *the* magnet to Killin is the fair Mary Cameron, the Perthshire belle. To be waited upon by her is indeed a privilege. "Describe her appearance?" More easily said than done, but I will try.

Rather above the middle height; there was a grace and dignity about her that would have befitted the position of a lady of high birth. Her manners were modest and unassuming, and she appeared to be quite unconscious of her beauty. Our admiration was excited by the luxuriant hair of a rich golden tint, the hazel eye, and regular features, and most of all by the winning smile which lit up her face when speaking. We could not doubt that an unselfish desire to please was the motive that influenced the active movements of our Hebe.

We gave ourselves the credit of having discovered this lily of the mountains, but the poetical effusions addressed to her in the visitors' book proved that we were not her only admirers.

This then was the reason why that good-looking fellow P. had trundled along in such a hurry yesterday. Sly dog! he wanted to

---

* Ben Lawyers is 4,015 feet in height. The ascent is very easy, and the view from the summit varied and magnificent. It has many interesting geological features. See Geikie's "Scotland."

get the weather gauge of me. He succeeded, too, and what is more, I failed to cut him out.

10.15 a.m. Left Killin, taking the north road by Loch Tay. It rose gradually, and was very heavy for the first four miles, but when it commenced to slope towards the East it became firm and good, and we had a splendid spin to Kenmore. The north road was selected, because we had heard that it would be better for our machines than the other; owing to its height, however, the lake is not seen to advantage from it.

The loch contracted towards the East end,* the bare slopes giving place to Drummond Hill and other splendidly wooded heights, and a distant vista of the Tay valley gave us an inkling of pleasures to come. The approach to Kenmore, cut out from the rock and ornamented by noble trees, was very fine.

The village is remarkable for the neatness of its cottages, and also for the tourist prices at the inn. We were tempted to partake of the good things on the table, but P. thought it wise to test the charges by calling for a pint of beer—eightpence ! ! This was sufficient; bidding them good-bye, we rode up the hill for Aberfeldy.

After pausing to admire Taymouth Castle and its princely environs, we rambled along, drinking in all the beauties of this lovely neighbourhood, which we were fortunate enough to see in bright sunshine, and at a time when rhododendrons and the graceful laburnums were in full bloom. P. was in ecstacies, and declared that it eclipsed the Trossachs.

Tourists, in crowds, now met us at every turn of the road to Aberfeldy,† where we obtained the economical meal we were in search of at the "Temperance" hotel, and after a look round from the quaint old bridge, we pursued our journey. The road *via* Loggerait was undulating and rather stony, and the scenery tame When within two miles of Dunkeld, it became more diversified. We put our steeds away at the "Royal" (Dunkeld), and after tea strolled on to the bridge. It was a beautiful evening, and the prospect of the noble Tay, the fine hill screens, and the Cathedral‡ nestling in dense foliage, was simply exquisite. We lingered about until dark, then returned to the hotel and wrote up our journals.

* "Lawyers" Inn, about half way along the lake, is the best starting point for ascending Mount Lawyers.
† Moness Falls are about two miles from the town. Charge, 1s. 6d.
‡ The Cathedral was gutted and defaced at the Reformation.

PUNISHMENT FOR DRUNKARDS.

I noted that we had heard the Gaelic language for the first time at Killin. Our vehicles, mine in particular, continued to be the source of much excitement. For instance, to-day, when near Kenmore, I saw a man jump off a wall and begin to dance about and snap his fingers; thinking him to be out of his mind, I prepared for emergencies. Poor fellow, it was only his way of showing delight at seeing so great a novelty. Owing to my having put on the india-rubber solution in a hurry at Stirling, it had not answered well, and I had to keep the tyre in its place with leather bootlaces, which required constant attention. This evening I carefully cleaned out the felloe, and spread the solution thinly and uniformly, allowing it 17 hours to harden.

DISTANCE.

Killin to Kenmore	..	.. 16 miles.	Rideable hills; good surface
Kenmore to Aberfeldy	..	.. 6 ,,	Splendid road; lovely scenery.
Aberfeldy to Dunkeld	..	.. 16 ,,	Level and good.
Total		.. 38 ,,	

Bright sunshiny day.

NINETEENTH DAY.

DUNKELD, COUPAR ANGUS, FORFAR, BRECHIN.

THE Rumbling Bridge is three miles on the Crieff road; we walked there because the ostler thought it too steep for our machines, but I beg to inform wheelmen that the hill is rideable, and also to recommend them not to omit seeing this romantic spot. The pendant ivy, ferns, moss, and picturesque chaos of rocks look exactly as if they had been arranged for effect. We were only just in time to enjoy a quiet view, for on our way back we met scores of Dundee holiday folk.

12.15 p.m. Left Dunkeld for Coupar Angus. Turning just before reaching the Bridge, we followed the left bank of the Tay for some distance, when a mile of hill had to be walked up. After surmounting that, we enjoyed a splendid spin of nine miles through Carputh to Meiklons. In a field near this hamlet we saw a carved pillar, to which was attached an iron collar. This, in by-gone days, was used to restrain and disgrace the unlucky individual who so far forgot himself on market days as to get drunk. Wheeled to the left here, the running being heavy until we hit off the highway between Blairgowrie and Coupar Augus; then bearing to the right, we worked up an incline to the latter town, and at 2.0 p.m. discussed a well-cooked meal at the "Royal" hotel.

Our course from Dunkeld, although rapid, having been very erratic, I asked if we could have done better, and was told that we had come perfectly right.

3.45 p.m. Journeyed from Coupar Angus to Glammis, through a flat open country. Being uncertain of the road at one point, I applied to a little girl for information. She first murmured softly, " I dinna ken;" then observing that we were "foreigners," she corrected herself and said, " I don't know."

Having obtained an order from the agent, who politely invited us to afternoon tea, we cycled through Glammis Park to the antique chateau, a lofty pile, with numerous pepper-pot turrets. The housekeeper did the honours, and explained that the tapestry, furniture, and everything in the interior, even to the lady's spinning wheel in the drawing room, was kept exactly as it had been handed down from generation to generation. In fact, while wandering from room to room, it seemed to us as though the world's history had been rolled back five or six hundred years for our especial benefit. We were shown the room in which King Malcolm died,* his bedstead and curtains bearing the date 1083—

Prince Charlie's bed and boots.

The coat Claverhouse was wearing when shot.

Some needlework by Queen Mary, &c., &c.

There are many secret stair-cases, and our curiosity was greatly excited about a mysterious chamber in which it is supposed that certain former occupants of the castle are doomed to play at cards until the Day of Judgment. This apartment is not open to the public!

After enjoying an excellent view of Forfar and Strathmore from the roof, we left the grounds by a different gate, and, as it was getting late, P. ran on to secure rooms at Brechin.

I was riding at a moderate pace through the suburbs of Forfar, when observing some little girls dancing in the road ahead of me, I repeatedly sounded my gong. All cleared off except one little

* According to tradition, Malcolm II. was murdered in this Castle.

AN ACCIDENT.

thing about seven years old. As she still continued to act the part of a teetotum, I shouted, whereupon she ceased to turn round and made to the right. I steered to the left, when suddenly she darted in front of me. In an instant she was down, and *bump, bump, bump, went the three wheels over her!!* Horror stricken I leapt off (my tricycle did not capsize) to pick up the mangled remains.

These Scotch children *are* chips of the old block; she was off like a bird before I could get near her, but once within the shadow of her own home, a torrent of tears burst forth. I hastened there and enquired for her mother. She was out. Finding that the child had only sustained a few scratches, I thought that a silver coin might prove a sovereign remedy, and tendered one to a woman who now came to the front. By her direction I gave it to the sufferer's sister, who looked at me as much as to say, "I wish you would run over sissy every day." I, who had expected to be torn to pieces by an infuriated mob, was surprised to find that the bystanders were indignant with the poor little dear for getting in my way.

Feeling very hungry, I stopped at a confectioner's shop to have something to eat. My "Cheylesmore" immediately became the centre of attraction to a vast crowd, and as they were beginning to pull it about, I was obliged to seize a bun and be off. At the outskirts of the town a number of people were playing at cricket; directly they sighted me, they one and all dropped their gear, and rushed in my direction with yells of delight, but in self defence I was obliged to distance them.

Although the road was fairly level, it had been rutty and loose all the way from Coupar Angus to a bridge across the Esk, about five miles from Brechin; from that point it improved to the town, where, at 9.15 p.m., I found P. at the "Crown" inn.

Over our evening pipe, P. told me that, while I was hunting up the agent at Glammis, he had had an amusing conversation with the lodge-keeper's wife.

He described her as being a stout, merry-eyed little woman, with a wonderful complexion, and who evidently looked upon him as a strange being, from a stranger country, on the strangest vehicle. She began by asking—

" Where have you come from on that queer machine ? "

" England," replied P.

" That's where the Southrons live, isn't it ? "

"Yes, and I have come from a Southern county, Kent."
"Aye, and are the people the same there as they are hereabouts?'
"Oh yes, much about the same—not quite so good looking."
"Are there any fields and crops there?"
"Bless you, yes, why it's called the Garden of England."
"Sheep, too?"
"Lots of them, only they have white-faces."
"Eh! but you ain't got coos as weel?"

At this moment I appeared, and broke in upon the conversation.

DISTANCE.

Dunkeld to Coupar Angus	.. 15 miles.	Erratic, but rideable; surfac excellent.
Coupar Angus to Forfar	.. 18 ,,	Level; rather loose.
Forfar to Brechin	.. .. 13 ,,	Level; rather loose.
Total	.. 46 ,,	

Very fine.

TWENTIETH DAY.

BRECHIN, DUNNOTTAR, KINEFF, MONTROSE.

CONTINUOUS rain had kept us prisoners at Brechin all yesterday. It cleared in the evening, and we walked to the beautiful little cemetery, which is kept like a Botanical Garden, then visited the cathedral and the adjacent round tower.* The early morning to-day was employed in inspecting Brechin Castle; it is prettily situated on the precipitous banks of the South Esk, and has made its mark in history.

9 a.m. Left Brechin for Stonehaven. The first five miles of the road, from being confined by trees and hedges, was very muddy, but further on the country became open and the running splendid. Our way lay along the tops of the hills above Strathmore, thus affording us a fine view of that fertile vale.

The last four miles into Stonehaven was done in grand style— L.O.H. It was noon, and P. was inclined to have something to

* This famous round tower is quite a distinct erection from the Cathedral; it is constructed of large stones running round in sloping courses, which rise above each other like a screw forming one spiral course from top to bottom. The East side is perpendicular, but it is about 3 feet off the plumb line on the West. Height 103ft., circumference 50ft. Tradition ascribes the erection of this singular building to the Picts.

eat; I, on the contrary, was in a fever to see Dunnottar before the threatening rain came on, so P. good naturedly gave way to my wishes, and after working our machines up a mile of hill, we left them at a farm house.

Not doubting that the ruins would be open and tenantless, I had not made any enquiries about them, my only anxiety being to get there. We were surprised to find the entrance locked, and were still more astonished when told that there was no admittance without a bookseller's pass. This was very provoking, and I became painfully conscious that my impulsiveness had as usual caused me to make a mess of it. As P. was not keen about seeing the Castle, I agreed to count it as being "done," but before many minutes had elapsed I confessed to him that if Dunnottar was thus neglected, I should reproach myself ever after.

Again P. conceded to my wishes, remarking, "Well, having come thirty miles out of our way on purpose to see it, perhaps it would be rather absurd to be too lazy to go back one."

In a very short time we had our passes in our pockets (1s.), and were being waited upon by a merry bare-armed lassie, who not only cooked and laid our luncheon with celerity and dexterity, but also served us with some smart repartees as occasions presented themselves. That aid to digestion, risibility, soon left us free to resume our travels, and once again we walked up the steep path which is the only approach to Dunnottar.* The isolated rock on which it is built is the most remarkable mass of conglomerate that I have ever seen. The pebbles are quite round, and it shows the different stages of construction most clearly.

* Dunnottar was built by Sir William Keith during the wars between England and Scotland, in the reign of Edward I. In 1296 it was taken from the English by Sir William Wallace. Edward III. retook it, only to be re-captured by Sir Andrew Murray, Regent of Scotland. During the time of the Commonwealth it was selected, as the strongest place in the kingdom, for the preservation of the Regalia. The garrison, under the command of Ogilvy of Barras, held out as long as they could against the English, but were ultimately reduced by famine. Previous to this, however, the Regalia were conveyed by stratagem in the following manner. Mrs. Granger, wife of the minister of Kineff, obtained permission to visit Mrs. Ogilvy, who entrusted her with the crown, which she concealed in her lap; while the sceptre and sword, wrapt up in bundles of flax, were placed on the back of a female domestic. The English General himself is said to have courteously placed Mrs. Granger in her saddle, little dreaming of the treasure she had about her person. On the Castle being taken in 1652, Mrs. Ogilvy would not divulge the secret, and died in close confinement. The Regalia was kept in the double-bottomed bed, and under the pulpit, at Kineff, until the restoration. At the Union the Regalia was stowed away in a chest in Edinburgh. It was rumoured for years that it had been removed to England, until George IV. issued a warrant for a search. The chest in which they were supposed to be returned a hollow sound to the stroke of the hammer, but the joy was extreme when, the ponderous lid being forced open the Regalia was found exactly as it had been left in 1797.

Hitherto, guides had been carefully eschewed by us, but here we were obliged to go round with the old man in charge. He told us how he used to play about the ruin in his youth, and how during his lengthened service as a soldier, he had treasured in his memory every nook and corner of the dear old place. Now, at the ripe age of eighty years, he had reached the height of his ambition, namely, to spend the decline of his life among the stones he loved so well. He was a great deal too fond of them to please us, for, impervious to even the broadest hint, the old gentleman continued to spin us long benders about every little detail. This we had to endure, for neither of us had the heart to cut him short. In good faith, all he related would have greatly interested us had we not been in a tearing hurry to get on.

Our attention was chiefly attracted by—

(1). The room in which the Regalia had been kept.

(2). The opening through which Wallace and his gallant followers entered, and took the fort.

(3). The curious portholes.

(4). The Well,—the great life sustainer during the lengthened sieges of the Castle.

(5). The Covenanters' Dungeon.* In this place certain Covenanters, huddled together like the victims in the Black Hole of Calcutta, were dying of thirst: when, as the story goes, in answer to their prayers a spring of water gushed from the rock and relieved their sufferings. It is there still; we drank of it, and noticed a peculiar mineral taste, which cannot be accounted for by analysts, so our guide informed us. In one corner of the den we saw the spot where the unhappy prisoners had undermined the wall and escaped from their confinement, only to be shot or recaptured.†

When all had been seen, P. declared that it would have been a thousand pities to have given this historical place the go-by. After " remembering " our venerable cicerone, we sought out our ever willing and ready steeds, and turned their heads towards Montrose.

The strong wind, which had so materially assisted us from Brechin to Stonehaven, had now to be contended with, but the splendid condition of the track made up for this disadvantage. Being

---

* In 1685, 167 of the Covenanters were thrust into this vault, where many of them died.

† " Some hung on crags, right dolefully to dee,
Some lap, some fell, some fluttered in the sea."

anxious to trace the Regalia through all its remarkable adventures, I parted company from P. at a hamlet about 5 miles from Dunnottar, and went down by a steep rough road to the quaint village Kineff, on the edge of the Cliff. I called on the minister, who very kindly showed me the room in the Manse (still called the Regalia Room), in which it had at first been secreted; then proceeding to the Kirk, he pointed out the place in front of the pulpit where it had been kept in safety for so many years. A tablet has been erected to Granger; the following is a translation of the inscription as given me by my reverend friend :—

> "Behold the spot where Granger's ashes lie,
> Who, from besieged Dunnottar, safe conveyed
> The insignia of Scotland's royalty,
> And in this hallowed ground in secret laid,
> Where now he rests himself; Heaven shall bestow
> Meet recompense on such desert as his—
> He, who his country's honour saved below,
> Now wields a sceptre in the realms of bliss."

I was surprised to find that, in spite of all that is to be seen and heard here, Kineff is seldom visited by tourists.

Another bye-way took me into the high road, which undulates on a line parallel to the coast. From Bervie, a long incline led me up to an elevated plateau, from whence, at a distance of eight miles, Montrose, on a low peninsular, could be clearly distinguished, also a plain stretching for miles to the Southward.

There was a pleasant slope of three miles from the high land to the level ground. The only noticeable object during the remaining five was the fine bridge over the North Esk.

On reaching Montrose, I was glad to see P.'s familiar form outside the "Queen's" hotel, where we roosted.

DISTANCE.

Brechin to Stonehaven ..	..	25 miles.	Splendid road; all hills rideable.
Stonehaven to Montrose	..	23 ,,	Splendid road.
Highway to Kineff and back ..		3 ,,	Bad.
Total	..	51 ,,	

Fine; strong Westerly wind.

TWENTY-FIRST DAY.

Montrose, Arbroath, Dundee, St. Andrews.

Montrose is noted for its cleanliness.

9 a.m. Crossed the suspension bridge, then turned to the right, and with difficulty worked up a long ascent to the top of the brae. From thence the road dipped down one side of the ravine in which Inverkeilor is situated, and up on the other side, then it became level, and continued so to Arbroath. The soil being of a light character, the surface of the road was very loose; the scenery, too, was bleak and monotonous.

The ruins of the Abbey* stand on the north side of the tower; they are very extensive, and the remnants show what an immense building it must have been. The most interesting object is the stone marking William the Lion's grave.† P., on being shown some of this monarch's bones, was intensely disgusted, and wanted to know why they couldn't "let the poor devil rest in peace!"

While riding about the grounds I had occasion to use the clutch-gear for the first time during the tour, and it revenged itself for this slight on my part by jamming, thus compelling me to take the crank gear to pieces, and giving me nearly an hour's dirty work before I could resume my journey.

Passing through Arbroath—a busy place—we traversed a flat uninteresting country, on a heavy road, and had Dundee and the ruins of Tay bridge in sight for some time before our arrival. Paddling by a beautiful Cemetery, we entered the town at 3.30, and rode through its well-paved streets to Lamb's "Temperance."

After some refreshment at this first-class hotel, we had a look at some of the principal buildings, and went into the Public Library; then, regardless of the rain which had now set in, we crossed by the 5.5. ferry to Newport. On landing, a steep hill had to be overcome; the rest of the way to St. Andrews was fairly level and the road good. By the time I had reached the Links the rain had ceased, and I saw a number of golf players intent on the game.

When I arrived at the "Cross Keys," P.—who had gone on ahead—was cleaning his bicycle. His good example caused me to set to

---

* Founded in 1178 by William the Lion. The dimensions were:—Length, 270ft.; breadth 45ft. There is still one entire tower at the N.W. corner, 70ft. high. At the Reformation it was destroyed by fire. The style of architecture was a combination of Saxon and Norman.

† I am told that William the Lion was not buried there at all.

work on my machine, so, throwing my mackintosh across the palings, I employed myself for half-an-hour or more in removing the mud and rust. I then passed into the hall, and seeing a waterproof which I took to be mine, I told "Boots" to hang it up to dry, and thought no more about it.

DISTANCE.

Montrose to Arbroath	..	12 miles.	Rather hilly and loose.
Arbroath to Dundee ..	..	17 „	Level; rather heavy.
Newport to St. Andrews	..	11 „	Very good.
Total		„ 40 „	

Showery afternoon.

TWENTY-SECOND DAY.

ST. ANDREWS, COUPAR FIFE.

In the forenoon we first visited the ruins of the Cathedral;* only one tower, and some parts of the wall, are standing. At the Castle, the window where Archbishop Sharpe sat to witness the burning of Wishart was pointed out to us, and the Parish Church† completed our sight-seeing.

St. Andrews is a clean and peaceful little town; there are good sands, and I should say that it would be a pleasant place to spend a month or two during the summer.

I had just trotted out my tricycle, when I remembered my waterproof, and sent Boots for it; he returned saying that it could not be found, and he thought that I had not brought it in.

"Why, don't you recollect my telling you to hang it up?" said I.

"Yes, sir, but the other gentleman said it belonged to him."

"Then where is mine? It must be somewhere," exclaimed I.

"Well, sir, I can't find it."

Without losing my temper I suggested to the landlord, who stood by, that he was responsible for articles lost in his house.

* The Cathedral was a magnificent Gothic structure; when entire it had six spires or turrets. One at the West end still remains, and is 100 feet in height. It was destroyed by the mob in 1559.

† In the Parish Church is a grand monument to Archbishop Sharpe, and the pulpit from which John Knox preached his celebrated sermon.

In the midst of the argument it flashed across me that I had left it on the palings in the back yard. While looking about there, the landlord quietly remarked, "Is that it?"

I leaned over the palings; and could just distinguish little bits of my unfortunate mackintosh mixed up with the straw and dirt of a hitherto unnoticed pig-stye. The nasty brutes had pulled it down and torn it to shreds.

In sorrow, I told P. that my brand-new and expensive waterproof had gone, not " to the dogs," but to the pigs!

Leaving St. Andrews, we returned four miles on the Newtown road, and turned off it to the left after crossing Eden river, pursuing our way to Coupar Fife. There we housed ourselves for the night, but not before we had got a good ducking in a heavy squall, which burst upon us.

DISTANCE.

St. Andrews to Coupar .. .. 9 miles. Very good road. Wet afternoon.

TWENTY-THIRD DAY.

COUPAR FIFE, FALKLAND, KIRCALDY, DUNFERMLINE.

AFTER breakfast, being cooped up by the rain, I set about replacing the garment which had come to such an untimely end. No more 50s. articles for me was my resolve, as I stepped into a shop having a golden calf for a sign. Out of many that were presented to me I selected a light and serviceable mackintosh, and demanded the price. Five shillings!! The bargain was instantaneously closed, and I may here mention that this marvel of cheapness, owing to my preserving it in a case when not in use, survived the whole tour.

Noon. Took our departure from Coupar Fife, and traversed the ups and downs of the Kircaldy road to a hamlet called Kettle. There we struck off for Falkland, a pretty village under the Lomond hills. We obtained an order for the Palace,* in which, however, there was little of interest to be seen; then, being, as usual, on the look-out for a cheap meal, we ordered a beefsteak at the "Commercial."

* A favourite resort of James VI.

After having been kept waiting ever so long the meat appeared, but it was nearly cold before the potatoes were brought in. We then set to work, only to find that we could not make our teeth meet through the steak, so we had to make the best of it on bread and cheese, and rang for the bill. The stereotyped half-a-crown again! We felt ripe for a row, but the pretty and innocent face of our little waitress saved her mother from so dire a catastrophe.

We found our way to the Kircaldy road again by one which ran along the foot of Lomond hill, and paddled through an undulating fertile country to Dysart, Pathead, and Kircaldy, which together form one continuous town three miles in length. The ill-paved streets were too rough for riding, so there was no escape from the ever-increasing crowd of admirers, whose attentions I fear we did not appreciate.

There being a doubt concerning the best way to Dunfermline, we asked the opinion of four different people. Two gentlemen strongly advised us to go round by Burntisland; on the other hand, two coach-drivers would have us go by Kiltree. Deciding for the latter we turned to the right at the South end of Kircaldy.

The road was steep at first, and continued to rise at different gradients for three miles, it then dipped down to a vale among the hills. Turning to the left we crossed the level sward, then ran down a long decline to a reservoir in the hollow. On a rise just above this we had a pretty rural scene before us, knolls, clumps of trees, cultivated slopes, and pasture land dotted by sheep and cattle, with flashes of blue water here and there.

After running down hill for some distance we turned sharp to the right on to the main road from Burntisland to Kinross, and a stiff ascent took us to the summit of the range, from whence was a grand view of the noble Forth and its islands. On the opposite shore Edinburgh, Leith, Grantown, Newhaven, and Portobello seemed to be one immense city, the castle proudly overlooking the whole.

While standing here my feelings were stirred at the thought of the mighty wave of human life that was surging so near me, bearing onwards thousands of my fellow creatures with their manifold joys and sorrows.

A few yards further showed the inland view, with the tall chimneys and church steeples, and Dunfermline on an eminence in the distance. The road, which all the way from Kircaldy had been hilly, loose, and stony, now descended into the valley bay succession of abrupt dips of a dangerous nature, it then undulated to Crossgates. Being much fagged we had arranged to sleep at that place, if possible, but finding it to be a mining village we pushed on the remaining three and a-half miles to Dunfermline.

I asked a policeman to recommend an inn; he directed me to "White's" hotel in a certain street. On our way down the name Wright attracted my attention, and as it answered his description, we hurried in to escape the crowd. It proved to be a mistake but, although the house was small, the people were civil, everything was very clean, and we could not have done better.

I felt more fatigue after this day's journey than on any occasion since leaving Alnwick. The roads were bad enough, but the strong gale which had been against us nearly all day was still more distressing.

DISTANCE.

Coupar Fife to Kircaldy, via
Falkland .. .. .. 21 miles.
Kircaldy to Dunfermline .. 14 „
Total .. 35 „

Fine; strong wind against.

TWENTY-FOURTH DAY.
DUNFERMLINE, KINROSS.

WHILST struggling against the strong wind yesterday, we had consoled ourselves by imagining how gaily our vehicles would run before it on leaving Dunfermline. Unfortunately this morning there was a light air from the opposite direction, and a drizzling rain. Visited the Abbey* after breakfast. It is on the brink of a pretty glen, and the adjoining ruins of the Palace partially concealed in dense foliage had a most romantic effect. The East end of the Abbey has been rebuilt, and is used as a Kirk. The plain deal pews covered with dirty finger marks, and a gallows-like pulpit formed, in our opinion, an unseemly contrast to the magnificent architecture. We were shown the spot under which Robert Bruce's skeleton is said to have been found. In the nave are two pillars

* Dunfermline was the favourite residence of the Scottish Kings, and is associated with Margaret, the canonized Queen of Malcolm of Canmore, who fled to Scotland when William the Conqueror ascended the English throne. She conferred the name of Queen's Ferry on that well-known passage across the Forth. Both Malcolm and Margaret are interred in the Abbey. The Abbey was endowed by David I. The Abbots were mitred by the express permission of the Pope. It was burnt by Edward I., and again destroyed by the Reformers in 1560. The modern Church is attached to the old one, but its Gothic design presents a strange contrast to the sombre Saxon style of the old chancel.

marked with zig-zag lines in such a manner as to produce an optical illusion. At one point of view the lower part appears to be of greater diameter than the upper; at another, the effect is exactly the reverse. The stone work of the balustrade at the top of the tower consists of letters, which form the words " King Robert the Bruce." After promenading this active thriving town, we prepared for a start, the rain having ceased.

3 p.m. Returned to Crossgates, and took the highway Northward. In spite of the Scotch mist which soon enveloped us, we quite enjoyed the run to Kinross, the surface of the road being firm, smooth, and of a peculiarly springy nature; moreover, the day was calm—a great boon to us after yesterday's buffetting.

4.20 p.m. Arrived at Kinross, and giving the fashionable hotel a wide berth, we presently came to the "Salutation." Neither the name nor the exterior of the inn took our fancy, but the rooms on inspection proved satisfactory, and we settled down for the evening. Later on it cleared up, and we walked down and had a look at the Castle.*

DISTANCE.
Dunfermline to Kinross .. .. 13 miles.
Scotch mist.

TWENTY-FIFTH DAY.
KINROSS, PERTH, CRIEFF.

HEAVY rain. At noon P.—who refused to believe in my prophecy that it would be fine—started for Crieff wishing to get there early. 12.30. I left Kinross under a blue sky. The road was dead level to Glen Farg, but the tenacious mud played great havoc with my poor tyre, and I had not gone far before a bit of it came loose; I immediately dismounted and tied it on. A mile further, and another inch was sucked out of the felloe. I stopped again to secure that, and so on through the day, things getting worse and worse as I proceeded, until at last it was tied all round. By that time the first bit of string had worn through, &c., &c. Very trying to the temper.

* The unfortunate Queen Mary was kept a prisoner within these walls after her surrender at Carberry Hill. Her escape was accomplished after somewhat less than eleven months of captivity. It was the habit of the Castellair to have the key of the Castle gate placed on a table beside him when at supper. The page (William Douglas) who served at table contrived in placing a plate before him to drop a napkin on the key, and in lifting the napkin to lift the key with it. He then slipped out with the Queen. They gained the gate unperceived, locked it behind them, and put off in the boat which lay at hand for the use of the garrison, the Queen herself handling an oar.—*Royal School History of Scotland.*

The run of four miles through Glen Farg was rendered charming by the tender beauty of its wooded cliffs, and it was at just the right angle for L.O.H. From the foot of the glen a verdant plain extended for two miles to Bridge Earnhead. I then had to walk nearly two miles up Moncrieff Hill, and was riding the latter part of the ascent, when suddenly the view,* so graphically described in the Fair Maid of Perth, lay before me. The following is an extract from that book :—

He beheld, stretching beneath him, the valley of the Tay, traversed by its ample and lordly stream; the town of Perth, with its two large meadows or inches, its steeples and its towers; the hills of Moncrieffe and Kinnoul faintly rising into picturesque rocks, partly clothed with woods; the rich margin of the river, studded with elegant mansions; the distant view of the huge Grampian mountains, the Northern screen of this exquisite landscape.

I kept to the West side of Perth, and took some refreshment at the Railway Station. I then struck into the Crieff road, and passed close to Huntingtower,† which I did not think worth paying half-a-crown to see. The road which, although muddy, had been very good from Kinross, now narrowed, deteriorated, and was against the collar more or less for the last ten miles to Crieff. What with this, an adverse wind, and the shaky state of my bandaged tyre, I was heartily glad at 6.15 to find myself once more under my friend's hospitable roof, where P. had already established himself.

DISTANCE.

Kinross to Perth	17 miles.
Perth to Crieff	17 ,,
Total ..	34 ,,

Fine while travelling, then wet.

RETROSPECT.

BOTH P. and myself thoroughly enjoyed the tour we had taken together. On the whole the weather had been most favourable, permitting us to see everything at its best. The beauty of the scenery, and the excellent condition of the roads, had far exceeded our most sanguine expectations.

* The ancient Romans, in their passage over the same ground, hailed the scenery with "Ecce Tiber!" "Ecce Campus Martius!"
† Celebrated for the Raid of Ruthven.

The attention of the two "foreigners" was chiefly attracted by—

(1.) The abundance of pure water provided for man and beast, not only in towns and villages, but even in the out-of-the-way places where troughs full are frequently to be seen by the road side.

(2.) The unvarying civility of the lower classes.

(3.) In England any imposing detached building is pretty certain to be either a lunatic asylum or a workhouse. In Scotland it is the hydropathic establishment. These magnificent structures are nothing more nor less than temperance hotels on a large scale. Their low prices (three guineas a week, including baths) and excellent arrangements have rendered them very popular, and they are generally crammed during the season.

(4.) We thought that the use of soup plates for pudding, although a novelty, was a sensible fashion, as milk could be used *ad lib.*; but what surprised us more than anything else I have mentioned was to see our Scotch friends *peppering* their strawberries and cream. It was some time before I could make up my mind to try the experiment, but on doing so I fancied that it did bring out the flavour.

BICYCLE *v.* TRICYCLE.

My opinion concerning the great advantage of the tricycle on a long tour has been rather shaken by the admirable way in which P. has handled his Bicycle.

(1.) He always had the speed of me.

(2.) He has had less trouble in cleaning and stowing away.

(3.) By means of an iron framework—secured to the machine by a double hook, fitted to the handle-bar—he has been enabled to carry almost as much luggage as myself.

However, although my machine carried extra weight (*vide* first day), and had not all the latest improvements, I did not cause P. much delay. Therefore, as I consider him to be an exceptionally clever bicyclist, I would still advise the majority of tourists to take to the tricycle.

PART III.

T., who had answered my advertisement, and whom I had subsequently seen, had promised to meet me at Perth, on July 15th. That day being now close at hand, P. signified his intention of returning to England. To my suggestion that we should all go together for some distance, he replied with the old adage, "Two is company, three is none," but I persuaded him to take a run to the north on his own account before going home.

We parted.

From the first day of my tour I became aware that my strengthened tricycle was too heavy for my light weight in this hilly country, and I therefore ordered a new "Cheylesmore" of the ordinary weight, with crank ball bearings, to be sent to Crieff by July 10th.

On July 13th I heard that the machine could not be despatched before the 20th. This news decided me to go on with the old one for the present, every day being precious. I set to work to take the whole thing to pieces, and after thoroughly cleaning it I once more stuck on the intractable tyre with india-rubber solution. I should have sent for the proper composition long ago, had I not been expecting to get a new vehicle.

On July 14th I heard from T., to say that he had arrived at Perth, but as he was minus his tricycle, and was not sure when it would turn up, he recommended me to go on, and leave him to overtake me by rail. The weather being favourable, I fell in with his plan, and having sent him a programme of my intended movements, I, on July 15th, bade farewell to my friends at Crieff.

TWENTY-SIXTH DAY.

Crieff, Dunkeld, Blair Athole.

ELEVEN a.m. Began the journey by a continuous ascent, and turned to the left at Monzie. About two hundred yards beyond that village the road forks; took the right up the brae. Cyclists are advised to walk up this long incline. Near the top is a fine vista of the pastoral vale to the S.W., with pretty Comrie lying under the hills. Passing the tempting looking road to the right at the sixth milestone, I entered Sma Glen, which is flanked by high and rugged cliffs. These acted as a funnel to the wind, and in some places it was difficult even to walk against it.

Near the head of the pass is a large stone, which is supposed to have once covered Ossian's tomb.

" Ossian, last of all his race,
Lies buried in this lonely place."

The road now crosses the stream, and striking over a rough brae, slopes down to Amulree, a hamlet in a dreary waste, possessing an inn. About two miles from Amulree the road again forks. The left goes to Aberfeldy; the right, which I followed, declines through Stath Bruan to Dunkeld, the scenery becoming more and more pleasing as the town is approached.

I lunched at Dunkeld,* then rode up the hill by the Duke of Athole's park, and through magnificent covers of birch and larch. From thence, a verdant strath, watered by the Tummel, could be seen stretching away to the Grampian range. I enjoyed about nine miles of level road before reaching Pitlochrie, a clean village with a fine hydropathic establishment. This favourite place was already alive with tourists.

The cyclist will find that the reputed charms of the scenery from Pitlochrie, through the pass of Killiecrankie, are not by any means exaggerated. Its characteristic is sylvan beauty.

I stopped at the guide's house, and, while waiting for the "gude mon," his buxom spouse entertained me by displaying her curiosities. Amongst other things was the skin of a large snake from her native home, Brisbane (Australia). On hearing I was well acquainted with that town she almost embraced me in her enthusiasm, and

*Visit the Duke of Athole's grounds. The road to Blairgowrie is hilly, but the scenery is very fine.

poured forth a volley of questions ; after which she insisted upon my partaking of her hospitality in the shape of unlimited milk and oatcake.

On receiving my shilling her husband took me to the Queen's View, pointed out the "Soldier's Leap," and sang some Gaelic songs as per routine. I must confess to having been rather disappointed with this particular part of the glen. The stone which marks the spot where Claverhouse was killed lies at some little distance from the road.

I asked my guide, who was equally well acquainted with English and Gaelic, which language he considered the more expressive. He replied, that when speaking on any subject that required explanation, he could make himself more clearly understood in Gaelic.

My tyre having played "fast and loose" with me for so long, the crank gear now got out of order by way of variety. Constant friction had caused the right cog wheel to revolve loosely on the crank shaft, thus giving it play to cant and jam, which greatly increased the labour of driving.

On reaching Blair I at once went to a blacksmith, and took the cam arrangement to pieces for his inspection. He put on a thin

A VISIT TO THE BLACKSMITH.

zinc washer, which had the effect of making the wheel revolve more truly.

It was 9.30 before my steed was housed at the Tilt Bridge Hotel.

DISTANCE.

Crieff to Dunkeld	.. .. 22 miles.	Very good road.
Dunkeld to Pitlochrie	.. .. 11½ „	Capital running.
Pitlochrie to Blair	.. .. 8½ „	Delightful ride.
Total	.. 42 „	

Bright sunshiny day.

TWENTY-SEVENTH DAY.

BLAIR ATHOLE, DALWHINNIE, LOCH LAGGAN, ROY BRIDGE.

At the hotel I made the acquaintance of a gentleman on a pedestrian tour, and we agreed to visit the Bruan Falls together.

8.15 a.m. Left Blair,[*] soon overtaking my friend, to whom I had given a quarter of an hour's start, and we jogged on together three miles, until we reached a farmhouse, where I left my tricycle. Passing through the entrance gate (6d.), we walked up one side of

[*] A charming neighbourhood. By all accounts the falls of Fender and Tummel are worth seeing, and Glen Tilt is grand.

the falls and down the other, taking views from both summer-houses. These falls will be pretty enough by-and-by, when the foliage is thicker, but at present they hardly realise one's expectations.

Parting from my temporary companion, I resumed my journey towards Dalwhinnie, when the road at once became narrow and stony. After undulating for a mile or two, it ascended through a defile, which became more and more dreary as I advanced.

11 a.m. Arrived at Dalnacardoch. Two or three cottages and one large house, which I must warn cyclists is an inn no more, or they may have the same sad experience as P.

In a letter he told me that shortly after he left Blair a drenching rain set in, but disregarding this he pushed on to Dalnacardoch, expecting to find accommodation for the night, which was coming on. On arriving there just before dark, he was nonplussed at finding that the inn had been done away with for eighteen years, and he had the choice of going back eleven miles, or forward fourteen. He preferred the latter.

I succeeded in getting some light refreshment, and on I went. Thus far I had managed to escape the fresh metal by keeping on the edge of the road; but from this point the surface of the "highway to the Highlands" became almost as bad as that between Tyndrum and Dalmally, the only difference being that it was firmer, and that the loose stones were not quite so large. To make the matter worse, I had to contend with a constant incline and a strong head wind, while the dismal solitude and a searching shower made me pretty miserable. Altogether it seemed the longest fourteen miles I had ever cycled.

Even Dalwhinnie, three houses on a bare plain, surrounded by most uninteresting hills, was to me a very pleasant sight, and I was soon set up again by a hot meal at this hotel, which stands higher than any in Scotland. Some anglers were staying in the house, and getting very good sport in Loch Ericht.

3.15 p.m. Started for Loch Laggan.

Turned to the left after crossing the bridge half a mile from the hotel, and had some difficulty in pushing my tricycle up the steep brae, which is conspicuous from Dalwhinnie. The surface now changed to sand, alternately hard and soft, and I experienced steep ups and downs, principally the latter, for from four to five miles.

MISTAKEN.

Before descending into it I had a very good view of Laggan Vale and its village. It was pleasant to see green fields and a sprinkling of trees again. The road now dipped down through Cartlig. About a mile beyond that hamlet I turned to the left and ran between ranges of hills, the wooded slope of Lochaber being on the right.

The road and scenery now changed for the better, and the view about three miles from Loch Laggan,[*] being of a similar nature, is almost as lovely as the Trossachs.

When about two miles from the lake I saw a house on an eminence, and knowing an inn to be near, I took this to be it. To make sure, I asked a boy, who confirmed my supposition.

Putting my tricycle into the yard, I calmly walked into the parlour and rang the bell. When the maid appeared I ordered tea, and asked how long she would be about it. On her replying, "Half-an-hour," I said, "Oh, come, I can't wait so long as that. Look alive, I'm in a hurry." Promising to bring it as soon as possible, she disappeared, but the next minute a very dignified matron came in, saying, "This is not an hotel, sir; it's a private house."

Moved by my apologies, she took compassion on my disappointed looks, and brought in a jug of milk. I don't know whether it was cream or what, but a more delicious draught I have never taken. It seemed fairly to melt in my mouth. Being thus fortified, I did not stop at Loch Laggan Inn, attractive though it was, but pushed on for Moy.

The spin along the margin of the lake, through birch and rowan was very enjoyable. I understand that the fishing is good, and that the antiquary finds plenty to interest him in the vicinity. On losing the shelter of the trees towards the west end of the loch, the strong headwind began to tell upon me, and I was glad to rest myself at Moy inn, which, although small, afforded me an ample tea for eighteenpence.

About 7.30 I was off again.

The bleak sides of Glen Spean gradually incline to one another until they almost meet at Tulloch; here the Spean river makes a fine dash through a narrow channel. For a mile or two beyond Tulloch the road runs horizontally on a raised beach, and I

---
[*] "A very good trouting loch. The tenant of Loch Laggan hotel has liberty for his guests to fish the loch. The best months are from June to September."—*Sportsman's Guide.*

clearly traced the corresponding one on the opposite side of the gully. Mountains now showed themselves ahead, fine fellows with grand precipices. Patches of snow were still lying on Mount Ardnoch.

A decline of three or four miles through feathery copses carried me to Roy Bridge inn.

DISTANCE.

Blair to Dalnacardoch	11 miles.	Loose; stony.
Balnacardoch to Dalwhinnie ..	14 „	One of the few bad roads in Scotland.
Dalwhinnie to Loch Laggan inn	12 „	Good on the whole, but hilly and soft in places.
Loch Laggan inn to Roy Bridge	25 „	Excellent; hard gravel.
Total ..	62 „	

Strong wind ahead; one shower, otherwise fine.

TWENTY-EIGHTH DAY.
GLEN ROY, FORT WILLIAM.

BRIDGE of Roy (a post-office and a few scattered houses) is on a small plain at the junction of Glen Roy and Glen Spean. The inn is but little frequented, and though the landlord was civil, I am sorry to add that the cooking and attendance were indifferent.

After breakfast I trudged up Glen Roy, the lower part of which is a sheep-walk. Having gone three miles, I came to a fenced-in stone, on which a cup was roughly carved. It appears that Mass had once been said there, and the spot has since been guarded as holy ground.

A mile beyond this I had an excellent view of the three celebrated parallel roads. They were clearly marked on the steep sides of the glen, which bent to the right from the point where they commenced —five miles from the inn. So remarkable was their appearance that it seemed as if someone had gone up on each side of the glen and traced them with a pair of gigantic rulers. I walked up to and along all three roads, noticing that their counterparts were equally distinct. They are supposed to be raised beaches or terraces, formed either by the action of the sea as the land rose, or by a pent-up loch, which released itself in stages. The height of the lowest terrace from the valley is about five hundred feet (500ft.). From that to the second, 212ft. From the second to the upper 82ft. I made them all about the same width—viz., 20ft.

While pursuing my investigations, heavy rain set in, and on my return I had to wade through streams which I had easily stepped over an hour before. I may mention that this road is just cycleable; but, as it is sandy, I should advise those who have time to go on foot.

My afternoon was unpleasantly disturbed by a drunken farmer, who persisted in relating not only his own private affairs and speculations, but those of his neighbours as well. I feigned deafness, and resorted to other artifices to boom him off, but eventually was obliged to lock the door to keep him out of the parlour.

7 p.m. The rain having ceased, I determined to escape from this comfortless inn, so I packed up my traps and got under way. The mountains looked uncommonly grand, and their summits being swathed in clouds, their apparent height was greatly increased. For three miles, trees afforded some protection from the wind; but I felt the full force of it across the open moor, and the road being very soft from the recent rain, it was hard work getting over the irregular ground between Spean Bridge and Fort William.

On the way I amused myself by stalking grouse, which just here were very numerous. My wheels were sometimes within a few feet of them before they became aware of the proximity of their natural enemy.

My first sight of Fort William on low land by the seaside was not encouraging. I located myself at the "Macdonald Arms," a wee inn, with a tariff to correspond.

DISTANCE.

Roy Bridge to Spean Bridge	3½ miles.	Good.
Spean Bridge to Fort William..	9½ ,,	Ups and downs, good.
Total	13 ,,	

Wet afternoon; fine evening.

TWENTY-NINTH DAY.

FORT WILLIAM, SPEAN BRIDGE, INVERGARRY, TOMDOUN.

My principal object in visiting Fort William was to ascend the highest mountain in Great Britain. In connection with this I asked two questions this morning.

Q. When was the summit of Ben Nevis last visible?

A. We have not seen it for a month.

Q. What do you think of the weather?
A. Impossible to say. Last Saturday is the only fine day we have had for a long time.

The absurdity of waiting for an opportunity for carrying out my wishes was only too apparent. I walked about, and finding that Fort William did not improve on acquaintance, and moreover had an air of gloom which was depressing, I resolved to give up Glencoe and other projected excursions, and to get away at once.

11 a.m. Started for Invergarry.

The ruins of Inverlochy Castle can be clearly seen from the road. I lunched at Spean Bridge, a great improvement on Roy Inn; and as there is only three miles between them, I recommend the tourist to put up here.

The River Spean at the bridge is a fine sight. After crossing it I turned to the left, walked up a long steep brae, and had from the top an effective bird's-eye view of the Great Glen.

A splendid spin of three miles took me down to the shores of Loch Lochie, where an excellent road has been cut out of the hillside close to the water's edge, along which I ran merrily until checked by the spates which cross the path towards the east end.

Beyond the loch the road follows the canal; having crossed it by a bridge I went on by the north side of Loch Oich. The road now gradually rose and trended to the left, until about a mile from Invergarry, when it turned sharp to the right by the river Garry. Not having expected to see anything in particular, I was all the more delighted to find myself in a lovely neighbourhood.

On coming to the bridge over the Garry, I can only describe the beauty of the scene by saying that here Nature has arrayed herself in her wildest charms.

I found Invergarry inn half a mile farther along the north bank. I had tea with an elderly gentleman, who appeared to go in for enjoying life, hunting all the winter and fishing all the summer. From him I gained the following information:—(1) Glengarry caps are named from this glen; (2) the Garry falls should on no account be missed; (3) Tomdoun inn is a good one, and situated in the finest valley in Scotland; (4) the roads on the west coast would be too hilly for my tricycle.

7.30. a.m. All the inhabitants turned out to see me start, a tricycle never having been seen here before. The neat cottages about here assist to ornament the glen. About three miles from the inn, and just before sighting Loch Garry,* I left my machine by the roadside and walked through the wood to the falls.

There is no real fall, but a tremendous rush of water through a very narrow channel, the south side of which is a highly picturesque crag, about 200 feet high. The turbulent surface of the river, the splendid trees, the graceful ferns and mossy banks, together with the lichen-covered rocks, rendered this the most superb view of its kind that I had yet seen.

Having regained my steed, I paddled by Loch Garry. At first it was like riding through a park, but towards the west end the trees ceased, and the upper part of the river was a poor insipid stream, with low banks and haughs. The road, which from Spean Bridge had consisted of hard sand, now became soft, and covered with fresh metal.

Hereabouts I began to look out for the " finest valley in Scotland," but bleaker and bleaker became the way, until Tomdoun,† a solitary inn, was reached at 9.30. It was being enlarged, which was unfortunate, but as I was the only lodger I managed pretty well. While they were preparing my meal I took a survey of this wild place among the hills, and while watching the national game of " throwing the hammer," I felt that I was really in the Highlands.

I had been expecting T. to turn up ever since I started from Crieff, and thought that I should certainly have come across him either at Spean Bridge or at Invergarry. I only wished that he could have been with me to have shared the pleasures of the day.

DISTANCE.

Fort William to Spean Bridge .. 9¼ miles. Ups and downs; good.
Spean Bridge to Invergarry Inn 16 ,, Splendid run by the lake side.
Invergarry Inn to Tomdoun .. 10½ ,, Excellent road.

Total .. 36 ,,

Fine day.

THIRTIETH DAY.

TOMDOUN, GLEN SHIEL, KYLE RHEA, BROADFORD (SKYE).

ALTHOUGH I had arrived late, I decided to make an early start in the morning, and was called at seven; but as the festive rat had

*"The innkeeper gives the fishing, and provides boats free. Abundance of fine heavy trout, and some salmon. Best months May to August."—*Sportsman's Guide.*
†I met a party who had taken splendid baskets in Loch Quoich, and adjacent streams.

kept me awake the best part of the night, I gladly availed myself of the excuse that it was raining, to turn over on the other side and " drive my pigs to market " again.

10 a.m. Started for Cluny. The track struck over a wild mountain range, and I had to walk the greater part of six miles up-hill on soft gravel, then managed to ride across to the northern slope, where I paused for a few minutes to look about me. Mountains, mountains, everywhere.

I rode down into Cluny valley; but as the descent is very precipitous, and there are some awkward corners, I should advise the cyclist not to attempt it. There may have been a few sheep, but to my recollection I did not see a living creature, nor any signs of life from the time I left Tomdoun until I arrived at Cluny. This little inn stands by itself in a dreary situation, and I did not meet with a cheery reception; in fact it was some time before I could make any one hear. The charge for my slight refreshment was high; this I did not so much grudge, as customers must be few and far between in this remote spot.

From Cluny there was a gentle ascent of two miles, the glen up to that point being monotonous. From thence it became extremely narrow, the rugged mountains rising on both sides like gigantic walls, and in some places almost overhanging the road; two or three of the peaks were very singularly shaped. The winding road declined at a pleasant angle, thus enabling me to devote my whole attention to the impressive grandeur of the scene. Some friends, whom I met afterwards, told me that having seen both, they considered Glen Shiel to be almost, if not quite, equal to Glencoe.

At the foot of the pass I came on to a rich haugh, with some shrubs and bushes, and the stream which had flowed rapidly through the glen became a quiet river. There were two or three anglers at the little loch, from whence I ran on level ground to Shiel inn.* There is a wonderful cave somewhere about, but I had not time to see it.

I lunched with an Englishman, who, together with some others, was staying in this secluded place for fishing, and having excellent sport. He laughed heartily at the idea of my attempting to reach Kyle Rhea, and rising from his seat he pointed to a part of the road which could be seen high up on the mountain range, saying:—

---

* The Shiel can be fished for a small charge by residing at Shiel hotel. Rod season from February 11th to October 31st.

HARD CLIMBING.

" How are you going to push your tricycle up there ? I have been that way and know it to be impossible, and as for travelling in Skye as you propose, take my advice and give it up."

I thanked him, but said I should try it on.

3 p.m. Left Shiel inn, the whole household turning out to watch the start, and expressing their opinion that they would soon see me back again.

I turned to the left and managed to ride a short distance, but the gradient becoming more severe, I dismounted, and eventually succeeded in pushing my tricycle up the zigzag road to the summit.

No doubt my late companion would have been amused to see me struggling with my vehicle on some of the steep bits, rendered all the more arduous by the loose gravelly surface. It was indeed hard work. I had to make many halts, and was fairly drenched with perspiration before I drew a long sigh of relief at the top.

While fetching my breath I had a bird's-eye view of Loch Duich; there is about half a mile of arable land along its northern margin, studded with farm-houses.

Having regained my wind I commenced the descent on the other side, and a very remarkable one for a cyclist it was. The side of the glen (More) was very precipitous, and along this a road had been constructed without any parapet or protection whatever, thus I had a vertical wall on one side and a sheer precipice on the other.

I was aware that any slight inattention on my part, or any derangement in the machine, might launch me a distance of five hundred feet or more ;* but as the road was good, declined gently and appeared to be straight, I did not hesitate to cock my legs up and run down. This I did with the utmost caution, and soon found there were some nasty turnings which I had not seen, and the cyclist who has not every confidence in himself and his vehicle should not think of following my example. I ran for nearly, if not quite, six miles, without putting foot to pedal, except for an occasional stroke or two, which I did more to relieve my cramped muscles than for any other reason.

At Bernera I asked three old women the way to Kyle Rhea Ferry. They being speechless, either from astonishment or from not under-

* This Pass of Mam Rattachan is 2,000 ft. above sea level. Johnson, when travelling there, thus described it, "*a terrible steep to climb*, notwithstanding the road is formed slanting along it."

standing English, I took the broader road to the left; when told of my mistake I returned, and quickly covered the mile and a-half that lay between me and the Ferry House.

I was thankful to find smooth water and a slack tide, which enabled me to cross to Skye in a small boat, my tricycle being carefully placed amidships (fare 1s.). On the way over I spied a road winding up a mountain, part of it seemed positively like the side of a house. I nervously asked,

" Where does that road lead to?"

" Broadford, sir."

He might have knocked me down with a feather as I gasped,

" That's where I'm bound."

" Indeed, I expect you'll have a job with that straight up-and-down bit," replied he, with a shrug of the shoulders.

At Shiel Inn I had made fun of my friend's gloomy prognostications, but having done two mountains already, I felt that this unlooked-for third was no joking matter; in fact, the grim-looking range, with its mantle of lowering clouds, seemed an insuperable barrier.

There is a wretched inn on each side of the ferry, and I had some milk and biscuits (charge, eightpence) at the dilapidated building on the Skye side. The landlady told me she could put up a lodger, but I do not myself advise anyone to sleep there.

5.30 p.m. Now came the real business of the day. The climb was steep from the first, and I had the " up-and-down" bit in view all the time, but kept hoping that it would appear less impracticable as I advanced; however, on reaching the foot it looked as bad as ever, and I calculated the angle to be about 70 deg.

Though I have since been told that this was impossible, the gradient was such as to make me fear that I should have to take my tricycle to pieces and carry it up bit by bit; notwithstanding I determined to have a good try first. Grasping the backbone near the little wheel with my right hand, and the frame with my left, I put my shoulder under the saddle, and hove, hove, hove, gaining a foot or so at a time, until after frequent spells I at length succeeded in surmounting this extraordinary bit of road. I rested between whiles by turning my tricycle sideways. The remainder of the ascent was comparatively easy.

AN ANXIOUS MOMENT.

From the top of Bein na-Caillach* I had a commanding view of Sleat Sound, the deep blue water being flecked with the white sails of the coasters.

Having mounted, I was just commencing to move, when a sudden squall burst upon me, and in a second I was being whirled along by a furious gust of wind. To my horror, I discovered that I was being carried at railway speed down a steep pitch, with only a low wall between me and a frightful precipice; moreover, the road twisted in and out in a succession of sharp corners. It was an anxious moment! Had I lost my head for a second nothing could have saved me.

I dared not put too much pressure on the brake, for fear my invalid tyre should pucker up, and cause us to take a double somersault into the yawning abyss. However, I managed to gimlet the machine round the angles, and gradually to bring it under control, when I sprang off, and did not attempt to ride again until the squall was over.

The inland view of Skye was dreary in the extreme—bare high land and bog, without a tree to relieve the monotony. I rode down three miles to the main road, but had to be careful even here, there being a deep cleft one side most of the way. Turning to the left, I had three more miles and a strong head wind, with heavy rain, to encounter before arriving at Broadford inn.†

It was not pleasant after all my toils to be told that I could not be lodged at the hotel, but should have to walk half a mile to and fro through the rain between that and a cottage where I was to sleep. Nine o'clock had struck before I sat down to tea. While toasting myself over the fire afterwards, I read a letter from home, saying that the heat in England was almost insufferable!

DISTANCE.

Tomdoun to Cluny	10¼ miles.	Mountainous, with loose surface.
Cluny to Shiel inn	12 ,,	Very good road; grand scenery.
Shiel inn to Kyle Rhea	11¼ ,,	Mountainous; be cautious.
Kyle Rhea to Broadford	12 ,,	Eight miles of mountain work, then level and good.
Total	46 ,,	

Wet evening.

*The height of this pass is calculated to be two thousand feet.
†Steam launches run to the Spar Cave and Loch Cornisk during the season.

THIRTY-FIRST DAY.
Broadford, Sligachan, Portree.

My room in the cottage was very clean and comfortable, and I managed to dodge the rain when going to and fro. During breakfast I asked my neighbour to tell me what places in Skye would best repay a visit. His reply was, "I have seen nothing. Continuous rain has kept me indoors for the whole fortnight I have been here, and now my holiday is up."

11 a.m. Taking advantage of a lull, I started for Sligachan, and although the rain soon came on again, the surface being good, I managed to get along very well. The road rose a little at first, then declined to the Sound of Scalpa, from thence it went over a hill and down to the head of Loch Ainort.

Here a perfect hurricane of wind and rain drove me into a cottage, or rather a bothie. A fine young fellow was sitting by a low peat fire, some of the smoke from which curled up through a rough wooden chimney, the rest found its way into the room; the windows were small, and the walls very thick. A dog crouched as close to the embers as he could without singeing his tail, and presently some fowls walked in and made themselves quite at home.

My host's story was a melancholy one. The bad weather had driven all the fish out of the bay. He had toiled through the last two nights and had caught nothing. On my remarking that his house seemed to be in a wild spot, he said that it was the stormiest place in Skye; the gusts on some occasions were terrific, making it unsafe for the mail-cart to travel, and he had known it to have been actually blown over.

After we had been chatting about a quarter of an hour, in came a bonnie lassie; I rose to shake hands with her, and she seated herself with all the ease and grace of a lady. " Your wife ? " said I to the man. " My sister," replied he. On my making some commonplace remark with the idea of drawing her out, she merely bowed and smiled, and her brother observed, "She has no English!" so I had recourse to the most eloquent language of all, that of the eye.

By-and-by, there being a slight pause in the war of the elements, I set forth again. My way was barred by a wall of mountains which rose just in front of me, the black storm-cloud which swirled about their sides making them look inexpressibly grand, I might almost say terrible. I had a tough job to get my tricycle on to the shoulder of Glamaig, the gradient being very severe, and the surface loose sand. From thence a gentle descent round the base led to Loch Sligachan.

I had believed the fisherman's mail cart story, from having yesterday experienced something of the kind myself, and I now had another practical illustration of the force of the wind in these passes.

I was running quietly down at about six miles an hour, when a sudden blast met me full in the face, and not only stopped my progress, but was positively sending me backwards, when I hopped off my machine in a quarter less than no time. Well it was that I did so, for a moment later another came sideways, and had I been mounted it might have blown me into the gully below, a matter of about one hundred feet.

The road round Loch Sligachan was level and in capital order, but I could hardly make any way against the wind and rain. The lonely inn stands on a bleak plain at the head of the loch, and while approaching I thought it to be the most uninviting-looking place I had ever set eyes upon.

A change of clothing and a hot meal served by an attentive waiter soon caused me to take a more cheerful view of things in general. In the smoking room afterwards, an Oxonian, travelling with his tutor, related their misfortunes. Three times had they started for Loch Coruisk, and on each occasion were driven back by the weather, and the Cuchullins, which they had specially wished to see, had not once been clear during their stay in Skye.

To hear all this was very discouraging to a poor cyclist, but wet or fine, I determined to go through with my programme. Presently, on looking out of the window, I saw a wee bit of blue sky, and gleefully declared to my friends that it was going to be fine. "Too good to be true," was their reply; but before long the sun burst forth and all was gladness.

Not a moment was to be lost. I slipped into my half-dried clothes and trotted out my rusty and travelled-stained vehicle. My friends wished to go to the top of the hill with me, and I was only too glad to have their company, so we all walked together for about two miles, frequently stopping to look back and admire the most magnificent mass of mountains in Scotland.

Wave after wave of the vapoury curtain rolled away before the breeze, until the jagged outlines stood out clearly against the sky, their sides being beautifully tinted by the evening sun. The student acted the part of an instructor to me, and said, "That singular peak on the right is the king of the group—Scour Na Gillean, or Gillies Hill, so named from two lads who were killed while attempting its ascent. The black wall in the centre, with a remarkably serrated outline, is Blaven; the red one next to it on the left, with the beetling brow, is Marscow; the sugarloaf one you know to be Glamaig." His enthusiasm was refreshing, and he declared that he had not on the continent seen anything to excel this view in grandeur.

Parting from these gentlemen at the top of the hill, I ran on a level for a mile or so, then down by some patches of cultivation to Portree Bay, and round by its shores to the town. The detached pinnacle commonly called the Old Man of Storr was very conspicuous in the distance, and looked like a sentinel on his post.*

As I came nearer, the appearance of Portree with the yachts lying in the harbour, had a very pleasing effect, and my advent into the town was of a lively description. The working population were basking in the sun after the toils of the day; on sighting me a shout arose, a simultaneous rush was made from all quarters in my direction, and an excited crowd escorted me to the door of the "Royal" hotel.

When walking to the post-office afterwards I heard several people discussing the latest arrival, and disputing as to the number of wheels, etc.

I had tea with the brothers F. (Cambridge men); they, like myself were bound for the Quirang, and being obliged to catch the afternoon steamer, intended making an early start in a dog-cart. In reply to an invitation to accompany them, I said I should be unable to keep pace, but we agreed to breakfast together.

DISTANCE.

Broadford to Sligachan ..	.. 15 miles.	Undulating, firm surface, one bad hill.
Sligachan to Portree ..	.. 9¼ ,,	Good.
Total	.. 24¼ ,,	

Wet morning; fine evening.

THIRTY-SECOND DAY.

PORTREE, QUIRANG, STAFFIN BAY, UIG.

8 A.M. The brothers went off saying "Good-bye; very sorry you can't come with us, but we may see something of you; probably you will be arriving as we are coming back."

---

*Prince Charlie's cave is about two miles by water. The Man of Storr is 7 miles of bad walking.

Five minutes later I followed, taking the first turning to the right, and I had not gone far before I espied the dog-cart going slowly up a hill about a mile ahead. "Ho, ho!" thought I, "If you are not going faster than that, and the road remains good, there is a chance of our seeing the mountain together after all, my friends." Suiting the action to the thought, I put on a spurt, and gradually overhauled and passed them. This proceeding put the driver on his mettle, for sounds of the whip met my ear, and on coming to a stony bit, they shot ahead of me.

When the road improved I again led, and regardless of consequences, drove on at my utmost speed. We passed and re-passed each other many times during the fifteen miles to Uig, and were neck and neck at the commencement of the slope to the inn. This told in my favour, and I was enjoying some milk and biscuits, and trying to look quite cool and unconcerned, when they drove up to the door a few minutes afterwards.

I was off again, and had got a good start before the fresh horse had been put to. From the head of the bay the road made a sweeping zigzag to the plateau above, where I turned to the right and struck straight across to the Quirang, a distance of seven miles. Not seeing the footpath leading to it, I thought I must find a track lower

THE QUIRANG.

down, and had got half way, when a shout from my friends above brought me to a standstill. On their beckoning me up, I pushed my machine clear of the road and rejoined them at the top of the hill.

Thence we walked along a path close to the foot of the cliff, until abreast of the Needle, when we scrambled up past it into the interior of the mount. After refreshing ourselves at the spring, we climbed on to the celebrated table. If the reader imagines that I am going to describe the wonders of the Quirang* in my own words, when the graphic pen of Miss Gordon Cumming has already done so, he is much mistaken. That lady, whose acquaintance I made at Crieff, has given me permission to quote her account, which is as follows:—

"It is a stupendous mass of rock (amygdaloidal trap, black rock speckled with white), the grassy hill ending abruptly in a precipitous rocky face, whence green banks slope down to the sea. Its general form, and that of its neighbour the Storr Rock, is much the same as the Salisbury Craigs. The Storr has one gigantic detached needle about 160ft. in height, which stands out clear against the sky like a huge horn. The Quirang, in addition to one giant needle, has a perfect wilderness of huge detached masses of rock of every conceivable form. These are striking enough even when seen in the height of sunshine, but after a rainy night, when fleecy white mists curl and wreath themselves like spirit drapery round each weird form, and vapours steam up from the grass at your very feet until you hardly know where you stand, and every object is magnified ten-fold, the feelings of awe and mystery become almost overpowering. Sometimes a fantastic white shroud suddenly hides the whole scene. Then a rift in the cloud shows you the blue sea lying in the calm sunlight far below, dotted with islands and perhaps the white sail of a yacht. Suddenly a fairy hand draws back the curtain, and close to you is a rock like a huge lion couchant, behind it a tall pillar with a kneeling figure, which reminds one of St. Simon Stylites. Another moment these have disappeared, but in their place three giant figures with curled wigs and flowing robes have slowly emerged from the mist. They are unmistakably a King and Queen and Lord Chancellor, who, however, stands uncourteously *dos à dos* to his sovereign, but facing a solemn and shadowy old Druid priest who sits gravely guarding his rock sanctuary.

*The Illustration in Black's Guide gives one a very good idea of the Quirang.

"Geologists say this strange formation is caused by the crumbling away of the shale and softer masses, leaving those that can withstand the wasting power of the elements."—"*From the Hebrides to the Himalayas.*"

We had a beautifully clear, calm day for our view. Between the crags we gained delightful peeps of Lewis Island, Cuchullins, and the mainland, where, on looking closely, we could just distinguish a white building nestling among the hills, which we guessed to be Gairloch hotel. While gazing on mountain beyond mountain, ridge beyond ridge, extending northward as far as the eye could reach, I was impressed with the magnitude of the task which lay before me.

After enjoying the prospect in peace and quietness for some minutes, up came a squad of outmanœuvred guides, who had failed to anticipate our early arrival. One old fellow evidently looked upon us as trespassers, and persisted in repeating his formula. If time had not done so, the incessant cackle of these pests would have driven us away from this spot, where the human voice seems out of place.

On our way down we passed the site of the hut which had once stood there to give shelter, and where also refreshment could be obtained. It had been blown down and never replaced. We found the ascent and descent easy, but in most instances it must be rather a dangerous undertaking, and as the Quirang (1000 ft.), from all accounts, is seldom clear for more than an hour or two at a time, the tourist is recommended to engage a guide to prevent accidents.

I parted from my companions at the foot of the hill, and regained my tricycle, when I began to suffer the consequences of all the bumps during my race. I knew all the time that my left tyre was getting shaky, and now on examination I found that it was once more loose all round. Securing it for the present I rode gently down to Staffin Bay,* where are a few cottages.

After digesting a very good omelette at the clean little inn, I tramped off to the Kilt Rock. To find this I went along the coast for two miles and a-half, crossed the stream which flows out of the loch, and followed it down. I was very much pleased with the Kilt Rock. Miss Gording Cumming writes thus about it:—

"A wonderful headland known as the Kilt Rock, by reason of the many-coloured strata of which it is composed. From the green sea upwards layers of oolite limestone, oolite freestone and shale, alternating with lines of grass, lie horizontally, while rising vertically from these is a great mass of red, brown, and yellow columnar basalt. So high are these pillars that they quite dwarf those of Staffa. Indeed, McCulloch calculates them to be five or six times the magnitude of those in the wonderful little isle."

The land about Staffin Bay is arable, but although it was now near the end of July, the cereals were only just above the ground. The miserable state of the bothies, and the scanty dress of the people spoke of dire poverty, but in spite of this they all appeared cheery and well-disposed.

During my tour I had everywhere noticed the fine-looking school buildings; even in this remote place there was one, and my curiosity was much excited to see how the education here was carried on. I stepped inside and saw two long rows of unkempt heads of hair above the desks, and double the number of bare legs and feet beneath.

The owners of the same showed me their books, and the schoolmaster offered to let them sing. The little dears looked very healthy and merry, but I fear that Burns would not have appreciated their rendering of "Scots wha hae" and "Auld lang syne."

On my return to the inn, the landlord spoke enthusiastically about some caves near at hand, and I found in the visitors' book

*Duntulon Castle is 7½ miles N.W. of Staffin Bay, and Flora Macdonald's grave 2 miles S.W. of that.

a remark to the effect that they were superior to Staffa. This problem I leave future tourists to solve. I can certainly recommend the Staffin Bay inn, and it is not such a rainy place as Sligachan or Broadford, for on returning there I heard that while I had enjoyed fine weather, they had experienced a succession of showers.

On my way back to Uig I had a good sight of the whole range of cliffs of which Quirang is a part, and I believe that they formed the original coast line, their extraordinary excavations being due to the action of the sea and the atmosphere combined.

I was not housed until 9 p.m., and felt that I had done a good day's work. Uig inn is very small, and I was told off to share a room with rather a rough-looking customer, but in answer to my appeal the arrangements were altered.

DISTANCE.

Portree to Uig	15 miles.	Good running.
Uig to Staffin Bay and back ..	19 ,,	Firm surface.
Total ..	34 ,,	

Calm; lovely day.

THIRTY-THIRD DAY.
UIG. DUNVEGAN. SLIGACHAN.

CALLED at a quarter to seven—blowing and raining—went to sleep again. Fine at nine, got up.

Uig Bay is very sheltered; there is quite a little town round its shores, which gives it a cheerful appearance.

My intended room-mate breakfasted with me. He had a most peculiar, high-pitched sing-song voice, but I soon came to the conclusion that he was a very well-informed and sensible fellow. Perhaps his high opinion of my late "feats," as he was good enough to call them, had something to do with this opinion.

Noon, started for Dunvegan. Returned on the Portree Road to the fourth milestone, then turned sharp to the right and ran round the head of Loch Snizort, and through the village. A few trees hereabouts relieved the dreary monotony of the scene. From Snizort to Dunvegan the road, following the erratic outline of the coast, consisted of a series of sharp twists and turns. While traversing its undulations through a bleak moorland, the only signs of life that met my eye were a few miserable huts and an occasional forlorn-looking inn. These bothies were very roughly protected from the weather, some only by turf roofs, these being secured by the remains of nets or fibres weighted with stones. Many had no chimneys, and the smoke streaming through every crevice gave them the appearance of being on fire.

I stopped at Tayinlone Inn for something to eat. Visitors being unlooked for so early in the year, I had to make a second breakfast or an early tea, I don't know which to call it, on tea, eggs, and scones. The landlord, who was building a boat for the coming season, told me, in answer to my questions, that the natives eked out their living by fishing and by making the most of their little crofts and their cows. The islanders, in his opinion, had fallen off in physique since they had given up porridge for sugar and tea. He said that his inn did not pay, except in the shooting season, when it was always full, in fact every room was already engaged.

Arrived at Dunvegan at 6.30 p.m. The only place between here and Snizort where I could possibly have gone wrong was at a point about three miles from this village, where several roads met; there I turned sharp to the left.

Having been informed both at Uig and at Tayinlone that the distance from Dunvegan to Sligachan was eleven miles, I had not hurried myself, intending to get in comfortably at about nine o'clock. On asking again at Dunvegan I was astounded to hear that the correct distance was twenty-four! This news put me in a dilemma. On the one hand the fine weather, the expectation of finding letters and of meeting T., made me wish to push on to Sligachan; on the other, the lateness of the hour, the need of refreshment, and twenty-four miles of unknown road to be done partly in the dark, caused me to hesitate.

At this moment a Yorkshireman, who was just going to have tea, invited me to take a seat at the table. I accepted his invitation, and on calling for my share of the bill I read the following:—

	s.	d.
Tea...	2	6
Washing hands	0	6
Total for one tea	3	0

This at once decided me to move on.

7.30 p.m. Left Dunvegan without seeing the Castle, and pursued a road that alternately rose and fell for eleven miles to Struan, the surface being excellent. It was a lovely evening, and the prospect of Loch Bracadale, with its islands and many promontories reflected in the still surface of the bay, had a very pleasing effect.

The red cliffs at the entrance—the highest in Skye—were very fine. I also had a good view of those singular flat-topped hills called McLeod's Tables; and I fancied I saw McLeod's Maidens. These are three pillar-rocks off the N.W. point of the bay: the sea, in breaking over them leaves a vapoury train, and it is commonly reported that the idea of flowing dresses was taken from this circumstance. I did not stop at Struan Inn, although I believe accommodation may be found there, but pushed on through Bracadale, and round an arm of the loch—this could almost be jumped by a pedestrian, but is a mile for the cyclist.

From the loch there was a very steep bit on to the spur of Ben Ghlas, whence I had a most romantic view. Far beneath lay the placid waters of Loch Harport, from the head of which the river Drynoch stole its way through the deep vale. Right ahead, dimly perceived in the twilight, the weird-like peaks of the Cuchillins shot up into the sky. Again I found myself on an Alpine road, with a cliff one side and an unguarded drop of unknown depth on the other.

As it was almost dark, I had to take every possible precaution. Fortunately, the road was perfect, and as I ran slowly down, the baying of a dog in the depth below was the only sound that broke upon the still night air. There were one or two very dangerous corners; at these I dismounted, and eventually got safely down to the level of the vale, where the road became heavy.

Darkness had now set in, but I managed to find my way along. In the deep gloom the various objects that I passed assumed all sorts of grotesque shapes and forms, causing me to think more about ghosts and bogies than I had ever done before.

Hurrah! the lights of the hotel at last.

I had never enjoyed refreshment more than I did at eleven o'clock that night at Sligachan.

DISTANCE.

Uig to Dunvegan	29 miles.	Good, firm road, patches of fresh metal.
Dunvegan to Sligachan	24 ,,	Hilly, but splendid surface most of the way.
Total ..	53 ,,	

Very fine day.

THIRTY-FOURTH DAY.
Sligachan to Loch Coruisk and Back.

The people at the hotel thought I had run some risk last night, and I must say that I do not think I would ride again under the same circumstances.

I was anxious to know how that splendidly engineered road came to be constructed, and learned that it was made during the famine year, in order to give the poor islanders work. An excellent idea admirably carried out.

My nocturnal journey had been undertaken under the impression that T. would be waiting for me, but, to my great surprise, nothing whatever had been heard of him. It now began to dawn upon me that that gentleman might prove to be a myth, and that I should have to travel 1,600 miles alone through the most solitary parts of Scotland. Something had to be done. Bright thought! Telegraph to the landlord of the hotel at Perth for news. A gentleman who was going to Portree kindly offered to take my message and bring me the answer.

This being off my mind, I started at noon on foot for Loch Coruisk, and all the parties having been made up I had to go alone. I had no difficulty in finding my way by the pony track, but as it led me over loose rock, or through streams and bog, the walk was anything but a pleasant one.

I commenced most carefully by stepping from rock to rock, jumping the pools, and making a detour round the boggy bits. Presently a stepping stone turned under my weight, and in I went up to my knees. After that I tramped straight through everything, sometimes over my ankles in black mud, at others nearly up to my middle in water. It is worth while paying ten shillings for a pony to avoid this inconvenience, and to be free to turn one's whole attention to the scenery.

Again I was most fortunate in my day, all the mountains being quite clear. The varying aspect of Scour na Gillean was quite a study in itself; save for a greenish tint in places it looked exactly as if it had been made of cast iron, and the different shapes its peaks assumed as I went along were most curious.

On gaining the top of the ridge at the head of the glen I saw a lake in front of me. Thinking it to be Coruisk, I was floundering towards it, when a guide from the brow of the hill on the right hailed me to come up that way. I afterwards noticed that two separate parties made exactly the same mistake.

On reaching the higher ridge, which is just below the conical peak of Trodhu, my attention was immediately arrested by the whole range of Cuchullins, now close at hand.

They are nearly all about the same height—namely, 3,000 feet—and their continuous and exquisitely marked outline was indeed a wonderful sight. They are all known by different names, the only one I remember being the " Small-pox" Mountain, so called from its mottled appearance.

But where was Coruisk? " That dark-looking pool in the valley below, can that be it?" asked I of a tourist.

" No, you must go round the side of the hill to yon point on the left to see it well," was the reply.

My walk had been so harassing that I did not feel inclined to go a step farther, but since it had to be done, away I went, scrambling over the rounded boulders, and barking my shins in the endeavour to keep to the faint track.*

*There is a splendid illustration of Coruisk in "From the Hebrides to the Himalayas."

Coruisk (corrie of the water) gradually opened out as I progressed, and the point being reached, I looked straight up the gorge in which the loch lies. It was certainly worth the trouble, but I was too high up to see it properly; if I went there again I should land at Loch Strathbaig, see Coruisk from below, and then walk over to Glen Sligachan.

I sat about half an hour on the point, and the stern grandeur of the scene grew upon me more and more the longer I remained. The rocks around showed signs of having been acted upon either by heat or glacier friction. Among the different specimens of rock scattered about I noticed quantities of a green stone which I had not seen before in my travels.

The fascination of the scene had drawn me half way down the valley, when it began to rain, and I made homewards. A slight film of mist began to hover over the windward end of the range, and I was much interested in watching the clouds first wreathing themselves about the highest peaks, then spreading until they all joined into one mass, which gradually stole down the sides lower and lower, darker and darker. The mountains, now swollen to imaginary proportions, assumed a frowning aspect, which generated in my mind feelings of admiration mingled with awe.

All this time I was getting wet, and the track was, without exception, the most trying to one's temper that I have ever walked upon. I did nothing but stumble, wade, get bogged, and flounder about the whole way back to the hotel, and I would rather go over a dozen mountains with my tricycle than experience another such toilsome expedition on foot.

Late at night my friend brought me two telegrams. One from the landlord of the Perth Hotel, saying that he did not know what had become of T., the other from the very man himself, dated Invergarry, to this effect:

"Am taken suddenly ill; must return to Inverness. Leave word of your movements. Hope to join you later on."

This was a great blow to me, for I felt as though I had had a double loss, being pretty sure that my old friend P., rather than let me go alone for so many miles, would have accompanied me himself.

Quite disheartened, I for a few minutes felt inclined to give the whole thing up, but a glance at my carefully planned programme stimulated me to renewed exertions.

Wet evening.

THIRTY-FIFTH DAY.
Sligachan, Broadford, Kyle Akin, Balmacarra, Strome Ferry.

It blew and rained furiously all night, and up to 10.30 this morning. After breakfast I passed an hour in watching the various parties driving off in the rain, and felt a secret satisfaction in being able to bide my time.

11 a.m. The weather held up. Left Sligachan for Broadford and Kyle Akin, and walked up the greater part of the incline round the base of Glamaig, and also down the sharp pitch to Loch Ainort, which is dangerous.

The margin of the Sound of Scalpa is fringed by trees, and the few houses about tend to enliven the neighbourhood. I noticed this the more from having lately travelled through the wilderness which constitutes the greater part of Skye. 1.30 p.m. Lunched at Broadford, then went on through the rain, which now recommenced, and a good road along the shore line took me to Kyle Akin. I found there a neat little village and a comfortable-looking hotel, which was pretty full, judging by the number of noses flattened against the window panes.

I crossed the ferry very well in the ordinary boat (1s.). The man told me that he had once had two bicyclists on board, who apparently are the only wheelmen who have ever visited Skye. I hope that in future cyclists will be induced to see the wonders of the island, for, although the roads are undoubtedly hilly, and fresh metal is generally put down in June and July, I can assure them that by avoiding the Kyle Rhea route they will be able to do the remaining 150 miles without much difficulty.

On landing in Ross-shire I found a road winding in and out among the picturesque cliffs near the beach for a mile or so; it then struck inland, and my eye was gladdened by the sight of some young plantations, and other signs of fertility. After dipping into a valley, I had a long stiff pull, or rather push, on to the southern extremity of the Loch Alsh range. From here I had a noble view. The side of the hill, which declined steeply to the sea, was densely wooded, almost up to the highest point, while here and there a house, or a meadow studded with sheep, peeped through the foliage. On the opposite side of the loch the Kintail and Skye mountains proudly reared their lofty heads into space.

I now rode nearly on a level for a couple of miles through larch groves, with fine beetling crags on the left, and presently found myself at Balmacarra, at the water edge.

Here I had some milk and biscuits, and was told that I might have come a shorter way through some private grounds, but I was content to have secured the scenery, which was a delightful combination of grandeur and soft beauty. The hotel seemed to be well appointed, but was quite empty owing to the unfavourable season. Tourists start from here for Glomach Falls, which by all accounts are very well worth seeing.

From Balmacarra I ran by the loch for a mile, with fine timbered heights rising abruptly on my other side. Taking the left road at the fork, which at once began to rise, I had a severe struggle before attaining the summit of another part of the Loch Alsh range, and was rewarded by the most charming view imaginable of Loch Duich.

The rain had now ceased, and there being a dead calm, the mist was lazily hanging about the high land which girds in and partially concealed the gleaming water of the lake. In this peculiar light it was quite a fairy scene.

Having reached the northern slope I found a steep descent into a verdant glen, and as its surface was cut up by spates, I dismounted and walked to the bottom. After riding along for two miles, the road led me over a ridge, and down a break-neck bit into Strome Ferry on Loch Carron. This loch is closely hemmed in by mountains, leaving barely room for the railway on its south and the road on its north side. The building space for the village is also very limited.

While putting my tricycle away in the hotel stable at eight p.m. I saw that this day's work had given the finishing touch to the tyre, which since my race to the Quirang had been a constant source of bother and anxiety. I was just thinking that if my new tricycle had not arrived I should have to apply a fresh dose of solution, and give it at least thirty-six hours to harden, when I heard an ostler exclaim to his mate, "Why there's just such another as that at the station."

He little thought what glorious news that was to me, and for a short time I felt afraid to go and see for myself, in case it should indeed be too good to be true. Presently I mustered up courage, and went to the station. Bravo! there it was, sure enough, and in spite of my somewhat mature age, I felt inclined to dance a fandango with delight. No more fear of accidents; no more delays from defective tyres. Joy! joy! Having gloated over my prize for some minutes, I returned to the hotel, which I had all to myself.

My five shilling waterproof had its first real test to-day, and proved itself to be equal to the occasion.

Distance.

Sligachan to Kyle Akin ..	23½ miles.	Capital road all the way except Glamaig Pass.
Kyle Akin to Strome Ferry ..	14 ,,	Big hills, but the road is good. Magnificent scenery.
Total ..	37½ ,,	

Two or three hours' rain.

THIRTY-SIXTH DAY.

The Smash.

Directly after breakfast I took my old tricycle to the station, and unpacked my new one. Observing that the maker had sent handles of the usual length—which were too short for me—I obtained the railway blacksmith's assistance to shift my old ones on to the new machine. While doing so we found that there was not sufficient thread to allow the nuts to tighten the steering handle, therefore it would be necessary to make a washer of some kind to fill up the space. I asked the blacksmith to make one of iron; he replied that he could not spare the time for the job, but suggested a leathern washer, which, in his opinion, would do as well; I agreed, and it was fitted accordingly, and on testing it, I found it to work well. The brake lever was too short, but there was no help for that. So, after packing up my old steed and bidding him a fond farewell, I returned to the hotel with my new treasure and had something to eat.

2.30. Crossed the ferry. The boat was inconveniently small; this, with a strong tide and a chopping sea, rendered the passage anything but pleasant. Having landed my vehicle in safety, a feeling of great relief came over me. All now appeared *couleur de rose*, for with a light machine in perfect order, mountains and other obstacles would give me no concern.

After walking up a short rise, I found myself on a narrow level road, constructed on the side of a hill which sloped precipitously down to the water, the drop averaging about a hundred feet. It was prettily wooded and ornamented with flowers and ferns, and the surface of the road was firm and smooth. This, with a bright sunshiny afternoon, put me into the highest spirits.

With a light heart I vaulted into the saddle, and, resisting the temptation to fly along, I paddled slowly for a mile to make sure that every part was working correctly. Being satisfied on this point, I was just getting into full swing, when an old woman appeared round a bend in the road. To clear her I sheered to the right, then tried to straighten up again. Horror! *The steering gear had jammed!*

Instinctively I gave it a tremendous wrench, and made a convulsive clutch at the brake, which, from its being too short, I missed. At the same instant I found myself making straight for the edge, at the rate of eight miles an hour. Just as the wheels were leaping into space I threw myself out to the right, and after the sensation of falling through the air, I felt a heavy shock, and found myself buried in foliage.

Crash, crash, crash!

It was my tricycle, bounding through the bushes like an elephant through the jungle. Then all was silent.

I now picked myself up, and, having mustered my limbs, and found them correct, I caught sight of the old woman standing on the road, with an expression on her face which seemed to say, "Very neatly done, my laddie!" and on she walked, without asking if my neck were broken, ny nose put out of joint, or anything. She evidently thought that I had been showing off for her special benefit.

I found my tricycle on its side, some way down the hill, in the middle of a bush. Fearing to know the worst, I "uprighted" it with faltering hands. Sure enough, there was the right wheel of my brand-new machine, which I had not yet ridden for half an hour, doubled up into a figure that it would have puzzled the keenest mathematician to describe.

As I surveyed the wreck of all my hopes, I moralised to the trees around me as to the sad end of my tour in Scotland. Then came the after-thought, Why should I despair? Better to go on with the old one than give up altogether. Better still! apparently it is only the wheel that is damaged, why not replace it with the one from the other tricycle? Certainly it is not of the same pattern, but it is the right size, and may do; at any rate, it is worth trying.

Acting on this, I detached the right wheel, concealed the machine and my traps as much as possible, and scrambled on to the road. But how was I to convey this awkwardly-shaped mass of steel? I first tried one way and then another, and finally ascertained that the best plan was to carry it on my back like a sack of potatoes.

The second milestone hard by told me that I should have to trudge that distance with it to the ferry. That I was glad to get there may readily be imagined; also that the weight of the wheel seemed doubled during the last mile of my enforced return. This being the ferryman's side of the water, I experienced no delay in getting a boat. While they were preparing it the landlord of the little inn came out, and not only sympathised with me over my disaster, but, what was more to the point, kindly sent a man to watch over my belongings.

On reaching Strome, I carried my disabled wheel to the station, and was more than satisfied to find my old steed still there. It did not take me long to exchange wheels and re-secure the crate. I next sent a telegram to the Coventry Machinists' Company, directing them to send a new wheel to Auchnasheen with all dispatch, then re-crossed the ferry.

Having often trundled a field gun wheel, I thought to manage this one in the same way, but I found that the weight of the ball bearings made it run awkwardly, so it had to go on my back. When that began to ache I tried it first with one hand, then with the other, and in the course of time the scene of the accident was reached.

I now saw with thankfulness what a fortunate place it had been for my mishap. If this had occurred a few yards back, nothing could have saved me from being precipitated a hundred and fifty feet on to the rocks beneath, whereas I had merely fallen a vertical height of about ten feet, the slope after that being gradual and covered with shrubs.

The man sent by the landlord assisted me to lift the vehicle on to road, and then, with considerable anxiety, I endeavoured to fit the wheel. Ah! it would not go home; a stud on the socket of the new carriage preventing it. Again my heart sank within me. However, I found that the nuts would keep the wheel on, and that if a hole were drilled in the adjusting collar all would yet be well.

I eagerly inquired for the nearest blacksmith. "You'll have to go back to Strome, for the only one I know of this side of the water is at Garve, forty miles off," was the reply. This was enough to try any one's temper; but while slowly returning to the ferry, I succeeded in checking my feelings of impatience by pondering over the singular good fortune that had attended this accident.

1st. Had I gone along the road, and selected the softest spot, I could not have chosen the place better. 2nd. In another hour or two my old tricycle would have gone off by rail. 3rd. The wheel could be made to fit, thus necessitating only a temporary delay. 4th. I had been able to telegraph, and if the new wheel was sent promptly to Auchnasheen, where it was on my programme to return after seeing Loch Maree, I should not lose much time after all. 5th. Not only was I unhurt, but positively I had not even a scratch to show.

On reaching Strome once more (7 p.m.), I just caught the blacksmith as he was returning from his duty on the line. He most good-naturedly agreed to work at my wheel until it was finished. While he was drilling a hole in the adjusting collar, and making me an iron washer in lieu of the leathern one which had been the cause of the smash, I cleaned the ball bearings of the old wheel, and thoroughly put it to rights.

At 10.15 all was finished, but it was a good deal later before I had removed the oil and dirt from my skin, and could sit down in clean clothes to enjoy my first taste of food since 1.30 p.m. After tea, noticing that the right spoon of the brake did not bear properly, I endeavoured to make it do so by tying on pieces of leather.

DISTANCE.

On wheels .. .. 4 miles.

A beautiful day.

THIRTY-SEVENTH DAY.

Strome Ferry, Auchnasheen, Loch Torridon, Kinlochewe.

Rain prevented my making the early start that I intended.

9.0 a.m. Crossed the ferry for the fifth and last time, and when passing the now familiar spot, I again felt thankful for the narrow escape that I had had. It was a splendid bit of road to Jean Town, and I found that, although my odd wheels made the machine look rather lobsided, they ran very well together.

At Jean Town I asked the way to Auchnasheen, and received the reply so often given to one's enquiries, " Oh, you can't go wrong." A mile farther, at the head of the loch, the broad road and telegraph wires turned to the right; a grass-covered one went straight on. Repeating to myself the remark, " You can't go wrong," I concluded that I should do so if I took the disused road, so chose the one which the wires followed. After travelling nearly a mile, I found myself at the railway station, where the road terminated, and back I had to go and take the green one after all.

This ran at first along the bottom, then undulated along the north side of Glen More, which is bleak and sparsely populated. I particularly noticed that the grassy slopes of the land and sea valley were exactly the same, and thought that the sea, at one time, had rolled much farther up the glen, but on reading "Geikie's Scenery of Scotland" afterwards, I found that his theory is exactly the reverse of this—viz., that the glen was first scooped out by glaciers, then the land settled down and let the sea in.

Three or four miles beyond the turning, the road came down and crossed the railway. There is a cottage at that point, and I give the cyclist a hint, gratis, to find some excuse to stop there, for, just as I passed, the most lovely fair-haired lassie I had seen in Scotland came out and favoured me with a smile, which "haunts me still." Like a muff, I had not the presence of mind to fall off or do something to cause a delay.

Beyond Craig the valley contracted, and a group of mountains showed themselves ahead, their characteristic being ugly precipices which glistened in the sunlight. After seven miles of dismal moor hills I spied a milestone, and calculated that it would show five miles to Auchnasheen. On coming to it I read: " 10 Auch...... " This was very discouraging, and I was thinking that I should never reach Loch Maree that day, when two or three houses came in sight, at which I enquired the distance to Auchnasheen.

" This *is* Auchnasheen," was the reply.

" The milestone must be wrong, for a little way back it was marked 10," said I.

" Yes, but that is from Auchanalt," rejoined my informant.

12.30. p.m. Arrived at the hotel adjoining the station, chiefly used for refreshment by tourists *en route* to Loch Maree.

After starting this morning I thought my tricycle was going very fast, but the cause of this was manifest at the first hill I came to, for I discovered that it had been geared for speed, instead of equal, as ordered. I now sent off another telegram, directing that the proper cogs should be sent with the wheel.

Auchnasheen is a shade or two more melancholy than Dalwhinnie which is saying a good deal.

2.30. p.m. Started for Loch Maree, with a strong head wind in my face. The surface of the road was hard gravel, and level, by the margin of Loch Rosque, a most uninteresting sheet of water. At the west end of Rosque I had a long, stiff ride and walk up the brae, and from the crest of the hill I had my first view of Loch Maree.* Having often been warned on no account to miss seeing this lake, I had worked myself up to the expectation that I should there enjoy the finest scenery in Scotland. There was undoubtedly a savage grandeur about the mountains and promontories, which sank sheer into the water, but the straight line of the loch and the genera formality of the scene were disappointing.

The first mile of the wild narrow pass (Dochart) should be executed with care, because it is rather steep, and there is an awkward drop on the left hand. The trees, fields, and a few scattered dwellings at the head of the loch, give it an agreeable and picturesque appearance. I turned to observe a hugh mass of granite with a remarkable white cliff on its summit (Ben Eay), which rose on my left. The last mile to Kinlochewe was cut up by spates.

I had some light refreshment at the hotel, and as it was very fine and only 4.30 p.m., I started for Loch Torridon with the intention of sleeping at the inn there. Turning to the left at the west end of

---

*Loch Maree is 18 miles in length, the greatest width being 2½ miles. There are twenty-seven islands, about which are many traditions. Fair fishing can be given by the Loch Maree and Kinlochewe hotel keepers.

Kinlochewe, I skirted the base of Ben Eay, and, getting round to the other side, I noticed that its knife-like ridge was jagged like a saw, and the peak looked exactly as if a gigantic pepper-pot had been capsized over it.

The gorge now headed westward, and, to my disgust, the wind, which I had thought to dodge, blew as hard against me as ever. After passing Loch Clair, which is ornamented by a fringe of indigenous trees, I came to the valley of a "Thousand Hills." I should think there were quite that number of wee conical mounds, which rise side by side in a comparatively small space.

The gorge now became closely hemmed in by Ben Linghach, Ben Lett, and other mountains. The east end view of the former was very striking, the tapering peak being capped with white quartz, and its dull red sides broken into lines of terraces, which, in the distance, looked like the flounces of a lady's dress. A mile farther brought me to the side of this mountain, which rises 1,500 or 2,000 feet almost vertically from the road. The valley was thickly strewn with ponderous masses of rock which, from time to time, had dislodged themselves from the terraces above. While riding along I noticed many overhanging and delicately-poised blocks which, apparently, might have at any moment toppled over and crushed me into a jelly.

Ben Lett, and his neighbours on the opposite side, also covered with *débris*, were very fine. Altogether, these stupendous works of nature created a deep impression upon me, which was intensified by the utter loneliness. Perfect silence reigned around; not a living creature was to be seen.

On reaching Loch Torridon I met the laird, and asked him if there was accommodation at the hotel. " Oh, yes! plenty," replied he. Thus reassured, I pursued my way up the hill, and from thence observed a fishing hamlet in the corner of the bay, overshadowed by the western extremity of Linghach. While scanning the different habitations, I thought their appearance somewhat similar, but decidedly inferior to the generality of South Sea Island huts. There was one meagre-looking stone building in the village, and another rather better one on the side of the hill. Taking the latter to be the hotel, I rapped at the door. No response. Being informed that it was the school-house, I proceeded to the other, which proved to be the sought-for inn.

I walked into the parlour—there was not nearly room enough to swing a cat—and, giving up all idea of sleeping there, had a primitive tea, consisting of eggs and oatcake. On requesting my bill there was a whispered consultation among the females outside, a slight squabble, which was fast approaching the scratching-face stage, when the landlord came in and settled the question by boldly demanding "two shillings." "A small fortune to you, my boy!" said I to myself. Having paid up, I entered into an amicable conversation with him, and learned that they obtained their provisions from the Glasgow steamer, which called once a month; also that during this bad season it was a difficult matter to make both ends meet. I asked him if he was not afraid of the ricketty-looking crags overhead, to this he replied that there had not been a landslip in his time. While discussing the peculiarities of Linghach, he informed me that its summit terminated in a ridge which was to narrow too walk on with safety.

Leaving him in charge of my tricycle—which, as usual, was surrounded by an excited crowd—I stepped into one of the poorest-looking huts. When my eyes had become accustomed to the dense smoke with which the interior was filled, I perceived an aged woman croning over the embers of a peat fire. The furniture consisted of a spinning wheel, a deal table, and an old chair. I asked her a question, but the reply being in Gaelic, I bowed myself out and entered another dwelling. In this I found a female employed in making potato and oatmeal cakes. In good English she related her sorrows with sufficient earnestness to draw a sixpence from the bottom of my purse.

Wishing these poor people better fortune, I started on my return to Kinlochewe. While repassing Linghach, it struck me that it looked more like a ruined fortress after a long siege than anything else, and also that it was a good illustration of Geikie's theory, which is quoted as follows : " The conical form of quartz mountains seems to me to be entirely due to subærial decay. A homogeneous rock, traversed with minute joints and cleavage lines, tends to break up into angular *débris*, hence the thick coating of rubbish on hundreds of Highland hills. As soon as this detritus is broken from the rock it begins a slow descent to the valley below. The upper part of the mountain is thus exposed to continual waste, while the sides are better protected. The result is that the mountain, worn away above and shielded under its ruins below, grows more and more tapering until it passes to a perfect cone."

When about half way I came to a broken-down chaise, which caused me to think that I was very fortunate in having only once experienced a similar mishap during my prolonged tour. The surface of the road was rather loose and stony, but as it is nearly level the whole way, the cyclist should not on any account fail to witness the sublime scenery about Loch Torridon.

9.15 p.m. Arrived at Kinlochewe, and managed to get a bed. During the evening I had a long talk with a mountain enthusiast, who appeared to know every notable peak in Scotland, and gave me a good deal of useful information about my future route.

N.B.—The piece of leather that I had secured to the spoon of the brake had worn through early in the day, the consequence being that the brake did not act efficiently, and the sharp edge cut into the tyre. I now put on a fresh bit of leather, and cut out a number for future use.

DISTANCE.

Strome Ferry to Auchnasheen ..	25 miles.	Splendid road, no hills.
Auchnasheen to Kinlochewe ..	9½ ,,	Hilly ; good surface.
Kinlochewe to Loch Torridon and back	24 ,,	Level ; rather loose and stony ; impressive scenery.
Total ..	58½	

Fine, but strong wind against.

THIRTY-EIGHTH DAY.
Kinlochewe, Poolewe, Gairloch, Auchnasheen.

From outside the hotel I had a capital view of Ben Slioch, which, rising straight up out of the lake, displays every rift and fissure in its deeply scored side. Its summit is peculiar, being shaped like a battlemented tower. Availing themselves of the fine day, a party had started off early to take it by storm, my enthusiastic friend leading the "forlorn hope."

9 a.m. Started for Gairloch. The road, which ran along the margin of the lake, was level and good for four miles, and I had peeps of stern grey mountains through the trees which fringed the road. After this I pedalled through a sandy wilderness among scattered granite boulders on an undulating and loose track, which, together with a strong wind, rendered the travelling anything but pleasant. Beyond Guidie Bridge I again ran through pretty woods and between mossy banks decked with flowers, and after several dismounts reached Loch Maree Hotel, perched on an eminence, and having a good look-out on the lake and its twenty-four islands grouped abreast this point.

At the eleventh milestone the road turned from the water and struck to the left up a long steep brae into a defile. After bowling along, cheerily O, for about four miles among green and treeless hills, I made my way through a narrow gulley between picturesque and variegated rocks, where brawled a lively burn, making at one point a pretty fall.

Here I dismounted, not liking the look of this bit of road. It was well that I did so, for, beside some sharp pitches, the road about half-way down turns at right angles, and there is only a low wall to prevent the cyclist from leaping into a chasm of greater depth than he would care to fathom.

At the foot of the hill I found myself in a secluded dell, with a wood to the left, and to the right a number of green and rocky hummocks, tossed about in the utmost disorder, while on the level ground each side of the burn, patches of corn were springing up. At the west end I entered a sylvan larch plantation, beautified by the purple heather in full bloom, and a few lichen-covered rocks scattered here and there near the now tranquil stream completed the charms of this paradise in the wilderness.

The surface of the road, which had been getting worse as I progressed, now became deep clayey mud, and I was obliged to walk up through the wood to the crest of the hill. I then ran down a long declivity to Gairloch, a sequestered little village in a deep ravine thickly mantled with foliage.

Near here, in a snug corner of the bay, passengers are landed from the Glasgow steamer. The road, now firm and good, led me up the west side of the ravine, and by the new kirk to the hotel, which is on the side of a bare sand-hill, commanding an extensive view of the bay and the islands of Lewis and Skye. The day being very clear, my old friends the Cuchullins and the Quirang Cliffs were distinctly seen in the offing.

This large hotel (quite a rival to the Langham) is generally full to overflowing in the season; therefore, the tourist should anticipate his arrival by telegraph. I was too early—12.30—for the *table d'hôte* luncheon, but the waiter soon brought me some hot soup and other dishes acceptable to the palate of a hungry cyclist. At the same time I feasted my mind with the unusual luxury of an English newspaper, glancing occasionally out of the window at the white sails of a yacht which was manœuvring about the bay.

2 p.m. Continued my journey to Poolewe. I climbed to the top the steep hill at the back of the hotel, then, seeing a dangerous

bit in front of me, did not mount until I had passed it. I now rode through a wild rocky gorge, between bare hills, on a tolerably good track for three miles. The road then began to descend gradually for a short distance to a rocky platform, from whence I really had a magnificent vista of Loch Maree. Now for the first time the scenery struck me as being truly grand, the finely-marked outline of the different points and headlands which jut into the lake giving it the variety which is so wanting from other points of view.

I had ridden down to the platform, but thinking it prudent to survey the road before tricycling farther, I walked on a few yards, and saw that it made a sudden plunge into the valley below. The wheelman is therefore cautioned not to ride down this deceptive hill. From the foot I jogged over a level but rather rough mile to the village of Poolewe, which is on a flat bit of ground at the head of Loch Ewe. There is nothing in particular to see except the river, which rushes furiously from Loch Maree into the sea, thus having a short life and a merry one.

I had an excellent tea, with toast, eggs, and jam, at the little inn, for the sum of one shilling, and should therefore recommend the cyclist to make it his head-quarters while in this neighbourhood. There is a road from Poolewe to Little Loch Broom, but I was informed that some parts of it are very bad indeed.

Feeling rather tired, I took a little snooze after tea, then, finding it to be 5 p.m., I hurried off with the idea of sleeping at Loch Maree Hotel, which had quite taken my fancy when passing it. When my eyes were fairly unbuttoned, I saw that a great change for the worse had taken place in the weather. Common sense prompted me to go back to my late comfortable quarters, but having started I felt loth to return even half a mile, so decided to make a dash for Gairloch.

On reaching the platform before mentioned I saw black storm-clouds hanging low on the mountain sides, and a heavy squall sweeping down the loch, so gaining the top of the hill I bustled along as fast as the condition of the road would permit. Presently the first few preliminary drops fell, then down it came thick and heavy, and my five-shilling waterproof was brought into requisition. Before long I felt a tiny stream gradually stealing down the back of my neck, quickly to be followed by others, and just as a brook is converted into a mighty river by tributary rills, so did my poor back soon become the bed of a Highland torrent.

A DOUBTFUL OFFER.

I found the descent to Gairloch too steep for safe riding. When nearing the hotel I argued within myself that, being very wet, I might just as well stick to the programme of sleeping at Loch Maree hotel, so I gave Gairloch the go-by. I had to plough my way through such deep mire that I am sure that potatoes might have been planted in the tracks of my wheels between the village of Gairloch and Kerrie waterfall, where mud gave place to sand.

Being too lazy to dismount, I risked the hill down to the eleventh milestone, but it was all right, for the loose surface kept the machine under control. The road was again very sticky through the wood to Loch Maree hotel, where I arrived at 8 o'clock.

In answer to my inquiry about a room the waiter said in a patronising manner that he thought he could get me a billet on a sofa or on the floor of the drawing-room. Thanking him for his condescension I said that, late as it was, I should prefer travelling ten miles further in order to get a comfortable bed at Kinlochewe.

"You'll find that quite full, I'm sure," replied he, "for *we* sent a large party there to-day."

"No matter, I'll chance it," said I, thinking this to be a ruse, for the hotel had been nearly empty when I left it in the morning. "Good night," and on I went.

The road was heavy, and the perpetual ups and downs were decidedly harassing in my tired condition, but I relieved my feelings somewhat by having a good growl at the singular ill luck that I had had with the wind during the day. All the way to Poolewe it had been strong from the west; no sooner did I start from there than it shifted right round to the east, and at the present moment myself I was bending nearly double in my endeavours to present as little surface as possible to the freshening squalls and blinding rain.

It was a comfort to get under the friendly shelter of the trees again. While riding silently along, a fine deer emerged from the lake side, and being unaware of my proximity gave me an opportunity of admiring his easy and graceful movements until he disappeared to the right.

9.45 p.m. Drew up at the door of Kinlochewe hotel and rang the bell. Although I had not attached much importance to the waiter's opinion, I must confess to a feeling of trepidation when the door opened and I put the question,

"Can you take me in?"

"*Quite full, sir;* but perhaps we can manage to give you a shake-down somewhere."

I was too wet and cold to like the idea of a shake-down. What was to be done now?

"Go on to Auchnasheen," prompted Obstinacy.

"All very well," replied Prudence, "but it is dark, it is late, the road is dangerous, you need refreshment."

I could only make up my mind promptly to one thing, and that was to have supper at once, which the attentive landlady prepared for me with all dispatch. While discussing this the arguments of Obstinacy prevailed, and I decided to chance everything for a warm bed, which I was sure to get at Auchnasheen.

11 p.m. Got under way. It was dark, but by stooping low I managed to make out the white sandy road a few yards ahead, and, having carefully noticed its features the day before, I knew pretty well where the bad bits lay. I got on pretty fairly, and although I could have ridden some way up through Glen Dochart, I thought it safer to walk past the chasm, and to the bottom of the steep hill on the other side.

It was indeed a wild night; the wind blew hard in my teeth, and every now and then, by way of keeping me awake, there would be a fresh hand to the bellows, bringing a pelting rain-squall. I am not at all superstitious, but I will candidly admit that while going through that gloomy pass, overhung by dark and strangely-shaped crags of rock, I felt a shudder pass through me more than once, whether from fear or cold I cannot tell. All that I can say is that I was uncommonly glad to see the gleam of Loch Rosque in the distance.

I now mounted and pedalled very slowly. A little pitch in the road gave me a nervous shock, so I got off again. "It's all right now," thought I; "here goes!" and, bounding into the saddle, I was beginning to get quite plucky, when the roar of a torrent met my ear; a second later its foaming waters were under my very nose. In sheer desperation I put my helm hard a starboard, and, luckily, hit upon the narrow bridge, my few remaining hairs literally standing on end. "*Arrectæque horrore comæ et vox faucibus hæsit.*"

"This kind of thing will never do!" gasped I, dismounting again.

On reaching the margin of the lake I once more tried my fortune in the saddle, and as the road became broader and more level, so I gradually increased the speed.

I thought Loch Rosque never would come to an end, and hoped I had seen the last of it several times, but it kept turning up, looking as long as ever. However, as all things good and bad come to an end, so did this romance of "Nauticus" in search of a pillow, and at one o'clock I reached Auchnasheen.

In the hotel all was silence and darkness. I rapped again and again. At length I saw the flicker of a candle, then a window opened and a gruff voice growled out, "Who's that?"

"A benighted traveller. Can I have a bed?"

"Yes."

Down banged the window and up flew my spirits. My tricycle and myself were both admitted. He, in spite of his prolonged exertions, required neither fish, flesh, nor fowl. I only wanted light refreshments, which the worthy landlord quickly set before me.

I fairly crowed with delight when my head touched the long-sought-for pillow.

DISTANCE.

Kinlochewe to Poolewe and back 51 miles. Hilly, surface rather loose and stony.
Poolewe to Auchnasheen .. 9½ „
Total .. 60½ „

Wind against all day. Very wet evening.

THIRTY-NINTH DAY.
Auchnasheen. Garve.

Turned out at 9 o'clock. Boots greeted me with, "Your clothes are in a fearful state, sir; it will take some hours before they are fit to wear." Happily everything in my bag was dry; so, after borrowing a velveteen coat from the landlord, I made quite a fashionable appearance in the coffee-room.

I breakfasted with a married couple, who were rather in a fog about their future movements. The husband used the plea of bad weather, and many seductive arguments, in the endeavour to persuade his better half to return home, and leave him to have his fling at Loch Maree.

She did not see it in the same light, and informed me confidentially that her dear John had heart-disease, and she did not like to let him out of her sight. Later on he disappeared for some time, much to her distress. She first of all imagined that he had been run over by the train that had passed an hour before he went out; and when I assured her that that was scarcely probable, she began to picture him lying dead in a ditch. In fact, she worked herself up into such a state of agitation, that, fearing the good woman would faint in my arms, I volunteered to go and hunt for him. The end of it was that he turned up all right, and, here allow me to tell those who say that "women *always* have the best of it," that, after giving his wife the strictest injunctions to go home by the next train, the husband went off in the coach.

While scribbling in my journal I heard that the train from Inverness would arrive in a few minutes. Now, thought I, if my wheel comes by this train it will be smart work on the part of the makers, and a happy finale to my chapter of accidents. I went out to the platform. Presently a shrill whistle announced the approach of the train. It stopped. I eagerly scanned the guard's van. Cheers! The wheel had arrived, and with it the spare cog for which I had telegraphed. Believe me, I did feel happy; if there had not been so many people on the platform I should have danced another fandango. All that was now necessary to put the machine in perfect condition was to exchange the right wheel for the new one, and to put the fresh cog on the left wheel. For this a blacksmith's services were required. I asked for one, but received the same reply as before—"None nearer than Garve."

I had now a problem to solve, a regular case of X and Y—viz.,

Having the right wheel geared for one speed, and the left for another, what will happen if I ride with them in that condition?

After nearly scratching my head off, Thought No. 1 suggested—

"It will be all right, because the faster wheel, by not allowing the cams of the slower to come into play, will convert it into a running wheel."

Thought No. 2 said—"No, it won't. You'll have the machine turning round and round, and throwing you into a ditch, over a precipice, or something."

Thought No. 1—"It won't."

No. 2—"I tell you it will."

No. 3—"Put on the wheel and try it in the yard."

No. 4—"What, in the rain! Thank you for nothing."

No. 5—"Disconnect one chain, then you will know for a certainty that there will be one driving and one running wheel."

Acting on the good advice of No. 5, I tied the left chain to the back of my tricycle, booked the old wheel to Coventry, and sat down to luncheon.

Auchnasheen means "place of storms," and it certainly kept up its reputation during the last twenty-four hours of my stay. It is situated at the junction of three glens, so that if the wind whispers from any direction it is pretty sure to howl at that unhappy place. This morning, on getting up, I found that the wind had freakishly shifted to the west again, and was blowing hard, with a succession of heavy rain squalls.

After luncheon, the weather being too unfavourable for a start, I employed myself by readjusting the steering apparatus. It had worked very well since leaving Strome Ferry, but by mistake I had misplaced one of the wheel washers.

2.30. p.m. The weather having "faired" a little, I got under way. Noticing that a knot of people had collected to see me off, I thought that it would be the correct thing for "Nauticus" to show them how to do it in style.

I put on a spurt, and was flying along gaily O! when, Tableau! and *"Nauticus" was to be seen on the broad of his back in the middle of the road, with his tricycle on the top of him!* To my mind, this proved in much too practical a way the truth of the oft-heard warning, "Pride will have a fall."

I felt dazed and half stunned for a few seconds, and could not make out what in the world had happened. On coming to, I uprighted the machine, and found that the lower nut, by working loose, had allowed the pinion-wheel to drop out of gear; whereupon, as quick as lightning, the machine had charged into the wire fencing which guarded the embankment, rebounding again like an india-rubber ball. I tightened the nut and went on, but had not gone a hundred yards farther before bang I went into the wall on the left!

This fairly alarmed me. "Good gracious!" cried I, aloud; "the thing's bewitched! Bother that old woman, she'll do for me yet! I shall break my neck in a minute; there's no railing now." In spite of the wind and rain, which were beating mercilessly upon me, down I had to go on my knees and take the whole of the steering arrangement to pieces to see what on earth was the matter.

Stupid fellow! I had put the pinion-wheel on upside down, and it took me about ten minutes screwing and unscrewing nuts, placing and re-placing washers, before I could proceed.

Feeling as limp as water, with all the swagger taken out of me, I was positively afraid to ride until a perfectly safe part of the road was reached. I then mounted, but, as the steering gear was always too tight or too loose, I was in a constant fever, and kept mounting and dismounting, tightening and loosening, until I found that more rapid progress could be made on foot.

The road ran nearly level through Strath Bran, a green wilderness supporting a few sheep. Beyond Auchanalt it undulated by the side of Loch Hular and another lochan, both prettily-lined with larch trees. The road dipped somewhat precipitously to the bridge, which crosses a roaring burn from Loch Fannich, then rose steeply on to a plateau overlooking the bold but picturesque banks of Loch Linchart.

The surface, which had consisted of rather soft gravel, now became hard and smooth, and as my tricycle was beginning to behave itself properly, I enjoyed a pleasant run of nearly four miles down to Garve. This cosy little village lies in a fertile vale, closely encompassed by high land, the sides of the hills being partially clothed with wood. The cyclist may allow two hours as the average time for this journey, but with my skittish steed it took me more than four to accomplish the sixteen miles.

My first idea on reaching Garve was to find the blacksmith about whom I had heard so much, and I made straight for his shop in order to catch him before he left work. Being out of the line of tourists, I did not think it worth while to engage a room at the hotel on my way. I rode up to the shop door, feeling how very dependent I had become on this important class of mechanics, especially now that they were so few and far between. I stepped inside, and asked the "gude mon" if he would do a job for me. "Yes," was his laconic reply, but directly he sighted my tricycle, with its network of wires and complicated fittings, his jaw fell, and he muttered,

"I know nought about them things."

"There is nothing difficult. I will explain what has to be done," said I.

After looking at it gloomily for a moment longer, he said, decidedly,

"No, I won't have anything to do with it."

"Lend me your tools, then, and I'll work at it myself," exclaimed I, in a huff.

"Oh, yes, you can have the tools," replied he, readily.

I set to, removed the left wheel, unscrewed the cog-plate, and was putting on the new one, when, seeing that I had not unearthed a nest of hobgoblins, he came to my assistance and volunteered to do the rest under my direction. I found that, from the new plates being larger than the others, the chains were too short, and we had to file the framework to make the crank fit. I now turned my attention to the brake, which had not fitted properly since the accident at Strome Ferry, but I had consoled myself with thinking that it would be all right when the new wheel arrived. After shipping that this morning, great was my astonishment at finding that the brake did not bear any better than on the old one. At the time this seemed unaccountable, but on consulting the blacksmith we both came to the conclusion that the framework of the machine had been sprung by the fall. Nothing could be done, so after all my fandango dances I was doomed to travel more than 1,100 miles on a tricycle, the wheels of which did not run truly, and having a brake which, to be of any service, must be continually covered with leather.

When this son of Vulcan had filed the sharp edge of the spoon for me, I gave him the fee which he had now fairly earned, and left for the inn. The colour of my hands reminded me of those minstrels who "never perform out of London," and I was looking forward to a good wash and other luxuries, as I put my steed into a stall at the hotel stables. Walking indoors, I asked to be shown my room.

"There are none vacant, sir."

"What, no room!" cried I, in dismay, "Who in the name of patience is staying in this out-of-the-way place?"

"A shooting party, sir, has engaged every bed in the house."

"Is there any other inn?"

"Not within some miles, sir."

"Then what *am* I to do" cried I, in despair.

"Mrs. Fraser, at the cottage, may be able to put you up."

It was with many misgivings that I arrived with my bag at the door of a very humble dwelling, which appeared to be undergoing a process of re-thatching and whitewashing. Mrs. Fraser had gone to kirk, but a neighbour kindly dug out the husband. In answer to my inquiry, he replied that he "never interfered with the missus,".

I FIND HOMELY QUARTERS.

and did not tell me whether she could take me in or not. She would be home soon, if I would wait. There being very little option in the matter, I did wait, and while doing so, ascertained that he worked on the roads, and began to pump him as to the condition of those I was about to traverse. Presently I happened to remark what a beautiful evening it was after the gale.

"Gale!" exclaimed he, "It has been calm and fine here all day."

After chatting until past nine o'clock, I was not a little pleased to hear him say, "Here comes the old 'ooman, now you ask her;" and away he went, evidently not wishing her to think he had taken any steps in the matter.

Assuming my blandest and most insinuating manner, I greeted her, put the all-important question, and breathlessly awaited the verdict, feeling that I would rather have coiled myself up like a dog before the kitchen fire than go any further to seek a night's lodging.

However, instead of treating me with distrust, as she might well have done in my dirty and dishevelled condition, she said, "Oh, sir, I hardly think my poor place is fit for a gentleman like you." "Dear me!" thought I, "how very observant these Scotch people are, to be sure!" Then, taking my cue from her, I assured the good woman that my tastes were exceedingly simple. She showed me into a

I

charming little room, containing a table covered with well-bound books, and quite a grand bed in the corner. She looked most pleased when I said that it would *do*, little knowing that a few minutes earlier I should have thanked her for a square yard of the floor. The dear old soul now took me under her wing, and had she been my mother she could not have concerned herself more for my comfort. She lighted a fire, and while I blew it into a good blaze with a pair of bellows, the dame busied herself in preparing my tea, apologising every now and then in a soft, sympathetic tone for not being able to give me a more hospitable reception.

After tea, while lounging in an easy-chair, and warming my toes over a cheerful fire, I felt more at home than I had done since starting on the tour.

DISTANCE.

Auchnasheen to Garve .. .. 16 miles. Very good road.
Wind and rain in the neighbourhood of Auchnasheen.

FORTIETH DAY.
GARVE, ULLAPOOL, INCHNADAMPH.

This morning I enjoyed another surprise. A fair damsel came in to lay and attend breakfast—the daughter, if you please, all smiles, and so pleasant. On requesting my bill, the young woman took so long in making it out that I was beginning to feel nervous about its length, when in she came, and hoped it would be satisfactory. I read as follows :

	s.	d.
Tea (two eggs, butter, and jam)	1	0
Bed, attendance, and fire	1	0
Breakfast (ham, eggs, jam, butter)	1	0
Total	3	0

My inclination was to give five times that amount, but on the principle that "business is business," I settled the bill as it stood, and gladly avail myself of the present opportunity of thanking Mrs. Fraser and her daughter, and wishing them every happiness. Fortunate is the cyclist who can secure a night's lodging under their roof.

There had been showers all the morning, and a heavy one had just ceased when I started for Ullapool at 8.30 a.m. I noticed that, owing to the sheltered situation of Garve Valley, the cereal crops were in splendid condition. From the west end of the village the road headed to the northward, through Strath Garve, and almost immediately began to ascend, continuing to do so more or less for fifteen miles. The loose gravelly surface was saturated with rain, and the strong wind made the travelling rather laboured—at least, such was evidently the opinion of a Hieland laddie who ran alongside of me for about a mile, for on parting he said, "Hoot mon, I dinna think meikle o' that!"

Here, as often before, I was bothered by cattle straying across the track. The silly brutes always stand with their heads lowered until one is within a few feet of them, then it is a toss up whether they are going to charge or to plunge right across my bows. Sheep sometimes annoyed me in the same manner. After some practice I found that barking like a dog acted effectually upon them, but to get any sort of active movement out of cattle I had to imitate the voice of a lion, which attempt generally resolved itself into a *roar* of laughter.

I rode by the side of a burn, between monotonous green banks, for five miles, when a few trees and a group of cottages (Kirkan) hove in sight, conspicuous amongst which was a corrugated iron shooting-box. The keeper, who was airing the dogs, said that birds were plentiful in that neighbourhood.

Six miles from Garve I took the left road at the fork, and although the surface now became firm and smooth, I had great difficulty in making any headway, until the road, having made a wide sweep round to the N.W., put me under the lee of the hills.

Ross-shire is specially distinguished by its groups of mountains, the summits of which are Alpine and rocky, while the lower parts stretch out in prolonged chasms and ridges. The groups are separated from each other either by wide table-lands or pastoral valleys. Dirrie More (the long steppe), on which I had now entered, is the principal of these. It is about twenty miles in length, and nearly dead straight, the monotony of the scenery being heightened by the sombre slopes with which the Strath is bounded.

After bowling along four miles I passed Alguish Inn; it appeared to have good accommodation for man and beast, but how the landlord manages to keep out of the County Court is a puzzle to me, for I don't remember meeting more than five persons between Garve and Loch Broom. In fact the gloomy solitude of Dirrie More is well known, and while riding along I was only reminded of my fellow-creatures by the grass-covered walls of habitations, long deserted, and by an occasional cairn marking the spot where some luckless traveller had perished in the snow. To traverse these lonely wilds on foot, where not even the bleating of a sheep breaks the perfect silence, would be intolerable, but my rapid movements caused a quick succession of fine mountain forms to pass before me, which fully occupied my attention.

Ben Wyvis was not quite up to my expectations, but I was much struck by the singular appearance of Ben Derag, which I had before me for some time. It sprang up from the plain like an island from the sea, and its resemblance to a broken-down crater reminded me of St. Paul's Island, which I once passed on the way to Australia.

The road by Loch Druin was execrable, necessitating a dismount. The fine peaks of the Dundonnel Hills are seen to advantage from this point. From the lodge at the west end of Druin I ran by a gradual descent through a wild rocky glen to Braemore, where it narrowed, and the clothing of young firs on either side showed that human skill was doing its best to reclaim the desert.

Having passed the entrance gate I was riding carefully down, when over a low wall to the left I spied a bridge, and immediately

A KINDLY HINT TO THE SCHOOLMASTER.

afterwards was brought to a standstill by the sight of a most extraordinary chasm or rent in the earth. I dismounted, and saw as much as I could of it from the road, very much wishing to get nearer, but the grounds being private, and seeing no one about, I reluctantly proceeded to walk down the remainder of this hill, which is dangerous.

About midway there was another rent on a much smaller scale, running at right angles to the road. Both chasms were quite vertical, and their bare mica-slate sides looked as if they had only been wrenched asunder the day before. Break a loaf of bread and place the several sides together until they nearly meet; this will give an idea of the jagged appearance of the fissure.

Passing Braemore stables at the foot of the hill, I entered upon charming Inverbroom Valley, where, after my long journey through the wilderness, it was pleasant to hear birds singing, to see waving cornfields and snug farmhouses, while sleek cattle and sheep browsed by the side of the murmuring stream, which discharged its waters into the sea. The contrast between the stern grandeur of the ruddy screen of mountains with which the valley was girdled and this pastoral beauty enhanced the effect of the scene. While riding along I was much struck by the appearance of Craig Vore, which rose vertically to a height of 1,145 feet not far from the road.

The splendid surface enabled me to fly all the stiff undulations between the head of the loch and Ullapool, a fishing-town containing many well-built houses. Its situation, on a low sandy point, rendered it visible for some time before I reached the hotel at 1.30 p.m.

The sole lodger in this excellent establishment was a commercial gent, who, having just arrived from London town, thought himself at the world's end. Presently a school inspectress joined me at luncheon, and I had the pleasure of taking a note from her to Inchnadamph. "A kindly hint to the schoolmaster," thought I, "to cram up something for the occasion."

While I was looking at a merry hay-making party in front of the hotel, a man explained that they literally have to "make hay while the sun shines," and be smart about it too, in the vicinity of the "Lake of Showers."

There is now a regular coach service between Garve and Ullapool, and on comparing times with the printed notice I found that my "Cheylesmore" had the best of it by a quarter of an hour.

4 p.m. Left Ullapool, once a flourishing place, but since the fish have left the bay many of the inhabitants have migrated also, leaving the remainder to get what they can out of their little crofts. After clearing the village I had to climb a steep hill, from the brow of which I had a superb retrospective view of the country I had lately passed through. Westward a fine bay, speckled with islands, lay mapped out before me, while immediately in front stood a grim, bare, and strangely-wrinkled mass of granite (Ben More).

From the brow the road plunged headlong into a snug little cove, in which rested a few fishing-huts. I rode by these and up through a narrow defile gorgeous with purple heather. On gaining a higher level I saw that the slopes on and around Ben More were thickly covered with rocky fragments of all shapes and sizes. "A rare place for a geologist to spend a happy day," was my inward remark. I now experienced a succession of long steep braes, through a bare, bleak country, occasionally passing a solitary shieling tenanted by the shepherd, whose sheep were scattered far and wide over the scanty herbage in their endeavours to find a dainty morsel.

It was interesting to watch the ever-changing features of Ben More, Coulbeg, Coulmore, and others, which were now shapeless, now symmetrical, so that there was something fresh to notice at nearly every revolution of my wheels. I managed to make very fair progress through this hilly region by spurting as far up each gradient as possible. I would then walk over the brow and down the steepest bit on the other side, then remount and run as far as I could up the next slope, and so on.

Fourteen miles from Ullapool the telegraph wires turned off to the left, and followed a branch road through a fine-looking pass. I felt doubtful about this, as there was only one track in my map (Black's "Sutherland"), and seeing a house, I went there to make inquiries. It proved to be a shooting-box with a keeper's cottage attached. I entered the latter, and learned that the left-hand road was a new route to Loch Inver. While resting here I had a good view of Fiddler's Peak, which my friend at Kinlochewe had told me to look out for; I thought it resembled a cone with a piece chopped out.

After leaving the cottage I walked up a stiff hill for a mile, then rode for two more on a narrow track through a wild glen, passing one or two lochans on the way. Turning a corner I suddenly found myself on the brink of a precipice, with a noble landscape spread out before me.

Away to the north-east stretched a verdant plain, enclosed by steep hills, and brightened by silvery Camaloch and other picturesque sheets of water. The scene was overlooked and frowned upon by the More Assynt range of mountains, some green and heathery, others of a dull white colour, like half-melted snow. The glow of the evening sun lighted up and showed out every detail with great distinctness, and while it was clear and fine with me, not five miles distant the sky was obscured by a pall of dense clouds, from which streaks of heavy rain were descending. Looking back, I could see the graceful forms of Coulbeg and others sketched against the sky. The *tout ensemble* was very impressive.

I had to exercise considerable caution in running round the cliff, and stopped several times to admire the fantastical crags which glistened over my head. Passing the hamlets Knochan and Elphin, I came to level ground at Ledmore, a straggling village. A mile of rough travelling brought me to the main road from Oykel Bridge, where I turned to the left. At this junction* I saw something which

---

*" Altnakealgac (two miles on the Oykel Bridge Road) is a capital head-quarters for the angler and sketcher. Lochs Borrolan, Cama, Urigile, and Beattie, the Ledmore and Ledberg rivers, besides many streams, can be conveniently fished from this Inn, and are all open to the tourist. One writer states, that in ten days during the month of August, he caught 105 dozen trout with the fly (some years ago). One day I killed, in three hours' fishing with the fly, 40 trout and 3 char in Loch Borrolan. There is a boat on Loch Urigile."— Young's "Sutherland."

appeared like a small dovecot; wondering what this could be used for, I inquired, and discovered that it was a letter-box. I afterwards noticed numbers of these at cross roads all over the country.

I now ran merrily down a gentle slope, through Glen Assynt, passing the Ledberg marble quarries and pretty Loch Awe. When about two miles from Inchnadamph, I rode along a splendid limestone ridge, about two hundred and fifty feet in height, and beautifully tapestried with ivy. 8.30 p.m. Reached the neat hotel at the head of Loch Assynt.

While putting away my tricycle I heard the landlord rating one of his men for being so long in driving to Loch Inver* and back. His reply was, "I could not go faster; the road was so bad that I feared for the springs of the dog-cart." As his master accepted his excuse, and also told me that the road would not do for my machine, I gave up my intended trip to Loch Inver, but from what I have since heard, I should advise the cyclist to try it, as the scenery will amply repay his labour.

There is generally one private room in these hotels, while in this instance it was already occupied, the coffee-room party consisting

*"Lochs Beanoch and Loch Skin a Skink are literally teeming with trout, and there are many lochs about the latter that have not yet been fished."—*Young's* "*Sutherland.*"

WEIGHING THE BASKET.

of a family, some anglers, and myself. After the family and myself had had tea the fishermen returned from their day's sport, and there was great excitement while weighing their basket.*

When I mentioned the fissure near Loch Broom, one of my companions remarked that the view from the bridge across the chasm was the most awe-inspiring he had ever witnessed, and as others may wish to see it, I append a short description, kindly given me by one who knows the locality well.

"Of the six principal ravines on the Braemore estate, the one most generally known is on the Garve and Ullapool road, called 'Corrie Halloch (ugly gully); height, 200 feet; width, 84 feet. The best view is obtained by passing through a wicket-gate from the public road, along a private path, to a point where the ravine, a waterfall of 135 feet deep, and the suspension-bridge above it, are seen together. During heavy floods, the thundering roar of the falling torrent, and the spray thrown high aloft, with its own rainbow in the midst, produces an effect really very grand, and probably not to be surpassed in Great Britain."

I may add that Mr. Fowler kindly permits the public to make use of the paths leading to the bridge.

Before midnight it came on to pour with rain.

N.B.—Although I had many views of Mount Suilven, it never took the beautiful cone shape which I had been prepared to admire.

DISTANCE.

Garve to Ullapool	32 miles	One or two bad places, otherwise an excellent road.
Ullapool to Inchnadamph..	26 ,,	Very hilly, but the surface is firm and good. Grand scenery.
Total	58 ,,	

Fine day. Wind against.

FORTY-FIRST DAY.
INCHNADAMPH, KYLE SKOU, SCOURIE.

I HAD gone to bed with the depressing consciousness that it was a stormy night, and that the bad weather was just as likely to last a week as not, which would be a serious matter for me while travelling through this lonely and mountainous district. Judge, then, of my

* "Good and varied fishing. I killed an average of 55 trout per day on Loch Awe. The angling season commences in June."—*Young's* "*Sutherland.*"

satisfaction on being awakened this morning by the light of the glorious sun, which came streaming in through my partially closed windows.

During the forenoon I went to see the subterranean burn (the Traligill) which, about a mile and a-half up stream, disappears under an overhanging rock, runs underground for about 600 yards, and then pops up again as lively as ever. At the top of the glen, about a mile and a-half further, there is a grand view of Ben More Assynt (3,281 feet, the highest mountain in Sutherland), and its stupendous precipices. It is said that the golden eagle is still to be seen swooping about its crags.

I attended the Gaelic service at the kirk, and listened attentively to what appeared to be a most eloquent and impassioned discourse without understanding a single word of it. A young fellow led the singing, which I tried to follow, but invariably found myself at the lower B when he had jumped to the upper E.

1.30. Left Inchnadamph for Scourie.

Not far from the inn I halted for a look round. The south side of Loch Assynt is lined by diversified high land of different coloured cliffs; this with a fringe of natural wood sets it off. Numerous rocky points jut into the lake; on one of these near at hand stand the picturesque ruins of Ardrech Castle, an historic building, Montrose having been enticed into it and kept a prisoner after his defeat in 1650. The grey sides of Quinag rise sheer from the Northern shore and form the predominant feature of the landscape.

As directed, I took the first turning to the right, and after slaving up a break-back hill I found myself at a farmhouse, where the road ended. Returning to the lakeside I went on to Skiag Bridge, and commenced the ascent. The first part was very severe, but I managed to ride the last half-mile to the crest of the ridge between Quinag (2,541 feet) and Glasven, which were close to me on each hand.

From this point I first took a bird's-eye view of Loch Assynt, which wants an island or two to enliven it. The view to the northward was savagely rugged and wildly beautiful. From my standpoint the mountain side, covered with colossal masses of débris, sloped down to Kyle Skou, a deep inlet branching off into Glen Dhu (dark glen) and Glen Coul. Away beyond this and all around to the east appeared a chaos of rugged elevations heaped about in endless confusion, as though there had been a general scrimmage. On the other hand the syren Atlantic wore a deceitful smile which seemed to promise eternal tranquility.

From the ridge the rough track dipped steeply down to a bridge across a stream. Here I stopped, and walked by its side through a gully brilliant with heather, and ornamented by elegant pinnacles of rock for a quarter of a mile, when a fine but nameless waterfall (100 feet?) came in sight.

Regaining my tricycle I mounted, but finding the path to be still dangerous I walked a little farther, then by using caution I was able to ride the rest of the way down by Unapool to the ferry. They can give a shake-down to two or three travellers at the primitive inn. As regards the situation, I will give the following quotation from Mr. Young's "Guide to Sutherland":—

"For an artist in search of Highland scenery of the wildest and grandest description there could be no better place than the Ferryhouse at Loch Kyle Skou." Again, "All round these lochs there is a ring of grand mountains, beginning with Ben Strome and sweeping round to Quinag on the south; the circle being filled up by Ben Leod, The Stack of Glen Coul, Ben Uie and Glasven."

While crossing the water (4d.) I questioned the ferryman concerning the little-known waterfall at the head of Glen Coul. He said that it was 500 feet high, and when full was in his opinion finer than Foyers. This fall must be viewed from a boat (fare five shillings). After landing on the north shore I rode a little, but the loose surface soon compelled me to dismount. After walking for about a mile I passed a well-built house with a garden and orchard; from thence the road began to rise. Presently a heavy shower drove me into a cottage, where I was welcomed by an elderly man and his wife, who gave me a chair by the fire. They were English, and the husband told me that he worked for the owner of the big house, but that it was only possible to cultivate plots of ground here and there, and even those were very unproductive.

Continuing, I walked up a long, steep ascent. From the top, Quinag, which from other points of view had shown either one, two, or three peaks, now bore the appearance of a gigantic *cul-de-sac*. I now realised the truth of the saying, "Sutherland is a county where no man who cannot climb like a goat and jump like a grasshopper should attempt to travel," for the whole way to Badcaul is composed of ranges and knolls of gneiss, with very little vegetation. I really cannot say how many times I mounted and dismounted during those seven or eight miles. The narrow road dodged in and out and up and down in a most remarkable manner, which I will attempt briefly to describe.

It first of all wriggled round numerous tarns* for about three-quarters of a mile, then descended steeply to a loch thick with reeds and water-lilies, with a fringe of birchwood ; then it ascended to another plateau and repeated itself. It next ran down to a small bay (Colva) on the coast. Up it rose again to a third plateau, where, after twisting and undulating by any number of lochans, with pretty peeps of the sea, it went precipitously down to Badcaul—a most lovely inlet, decked with twenty-four picturesque islet gems, on which the last rays of the sun were lingering.

While paddling through this lonely region I had fully expected to come upon flocks of wild fowl floating on the bosom of the lake, to surprise the osprey on its nest, or at any rate to see traces of the marten or wild cat. But no ; the most tempting cover was tenantless, and the impressive stillness of the calm evening air was unbroken even by the wheels of my tricycle, which travelled noiselessly over the sandy surface.

Near Badcaul there is a large storehouse for preserving the salmon which are taken in great quantities on the coast. The road, which had been narrow and rather heavy, now became wide and firm. After walking up a stiff hill out of the village for nearly a mile, I mounted and rattled along a mile of level and one of slope down to Scourie. This is a scattered township, situated close to the bay, and surrounded on all other sides by rugged ledges of bare rock. There were patches of oats and barley in between the knolls on the plain, but the place, on the whole, wore a bleak and sterile aspect.

I found a snug inn, but as its limited accommodation was already occupied by two fishing parties, I was told off to sleep in a cottage belonging to the hotel-keeper a mile away. I chummed with the Cambridge fishing—I beg their pardon, reading—party, and, as we were mutually interested in our different pastimes, the conversation flowed freely. The "coach" had been to these parts for several years in succession, and was very enthusiastic about the fresh air, fine scenery, and good sport. From his account I imagine that the veriest novice, by simply flogging the water, could quickly fill a basket. He strongly advised me not to leave the neighbourhood without seeing the wonderful cliffs of Handa Island, which range from six hundred to eight hundred feet. Finding, however, that this would entail a day's boating, I did not think " the game worth the candle."

* "There is a chain of fresh water lochs, in which the trout are numerous and excellent."—*Young.*

While remarking on the number of lochans and tarns that I had seen, he said that from the summit of Glasven no less than 240 could be counted.

I was now asked to give my experiences, and presently began to relate the triumph of my " Cheylesmore" over the Cantab's dog-cart in the race to Quirang, in spite of their conviction that I should be nowhere. On telling their names I saw an exchange of glances between my auditors, but being wrapped up in the narration of my own exploits, I continued to the end of my story, when one of them exclaimed, "Ha, ha! The youngest F. is one of my greatest friends." Fortunately I had not " put my foot in it."

Hearing that I was bound for Durness, they advised me to hurry on so as to arrive there before the party in the private room, who were going to make an early start for that place, otherwise I might have to sleep in Smoo Cave or some other damp spot. Thanking them for the hint, I determined to cut out the select ones if possible, but almost despaired of doing so, as it was now nearly midnight and I had the drawback of a distant bed.

Luckily, it was fine when I started off for the cottage, conducted by a damsel whose charms I could not distinguish in the darkness of the night. No sooner had she opened the door of my room than she fled from my presence like a streak of lightning, and I—poor I! —was left, like Alexander Selkirk, monarch of all I surveyed.

A joke's a joke, but I did not like being left alone with rats all night, and soon began to imagine all kinds of horrors. I first conjured up a scene of blood and murder, in which I was to play the part of the victim, but second thoughts told me that they do not go in for this kind of thing in Scotland. Visions of ghosts next passed before me; for these I prepared a warm reception in the shape of a heavy poker.

I had just tucked myself comfortably in, when it flashed across me, " Suppose I am taken suddenly ill?" But before I could settle what was to be done in such an emergency I fell into the arms of " Murphy."

DISTANCE.

Inchnadamph to Kyle Skou Ferry 9 miles. Mountainous, tolerably good surface.
Kyle Skou to Scourie .. .. 12 ,, A hilly, romantic ride.

Total .. 21 ,,

One shower, otherwise very fine.

FORTY-SECOND DAY.

Scourie, Rhiconich, Cape Wrath, Durness.

My timid guide rapped me up at 6.30, but as it was raining hard, I considered, on the principle of "bird in hand," that it would be wiser to make sure of another wee snooze in the bed I was in than to tear off through the wet on the chance of getting one, thirty miles away.

When I woke again the sun was out, and it was not long before I set off for the inn. On the way I inquired for the post-office, and was directed to a blacksmith's shop; at my request, the brawny-armed Cyclops left his bellows and handed me a welcome letter. The private party were having breakfast when I arrived, and I had barely time to gobble up mine before their carriage and pair drove up to the door.

I made tracks as soon as possible, and overtook the reading party with their books (of *flies*) by the side of Loch Baddindaroch; and while we were walking up the steep brae from the east end of that lake the carriage party joined us.

"Well," thought I, "is this to be another Quirang race, or will it be the second edition of the romance of 'Nauticus in search of a pillow'?"

I gained the top before the carriage, and off I went as hard as I could paddle down a narrow road of rather loose sand, which, after working its intricate way to level ground, made a very wide sweep round an arm of the sea, and through a boggy wilderness to the point whence the road branches off to Lairg. Here I turned to the left, passing a solitary shieling, and ran on to the bridge across the Laxford, which has the reputation of being one of the best salmon and trout rivers in the north.

The irregular outline of the sea loch, the variety of different crags and eminences partially clothed with shrubs, creepers, and heather, the rush of water issuing from between dark overhanging cliffs, with spiky Ben Stack and one or two other mountains in the background, formed an uncommonly romantic picture.

I could not remain long to enjoy it, for I expected every second to hear the dreaded sound of wheels, so I continued my way along the edge of Loch Laxford for half a mile, then headed north up a stiff hill. From the brow of this to Rhiconich the features of the road were similar to that between Kyle Skou and Badcaul—viz., a labyrinth of ponderous masses of granite, interspersed with numerous tarns teeming with trout; the gradients being less severe, the ride was all the more enjoyable. The white sand on which I had hitherto been travelling all along the west coast now changed to red.

11.30 a.m. Arrived at Rhiconich, on Loch Inchard, a singularly wild place, huge boulders acting the part of standing crops. There is apparently very little business done at this inn, for I broke the bank by requesting change for a shilling. Chuckling at the idea of having outstripped the carriage and pair thus far, I hastily swallowed some light refreshment, and bustled on as fast as I could up an incline of four miles.

After the first very steep bit the gradient became more easy by the side of the burn Achrisgill, which made one or two pretty falls. From the top of the hill the character of the country underwent an entire change, and I emerged on to a sombre moorland, shortly reaching Gualin (shoulder), a house at the watershed. A long inscription explained that this edifice was built to give shelter to any unfortunate traveller who might be caught in one of the fearful gales which sweep across this elevated and exposed situation. Let it be known, however, that it is now a shooting lodge, and masons were hard at work preparing it for the laird when I was there.

The Gualin commands an extensive view of the valley to the Kyle of Durness, through which I could see my track winding for several miles. On the right the detached mountains Foinaven (2,980 feet), Cranstackie (2,629 feet), and Ben Spionn (2,536 feet), rose boldly from the plain.

I now enjoyed a decline of five miles. The first part was steep, but the remainder being nearly level, with a good surface, I was able to tool along at a good pace. Passing the head of the Kyle, which is surrounded by heathery hills, I walked up an incline to a fine plateau, pleasant to the eye, with its verdant carpet of grass and patches of growing corn. Another mile, with cottages here and there, brought me to Durness Hotel, near the sea, at 2.15 p.m. I immediately engaged a room, and, while baiting my steed (oiling up), I informed the landlord that he might look for some gentlemen whom I had raced from Scourie and beaten.

J

3.0 p.m. Started for Cape Wrath. I had to return to the Kyle, and ride half a mile along its north shore to an eminence opposite the ferry-house. They keep a good look-out, for I had not been waving long before I saw them launching the boat, but the tide being very strong, it was some time before they got over. When they did arrive affairs did not look promising, for, not having noticed the tricycle, they had brought a cockleshell, which they declared would not carry my machine through the nasty rip of the tide. Being pressed for time, I could not wait an hour while they fetched another boat, so, after some persuasion, they consented to risk it.

After considerable difficulty, I managed to get my tricycle from the rocks into the restive boat; then, by pulling close up in shore, we succeeded in crossing the rip with no worse luck than shipping a few seas.

On landing, I first had to climb a long stiff brae, and from the top of the vertical cliffs which guard the Kyle on the south side I could clearly distinguish the many sandbanks and shoals which the rapidity of the current had deposited in different places.

The road now dipped suddenly down to a ravine, along the bottom of which ran an open burn. There was no help for it but to off with shoes and stockings and wade through. I found it no easy matter to force my " Cheylesmore " over the slippery boulders in the bed of the stream, and I nearly found myself on my nose once or twice while doing so.

After another long walk to the top of the ravine, I mounted and rode across an undulating desolate tract for three or four miles, the scenery being varied by a fine mountain on the left (Fashbein), and another (Skrisbein) on the right. The surface of the road in some places was very bad—loose sand with stones heaped on. About seven miles from the ferry, the road crossed another ravine (bridged), and I caught sight of a fine pinnacle rock standing out from the bold coast. Up and down again to the snug cove Clash Carnock, in which the stores for the light-house are landed when the weather permits.

One more heavy rise, and hurrah! the turretted buildings surrounding the light-house at last, all looking the picture of cleanliness! It was refreshing to witness the unfeigned delight of the children on seeing a new face in this remote place. The keeper showed me over the lighthouse, and when I signed my name " Nauticus," he looked doubtfully at me, as much as to say, " You are either a humbug or a 'dook' in disguise ! "

I had imposing views of the red granite cliffs which form this renowned headland. One of these, 600 feet in height, resembled the outer walls of a castle, but the magnificent front of the cliffs can only be seen in its true character from the sea. The following is Anderson's description of a view from a boat. ("Guide to the Highlands.")

"From that direction abrupt and threatening precipices, vast and huge fissures, caverns, and subterranean openings alternately appear in the utmost confusion, while the deep-sounding rush of the mighty waters, agitated by the tides among their resounding openings, the screams and never ceasing flight of innumerable sea fowl, and often the spoutings of a stray whale in his unwieldy gambols in the ocean, form altogether a scene which none who has witnessed it can ever forget."

The heavy clouds which had obscured the sky during the afternoon had dispersed, leaving the air unusually clear, so that I could make out Lewis Island and North Rona, distant forty miles. Feeling somewhat exhausted by the toils of the way and the strong head wind, I asked for some tea, which was kindly served by the keeper's wife, who confided to me that, having lately come from a populous district, she felt the loneliness of the situation extremely, and that the difficulty of educating and employing the children was a serious consideration.

Wishing her good luck, and waving an adieu to the youngsters, who were hard at work weeding the courtyard, I hastened back, chancing the hills in my hurry to reach the ferry before dark, which I succeeded in doing, after the most severe twenty-two miles' ride I had yet experienced. The time occupied was two hours and three-quarters from the ferry to the cape, and two hours and a quarter in returning.

I recrossed in a large boat, and as the tide suited, I landed comfortably on the stone slip. At 9.30 p.m., while riding along in the deep gloaming, a brilliant streak of light suddenly shot up from the west, and illuminated the sky for some time in a remarkable manner.

Reached the hotel at 10 p.m., and supped with the select party, who had stopped to fish in the Laxford river (so much for the race), and had killed two fine salmon and a number of trout in a short time. In the course of conversation it came out that the stalwart Highlander still clings to his old superstitions; for instance, on no account will he venture out alone after dark, lest a witch, in the form of a hare, should cross his path, a certain omen of evil.

DISTANCE.

Scourie to Rhiconich	.. ..	13 miles.	Romantic; undulating road; firm gravel surface.
Rhiconich to Durness	.. ..	14 ,,	Hilly; good surface.
Durness to Cape Wrath and back	27	,, ·	A series of big hills; bad road.
Total	.. ..	54 ,,	

Fine day. Wind mostly against.

FORTY-THIRD DAY.
DURNESS, RHICONICH, LAXFORD BRIDGE, OVERSKAIG INN.

AFTER breakfast I trudged off to Smoo Cave (one mile). The entrance to this celebrated limestone excavation has a fine vaulted roof; the interior can only be seen from a boat, which has to be lifted over a ledge of rock, the charge for this privilege being ten shillings. I asked the reason of this exorbitant demand, and received the answer, "Hardly any one comes." I ventured to suggest that if the tariff were lowered more money would be netted, for probably others, like myself, do not care to pay through the nose. After amusing myself by bringing out the echo I returned to the hotel, having a good view of the fine cliffs about Far-out Head on my way. Durness is an excellent head-quarters for the geologist, who will find a rich harvest of fossils in the neighbouring rocks.

9.45 a.m. Started for Lairg, and rattled along cheerily to the foot of Gualin Hill (eight miles). While tramping up this I had a striking view of Foinaven, which seemed to be a mountain within a mountain, it being white outside and green in. Ben Spionnadh also showed out majestically its characteristic being white quartzite, with a spur shooting off to the westward. The select party passed me in the carriage, and shortly afterwards I saw them, rod in hand, walking down to the River Dionard—not much to look at, but a good one for sport.

From the watershed the southern prospect was gloriously wild— a sea of rugged knolls with green between. At Rhiconich I got my change for the shilling, but fared badly in the eating line, salmon, tea, and eggs not being sufficiently substantial for me when taking such heavy exercise. The inn was nice and clean, but the visitors' book showed that the cyclist is not likely to be crowded out here.

BEN STACK.

2 p.m. Resumed my journey and much enjoyed the return trip through this part. The whole road commands one constant succession of romantic scenes, every turn disclosing some new point of interest.

At the junction of the roads near Laxford Bridge I turned to the left and ran by the bank of the river, the fine red cliffs contrasting charmingly with the different colours of the stream, the foliage, and the grey rocks above. After travelling over half a mile of level ground, I went over rather a steep brae and down to Loch Stack on the other side. The expression of the scene now entirely changed, and combined a happy mixture of severe grandeur and softened beauty.

Ben Stack—sometimes compared to the Matterhorn—reared his gnarled and lofty head directly above me. The north side of the loch was bounded by a guano-coloured, deeply-furrowed wall, five hundred feet in height and some miles in length (Arkle). On the bosom of the lake reposed a gem-like island, on which gleamed a tall white cross: this no doubt marks the last resting-place of a former owner of one of the peaceful homesteads which lay amid patches of vivid green on the western border.

Having ridden beneath a canopy of trees to the east end, I laboured up a hill, and after a mile of level, issued from the shade and descended through a wilder tract to Archpharie, a hamlet, and the Duke of Westminster's Lodge at the west end of Loch More. This is a plain sheet of water, girdled with timber, aud brightened by a belt of glittering sand. I had a capital spin of four miles to the other end, whence the road ascended a long, rough hill, through a defile, then it dipped down to Loch Merkland.

I now came upon another transformation scene, but this time, unfortunately, it was of a most melancholy description—viz., an insipid lake set in sombre hills. The road, too, was thickly covered with fresh metal, therefore Merkland does not afford me any pleasing reminiscences. Loch Shin, which I presently came to, was no better, and, to make matters worse, it commenced to drizzle, and of course the wind, as usual, was right ahead. This combination of circumstances caused me to heave-to at Overskaig Inn; but, perhaps, after all it was the best thing I could have done, for, on dismounting, I found that yesterday's exertions and to-day's insufficient nourishment had begun to tell upon me.

I was very glad to sit in dry clothes by a roaring fire, although I should have preferred the society of some anglers in the private room.

In fact, I was feeling for the first time a little lonesome, and the desolate scene from the window was fast giving me a fit of the blues; when, to change the current of my thoughts, I took up my journal and wrote as follows :—" Reached this little inn at six o'clock; no

other house in sight. Delayed on the way by the screw-nut of the Stanley head working loose; no tools to fit it. Stopped at Laxford Cottage, and astonished the woman by asking for a pair of tongs. On promising not to pinch her nose, she produced them, but as they did not bite properly, my "Cheylesmore" soon began to frisk about again."

DISTANCE.

Durness to Laxford Bridge	.. 20 miles.	
Laxford Bridge to Overskaig	.. 24 ,,	Undulating, most of the road being good.
Total	.. 44 ,,	

Very wet night.

FORTY-FOURTH DAY.
OVERSKAIG INN, ALTNAHARRA, TONGUE.

My dreams were disturbed by the howling of the wind, and the dashing and gurgling of the rain, which partially flooded my room; it seemed as though the frail tenement would be swept away by the extreme violence of the storm. On turning out in the morning, I saw Loch Shin lashed into great waves by the wind, which was blowing a perfect hurricane from the westward.

At 11 o'clock the coach arrived. How I pitied the wretched pleasure seekers, who, by means of handkerchiefs and scarfs, were endeavouring to keep their wigs on their heads and their expensive ivories from being blown down their throats. Even the poor horses' ears looked inside out.

At 11.30, the rain having ceased, I began to think about making a move. A gentleman remonstrated with me for presuming to travel on a tricycle in such weather, and I felt that he was right, but the prospect of being borne on the wings of the wind was too tempting to be resisted, so I decided to proceed to Lairg and wait there for the weather to moderate.

To make my machine as efficient as possible, I tightened up the Stanley head and secured leather to both spoons of the brake.

Away I went like an arrow from a bow, and, with the exception of an occasional shade of anxiety, I thoroughly enjoyed the novelty of being blown, not only along the level ground, but actually up some of the slopes as well; and without putting foot to pedal, except for a stroke or two, I soon overtook a trap which had started before me.

The road undulated gently along the north side of the loch, the surface being pretty good. About five miles from Lairg the result of the Duke of Sutherland's labours for the improvement of the land became apparent, the road widened and was well macadamised, and farm houses, fat cattle, and other signs of prosperity, appeared on all sides.

Three miles further, after crossing a wooden bridge, I came to the point where the road branches off to Altnaharra, and finding that the wind would still be slightly favourable, I determined to save time and distance by heading north at once. This abrupt alteration of my course brought about a corresponding change in the scenery, for I had now turned my back upon the rapidly increasing signs of civilization, and before me lay a vast heaving barren desert (Strath Terry). The line of the road was marked by tall black posts, placed there for the guidance of travellers in time of snow, which frequently lies at a depth of twenty or thirty feet for months together.

For the first two miles the road was level, with rather a loose surface; it then began to rise, and continued to do so at an easy gradient for some distance. At the same time it turned towards the wind; therefore, in spite of its now excellent condition, I not only had to dismount, but found considerable difficulty in pushing my way against the fury of the gale, which swept unchecked across the open plain. Nevertheless I found objects to beguile the way. To the left rose my old acquaintance, Ben More Assynt, and to the northward Klibreck (3,164 feet), the central and one of the most majestic of the numerous isolated mountains which characterise the county of Sutherland.

I rode occasionally when favoured by the configuration of the ground, and by-and-by found myself at Craske—two houses in a dell, with a forlorn-looking inn—where I stopped and had milk and scones. The woman said that she had no bedrooms to let, but, if necessary, the parlour could be turned into one.

From the top of the hill above Craske (commonly called Lord Reay's green table, from its flat top), I had a splendid spin of seven miles to Altnaharra. But I had my work cut out to keep the machine under control, for the wind was behind me again, and the brake-leathers being worn through, the furious blasts whirled me along at railway speed.

While scudding through narrow Strath Bagastie I came upon some men who were repairing the road, the surface of which for the last fifteen miles had been similar to one of the Kensington Garden walks. In my enthusiasm I warmly complimented the workmen, and pleased them immensely by saying that they, one and all, deserved a " leather medal with a hole in it " as a reward of merit for their zealous and successful labours.

Presently Loch Naver hove in sight. A canopy of clouds rested on the peaks at the western extremity, and the contrast between the

peculiar gloom which overshadowed that part of the lake and the brilliant sunshine which illuminated the remainder had a most romantic effect.

4.30 p.m. Reached Altnaharra, a wee village with a lodge. I went to the latter thinking it to be the hotel, but a gentleman in plush quickly undeceived me. Mine host of the excellent inn afforded me every information, and I took his advice to start off to Tongue instead of making for Erriboll, as intended.

Got away at 5.30. On the north side of the fine bridge which spans the River Mudale at the foot of the village, I came to three branch roads. The left leads to Erriboll, the right to Strath Naver. Selecting the middle one, I immediately commenced a long ascent, but contrived to ride the greater part of it.

I soon observed on my left front a most singular mountain (Ben Loyal), which assumed various fanciful forms as I advanced. At first I likened it to a gigantic tortoise, but from the crest of the hill it resembled a lion couchant. While descending I was trying to find some new comparison for it, when my spirited "Cheylesmore," taking advantage of my abstraction, bolted, and charged at headlong speed through a wild gorge confined by deep red cliffs to Loch Loyal, where I succeeded in reining him in. Then the brute took the sulks, and I positively had to force him *nolens volens* along the edge of that noble expanse of water.

It was sad to see here and there ruins of habitations and other signs of better times on both sides of the lake. After two miles I came to the only house between Altnaharra and Tongue; from thence the road turned to the left, and inclined up the side of a barrier of hills which screen the seaward view. While walking up this I caught a glimpse of Ben Loyal's western face, which revealed an awful precipice.

On gaining the summit I found myself on the confines of a peat-moss wilderness, which rolled away northward into dim distance without a break in its monotony. While pursuing my cheerless way along the ridge, with the impression on my mind that Tongue would, after all, be a wretched place, the Kyle, lighted up by all the glory of the departing sun, burst upon my astonished gaze.

Beautiful and refreshing to the eye were the fields of vivid green, the dark foliage running to the water's edge, and the picturesque little town nestling among the trees in the bosom of the deep valley beneath. Bold were the headlands which protected the waters of the Kyle from the billows of the Atlantic Ocean. Grand was the circle of cliffs which guarded it from the inland invader. Noble were the mountains Ben Hope and Ben Loyal, which overlooked the scene with a sublime majesty unparalleled in Scotland.

The descent as far as the turning to Thurso was rideable, below that it was very rough and precipitous.

7.45 p.m. Arrived at the most popular hotel in the north (Tongue).

DISTANCE.

Overskaig Inn to Altnaharra ..	34 miles.	No hills to speak of, and a splendid road nearly the whole way.
Altnaharra to Tongue	17 ,,	First-rate road, but hilly.
Total	51 ,,	

Furious gale, clear overhead.

FORTY-FIFTH DAY.
Tongue, Loch Hope, Altnaharra.

THINKING that the meals were arranged *table d'hôte* fashion, I joined two gentlemen at the breakfast table, and was about to accept some eggs and bacon, when the waitress rushed in exclaiming, " That's not for *you*, sir." Her tone implied that it was gross impertinence for a common cyclist to presume to share the meal of distinguished visitors. I apologised, but they insisted upon my partaking of their fare until mine was ready, and made themselves so sociable and agreeable that I took the first opportunity of finding out who they were. One of them proved to be the well-known editor of the *Scotsman*, who pays an annual visit to Tongue, for the sake of the splendid fishing in Loch Loyal and numerous lochs in the neighbourhood.

As it was pouring with rain, I sent off a telegram to London, then employed myself with refitting my tricycle; and having ascertained that the enormous strain caused by yesterday's wind had bent the right spoon of the brake, I had it straightened and a fresh stock of leathers made.

At 3.30 p.m. the weather cleared up, but as the reply to my telegram had not come, and the next stage of my journey was involved in a considerable amount of uncertainty, I gave up all idea of moving that day.

At four o'clock, just as the expected telegram was handed to me, I heard that a trap had started for the ferry. " Now's my chance," thought I. " Altnaharra can be done in four or five hours, but if I give the wind time to get up, I may be detained here for a week." I hurried down through a grove of fine trees to the water's edge, and thence to a sandy point, where I found that the owner of the trap had hoisted the flag, and that the boat was already under way.

While waiting I enjoyed an unrivalled view of bonnie Ben Loyal (2,506 feet), its elegant peaks showing out clearly against the sky.

My companion remarked that this mountain is termed the Queen of Sutherland, and assuredly it deserves its reputation. The prospect was rendered all the more pleasing by the picturesque ruins of Castle Varich. In the course of conversation I was advised to abandon Erriboll, and to take the new road by Loch Hope, as being shorter and better in every way.

There is no road round the Kyle, and the inconveniences of this ferry are manifold. The following are some of them:—

1. Half an hour to an hour must be allowed from the time the signal is made until the boat arrives, and about the same for crossing.

2. If it is not close upon high tide there will not be sufficient water for the large boat, therefore no one but a foot-passenger can get over at all, and he is obliged to display his agility by hopping from rock to rock for half a mile in order to reach an island, and then to risk his life in a cockleshell.

We were fortunate in getting the big boat, but I had to stow my tricycle close to the horse. On the way over it came on to blow in a contrary direction, which compelled us to make several tacks, so what with the whistling of the wind, the flapping of the canvas, the flanking of the sheets, the heel of the boat, and the horse's heels, we all had a pretty lively time of it, and I felt devoutly thankful to find myself on *terra firma* once more at 5.30 p.m.

After walking for two miles up a rugged steep incline, I came to a forbidding desert of bog land called the Moin, a place that I shall not forget in a hurry. There is an old and very true saying on board ship,

"When the rain's before the wind,
Your topsail halliards you must mind."

This was the case with me at that particular moment. It had been perfectly calm during the rain, but no sooner did it cease than a breeze sprang up and quickly increased to a gale. Of topsail halliards I had none, but my hat was quite enough for me to "mind." As to my tricycle, it was a positive encumbrance.

The road was good, and I knew that it had been constructed at an immense expense for the benefit of wayfarers like myself, and yet, ungrateful man, I did not appreciate it, but growled and grumbled all the way to Moin House (house on the moss). This, like Gualin, has been erected to shelter the storm-stricken traveller; and allow me to recommend these establishments to those who are always sighing for a "breath of fresh air."

From the house I rode two miles down to the brow of the dangerous dip leading to the Chain Ferry, where I stopped to admire the splendid view of Loch Hope. A beach of pearly white sand marked its varied outline, and the combined effect of wood, fields, and homesteads formed a very pleasing rural scene, reminding me of Loch Laggan in Inverness-shire. Only in this instance the high land was on a much grander scale, spiky, rugged Ben Hope (3,040 feet) being the chief feature in the landscape.

At the lodge just above the ferry I turned to the left along the north side of the lake. Heavy masses of cloud began to gather about the mountain tops, and two or three sharp short rain squalls came sweeping over the water, which added indeed to the effect of the scenery, but not to my comfort. The road was pretty good for a mile or two; then I encountered a series of troublesome ups and downs, and the surface became loose and rough.

I had not gone far before a sense of faintness crept over me. In the middle of the day, having made up my mind that, what between the rain and the ferry, there was no chance of getting away, I had reserved my appetite for dinner, and later on, in my anxiety to catch the boat, the subject of eating had not entered my head. This neglected feeling now began to show unpleasant signs of asserting itself, and on considering how it could be appeased, I came to the conclusion that, the nearest inn being about twenty miles off, the only thing to be done was to beg my bread by the wayside. I soon came to a bothie, but as it lay a short distance from the road, and did not look particularly inviting, I passed it by. I had cause to regret this, for no others appeared ahead, though several mocked me from the opposite side of the water. A shepherd of whom I made enquiries invited me to his hut, but this being the one I had left behind, time would not allow me to return.

At the east end of the loch I passed along the base of Ben Hope, a grand sight, terrace above terrace of wood and rock, crowned by stupendous peaks exquisitely broken. I had resolved to get refreshment at Cashildhu (a few scattered houses at the head of the lake), but on joining the road from Erriboll I found the surface so excellent that I determined to run on and take my chance.

I now entered Strath More, a deep valley in the heart of the hills; its grassy sides sloped up to a rampart of rock from whence enormous blocks had fallen, among which the road wound its way, and having spun along rapidly for two miles, a dwelling came in sight at last. Two men were outside the door, and one, whom I took to be the owner, told me to go in and make myself at home, at the same time requesting a ride on my tricycle. This I, as usual, declined, out being urged, gave in, on the principle that one good turn deserves another. My diplomacy, however, was rather thrown away, for it afterwards transpired that he did not belong to the place at all.

On entering, I was cordially received by the mistress, and a strapping wench was directed to set scones and milk before me. I made such havoc with the latter, that in spite of my declaring that my thirst was quenched, the good dame went off to milk the cow again. In her absence I carried on a mild flirtation with the maiden fair, and was much amused with her naïve remarks. Among other things she told me that she had not been further than thirty miles from her mother's apron-strings in her life; she had never seen a railway, and what was more, "didn't want to."

Presently the master (a shepherd) came in with five dogs, who stretched themselves in various attitudes before the fire. This led me to inquire as to the truth of several wonderful stories which I had heard about the collie. He said that these were chiefly exaggerations, but that he at least could bear witness to the fact that, although he had charge of some thousands of sheep, his dogs would always detect and drive away a stranger.

9.45 p.m. I resumed my journey on a road that was level and good for two miles to Mussel; from thence it inclined steadily up the north side of the glen for about three more. As I ascended, the murmur of the river beneath met my ear, and the rays of the moon gave just sufficient light to show that I was missing some fine mountain scenery.

The shepherd had made some remark about an open burn, but I was taken completely aback by finding myself on the edge of a broad rapid stream of unknown depth. No one enjoys a tub more than myself at the proper time, but at this hour of the night, with a tricycle in tow, the prospect was anything but inviting. However, off came my shoes and stockings, and in I went. Ugh! so cold! It was shallower than it looked, so I got across pretty easily. I then remembered that this very stream (Alt-na-Caillach) makes a splendid fall of 300 feet not very far from the ford, and that in the neighbourhood one of the most remarkable ruins in Scotland is to be seen, viz., the tower of Dun Dornadillo, which tradition says was once a Scotch king's hunting box.

It was now cloudy and pitch dark, and my attention was wholly occupied in trying to make out my way. About a mile above the ford I came to the watershed, and the road appeared to be level for some distance, then it gently declined. Having been told that there were no dangers, I ran along with confidence; occasionally getting on to the grassy edge, and once going flop into the ditch by the wayside, but altogether seeming to keep to the road by instinct.

When the clouds parted a little I endeavoured to make out what kind of country I was paddling through, and took it to be bog and open moor. At one place I passed two or three detached houses all in darkness, and by-and-by found myself being carried down a rather steep descent; at the same time I sighted a gleam of water, and presently rode by what proved to be Loch Meadie. On gaining the summit of a hill beyond that the moon shone out brilliantly, and my heart was gladdened by seeing before me the high land, which I recognised as that about Loch Naver. I now spurted ahead more rapidly, and just after calculating that Altnaharra could not be far off I sighted the bridge on my right. "Here we are," cried I; "but where are the three roads? Ah, there is one." I dismounted. "But it's too narrow; this cannot be the place. Yet that's the bridge, without doubt, its three arches stand out clearly enough. Still it can't be the right one."

Having come to this conclusion, I mounted and ran on in momentary expectation of seeing another bridge. No, not a sign of one;

and after a mile and a half of this I became alarmed. Why, where *am* I going? The wind is behind instead of ahead, as it has been all night, and by the pole star I am steering to the northward of east instead of due south. The high land, too, looks queer. Bother! I'm all wrong. What a fool I was to suppose that two bridges of that size would be close together in this out-of-the-way place! Of course that must have been Altnaharra, and here I am flying up Strath Naver as fast as I can go." Back I went, but it took me some time to do the one and a half miles against the wind.

Once more the three arches came in view, and leaving my machine by the wayside, I walked towards them with the intention of ascertaining my whereabouts. As I drew nearer so the bridge seemed to recede; then it changed altogether, and I found myself close to THREE WHITEWASHED BUILDINGS! Never in the whole course of my life had I been so absurdly deceived, for from the road I would have wagered any odds that a bridge was before me.

"I'll knock these people up," thought I, going to the house door. There were no blinds, nor any sign of its being inhabited, and after hammering and shouting for some time, I gave it up and returned to the road.

The question now was, whether I should take shelter in one of the sheds or go on. The night being very fine, I made up my mind to proceed as best I might until daylight, which could not be far off.

I pegged along at a good pace for about twenty minutes, when suddenly the bark of a dog, and immediately afterwards the voices of men, startled the midnight air. Welcome! thrice welcome sounds to a benighted traveller. With a voice tremulous from excitement I asked the distance and direction of Altnaharra, and should not have been surprised at any answer, so utterly bewildered had I become. Nevertheless I could hardly believe my ears on hearing "Two miles straight ahead;" therefore if I had only gone quietly on, and had not been led astray by the vision, I should have been in the land of Nod long ago. It turned out that these men had been celebrating a birthday at the hotel, and that they lived in the very house which I had been trying to take by storm.

In due course of time Altnaharra Hotel was reached, and hurrah! there was a light in one of the windows. I drew up at the door and tried to get in; it was locked. I rapped; no reply. Louder; still none. Having read of more than one ardent lover contriving to attract his lady's attention by throwing gravel at her window, I tried this dodge at the lighted one. I could only find mud and pebbles, and not wishing to break the glass, I began with the former. Being unsuccessful, I lobbed a pebble. Crack! "Enough to rouse the seven sleepers," thought I. After waiting a little while I tried again, and, although in my desire to save the window my aim was not very accurate, I succeeded in striking the pane several times, but all to no purpose. At last my patience became exhausted, and taking a stone in my fist, I banged at the door until the building echoed again. The effect was magical. Up flew the window, out popped a head, and a shrill voice from amid a forest of curl-papers demanded, "What's the matter?" On explaining my situation I was let in, leaving my accommodating steed under a tree, and retired to roost at 2.30 a.m.

DISTANCE.

Tongue to Altnaharra (via Loch Hope) .. .. 30 miles. Only one hill to speak of; very good surface, except by Loch Hope, which was newly made.

Wet morning. Fine but windy evening.

FORTY-SIXTH DAY.
Altnaharra, Betty Hill.

During last night's adventures I felt that the crank was working rather loosely, the last mile or so becoming much worse, but being intent on getting in, I did not care to stop and meddle with it in the dark. On examining the crank this morning I saw what a narrow escape I had had, for one pin of the clamp had dropped off, and the other was within an ace of doing so. If this had happened, the balls of the bearing would have fallen out into the road, and the machine would have been rendered useless. As there was no blacksmith nearer than Betty Hill, I secured the clamp with stout copper wire, which answered very fairly.

I waited until eleven o'clock, hoping that the weather would hold up, but it was still blowing and raining when I started at that time. After crossing the bridge I turned to the right on to a narrow stony road, and while paddling along the bleak banks of the river I realised the cheerless situation of Altnaharra; but the comforts of the hotel, and the excellent fishing in the adjacent lochs, render it a very desirable place for the angler, and the cyclist may think himself fortunate if he can get a bed there in the season.

The first mile or two by Loch Naver lay through a pretty wood, and as the sun was now shining brightly, the view of the fine lake, with Mount Klibreck in the background, was of a pleasing nature. This did not last long, for I soon emerged on to a rolling, treeless country.

From the head of Loch Naver the road ran with gentle undulations by the banks of the river, and if the surface had only been good I might have made rapid progress, for the wind was in my favour; but it became worse and worse, first stony, next soft and sandy, then a combination of both. I struggled onwards, but on the whole found myself more frequently on foot than in the saddle. Now came the open burns of which I had been warned. The first was of a tantalising width, and after wasting some time in trying to get my tricycle across without wetting my feet, I had to strip and wade through.

By-and-by I came to Syre, where they were building on both sides of the river, and observing a heavy squall brewing, I went into a large house, and found a party of men and women having dinner in the kitchen, which they invited me to share. I did not require any pressing, and thoroughly enjoyed some hotch-potch and oatcake, afterwards chatting with one of the men (a shepherd). He cautioned me not to pat the dogs, as their temper was uncertain, and said that he never caressed them himself, for they would soon be spoiled if he did. I learned from him that the feathery ornamental collie is of but little use for sheep, and he pointed out a smooth black-and-white dog as his best.

The deluge being at an end, I continued my journey, and almost immediately came to a foaming torrent about as wide as Oxford Street. It seemed impassable, but there was no option in the matter, and I knew that the late downpour would soon increase its volume.

I went very cautiously to work; gradually the little wheel disappeared, and higher and higher rose the water. When about midway, what with the rush of the current and the slippery stones, I lost my balance, and just recovered myself in time to escape a compulsory trip down stream. My tricycle, on the other hand, got wedged between two boulders, and would not budge either way, till by raising the hinder part I contrived to lever it safely to land. After this I growled no more about the provoking narrowness of any other stream.

I flattered myself that as the execrable road could not become worse, the chances were that it would improve, but this was a mistake, for the sand became deeper than ever, riding was out of the question, and I was surprised to see that this was a mail route, and that the car could manage to get over the ground.

The scenery on the whole was decidedly monotonous, but there were several pretty spots, and the pasturage on both sides of the river was excellent. The numerous ruins that I passed showed that this must have been a thriving valley at one time. Even now it is more thickly populated than any other that I had seen in Sutherland.

The jolting and bumping did not agree with my poor "Cheylesmore's" constitution, for the Stanley head worked loose, and the pin of the clamp had to be frequently re-secured. These drawbacks, and the difficulties of the way, combined to make this one of the most harassing days of my tour, and I was heartily glad when the sixth and last burn had been waded through. Had I gone on a little longer, I should have become quite smart in the exercise of off and on shoes and stockings. However, bright sunshine gave a golden lining to my cloud of hindrances; in this I was uncommonly fortunate, for heavy rain was close behind me all day.

On joining the road from Tongue I found a great improvement both in width and surface; it led me up a steep incline, and I had a pleasant run by a fine cliff with trees on each side of me. I soon caught sight of the sand hills about the mouth of the river, and a short descent took me to Chain Ferry. On the other side I climbed a stiff hill by the straggling village to the hotel at the summit, where in a moment I passed from summer into winter, for I was met by a bitter wind which set all my teeth chattering.

After engaging my room (5.30 p.m.) I took my tricycle to the blacksmith hard by, who, like his fellow at Garve, showed great reluctance to have anything to do with it. However, I coaxed him into trying some screws, and, as luck would have it, one fitted the clamp; meanwhile, I busied myself with the Stanley head, and soon had the satisfaction of seeing my machine ready for work again.

This simple-minded countryman won my heart and made me feel quite young again by frequently addressing me as "my laddie."

DISTANCE.

Altnaharra to Betty Hill .. 26 miles. Level, with a deep, sandy surface.
Six open burns.
Wet morning, showery afternoon.

FORTY-SEVENTH DAY.
BETTY HILL, THURSO, JOHN O'GROAT'S.

THIS inn, as I have said, stands in a very exposed situation. During the night the building fairly trembled with the violence of the wind, and in the morning the prospect from the window was the reverse of cheering. Heavy masses of nimbus cloud were chasing one another across the leaden sky, while sheets of rain partially obscured the bare sand-hills and the gloomy cliffs of this iron-bound coast.

Taking advantage of a lull, I started for John o'Groats at 8.15 a.m., and commenced my pleasure trip by walking down into and up out of a precipitous ravine. After riding a short distance over a peat moor, another steep gully had to be crossed, and my temper was acted upon in the same manner by torrents of rain and a rough road. My journey for the next ten miles may briefly be described as a succession of stiff braes on a bad surface, the redeeming points being a fair wind and occasional glimpses of fine coast scenery. In about an hour and a half I came to a number of scattered dwellings, a manse, and some limestone quarries.

"Bravo! here's Melvich!" exclaimed I ; but it was Strathy. Melvich, when reached, was more compact and boasted an hotel. Finding, however, that the bad weather was being left behind, I resisted the temptation to refresh the inner man, and pushed on for Thurso.

The next excitement was crossing the Halladale Ferry, where my "Cheylesmore" had to squeeze itself into a cobble. From the ferry we walked up a long rocky hill on to a bleak plateau; but the worst part of the day's work was over, for the gradients began to tone down, the surface to improve, and last, but not least, the sky was clear overhead.

I now passed the boundary of Sutherland, quite an event to me after all my varied experiences and adventures in that county. Beyond Reay the character of the country underwent an entire change, for although it still remained open and treeless, sand gave way to shale, and extensive fields of corn and other cereals formed a striking contrast to the patches of cultivation on the west coast. The road, too, became firm and good, buildings cropped up in all directions, and other signs tended to show that I was approaching the busy haunts of men.

From the top of a hill I came into full view of Thurso. The immense extent of monotonous country in the background gives the town a desolate appearance, but the bay and the bold red cliffs of Dunnet Head were very fine. I enjoyed a capital L. O. H. run of three miles to the Royal Hotel, where I halted at 1.15 p.m.

After luncheon I strolled through the broad streets of this neat little town, and feasted my eyes on the contents of the shop windows, with the usual result, *i.e.*, an irresistible inclination to buy something. In this case it was really necessary, for my boots were ready to drop from my feet, and other items of my toilette were in a dilapidated condition.

A day would have been well spent in visiting Holborn Head, the Clett Rock, and the magnificent cliff scenery in the neighbourhood, but, my time being limited, 3 p.m. found me paddling over the bridge. Having turned to the left I came to the Castle, ascended a hill to the right, and from thence made rapid progress along level ground. The whirl of vehicles and the number of people about made me feel like a country bumpkin in the Strand, so accustomed had I become to travelling for miles without meeting a soul.

About a mile and a half beyond Castletown a finger-post sent me to the left, and at Greenlands Farm, three miles farther, I again turned abruptly in the same direction on to a narrow road with a splendid surface. The cyclist is advised to take this (the lower) road, and for fear of missing it he should make frequent enquiries after leaving Castletown.

After running through a mixture of bog and cultivated ground for two or three miles, I arrived at Houna. This is a hamlet with an hotel so exactly like John o' Groat's that more than one deluded tourist has been known to give a graphic description to his friends of what he had seen at the celebrated house, when all the time he had never been there.

Avoiding this mare's nest, I turned to the right and worked on a semicircle of two miles to John o' Groat's Hotel, where I arrived at 5.30 p.m. I had quite expected to see some fellow-wheelmen here, and on finding the house empty was much disappointed, for I had met with the same luck at Betty Hill. However, the landlady was a host in herself, and her powers of persuasion overcame my intention of proceeding farther, so I settled myself down for the night.

I passed the evening in reading up the history of the old house, the remains of which—a green mound—was just in front of the window. It appears that once upon a time there were eight Dutch settlers of the name of Groat. These gentlemen used to hold an annual festive gathering to commemorate the arrival of their ancestor in Caithness, and to prevent the occasional quarrels about precedence on these occasions, one of them named John built an octagonal room with eight windows and doors, in which he placed a table of the same shape. At the next anniversary he invited each of his kinsmen to enter by a separate door and to sit at the head of the table; in this way he pleased them all, for each supposed himself to be in the place of honour.

DISTANCE.

Betty Hill to Thurso .. 32 miles. Rough and precipitous.
Thurso to John o' Groat's.. 21 ,, Good surface; no hills.

Total .. 53 ,,

Wet morning, but ran into fine weather.

FORTY-EIGHTH DAY.
John o'Groat's, Duncansbay Head, Wick.

The morning being moist and unpleasant, I thought it advisable to wait a little. The landlord recommended me to go off to Duncansbay Head, but as the view appeared very tame from outside the hotel, I pooh-poohed the idea, and said that I had seen Cape Wrath. Presently, having had some further talk about it, I thought it would be just as well to go, if only to kill time.

A walk of a mile and a half on soft ground brought me in sight of the Stacks, three "stately-pointed" rocks. At certain times of the tide, tremendous waves, called the "Bears of Duncansbay," roll between these rocks and the shore, a distance of about 500 yards; but just then Bruin was taking a siesta. I rambled along the cliffs, which are composed of Caithness flagstones; they do not reach the altitude of those at Cape Wrath, but the variety in the shades of colour (delicate pink to black) and their different stages of decay and ruin render them highly interesting.

I noticed in many places that the sea was slowly but surely undermining the cliff, and the swell, when rolling into these caverns, thundered and roared, and occasionally the compressed air made a report like a gun. There were many rocks of different shapes which had been detached by the action of the sea; one of these still maintained its hold on the mainland by a natural bridge, which had a very picturesque effect. This stone is so rich in fossil remains and shells that it pays to burn it for lime.

On reaching the Head, I came upon a stupendous chasm 500 feet in depth, and running 700 or 800 yards inland, and I was much surprised and impressed to find such a remarkable proof of the resistless power of the ever-rolling waves. Myriads of sea-birds were here to be seen, some making the rocks re-echo with their shrill cries, others circling overhead or taking a seaward flight, while numbers seated in rows on the ledges of the cliff were watching the more adventurous divers in the sea below. I could make out guillemots, razor-bills, kittiwakes, and puffins. All seemed to consider me as one of the crowd, but the puffins were the most cheeky; several of them squatted close by, and, twisting their oddly-shaped heads, looked at me out of the corner of their eyes as much as to say, "Pray who invited you to our pic-nic?" All this made me feel as though I were once more at "Kittiwake Fair" on Ascension Island.

DANGERS OF NAVIGATION.

I saw several small craft being carried along by the tide, which was racing by at the rate of seven or eight knots, and I had a striking proof of the dangers of navigation in these parts from seeing two wrecks on the west side of the Head. One lay high and dry on the beach, and the mastheads of the other (a steamer) were just showing above the surface of the water.

On my return to the hotel I made a note in the visitors' book advising everyone to pay a visit to Duncansbay Head, and shortly afterwards had the satisfaction of seeing two new arrivals shut up the book and start off at once.

In the afternoon a touring bicyclist came in; he had travelled over some of the same ground as myself, and on comparing notes I found that his opinion concerning the roads tallied with mine.

4 p.m. Although the weather had settled into a real Scotch mist I decided to make a move, and tear myself away from Mrs. McKenzie, who presented me with an envelope full of a kind of cowrie shell peculiar to this place, called Groatie buckies.

The road, which consisted of a succession of rideable undulations on a good surface, lay through a melancholy tract of moorland, with here and there a house and a plot of cultivation. The last two miles into Wick were level. The town looked imposing in the distance, but a nearer approach displayed narrow dirty streets, reeking of herrings.

I put up at the "Caledonian," but would advise the tourist to try the new hotel.

DISTANCE.

John o' Groat's to Wick .. 19 miles. Easy undulations, firm and smooth. Calm; Scotch mist.

FORTY-NINTH DAY.
WICK, HEMSDALE, GOLSPIE, DORNOCH.

THE population of Wick varies from 6,000 to 16,000 in the fishing season, and the narrow streets, this morning, teemed with crowds of people in sea faring costume, bound for the wharves.

8.15 a.m. Started for Hemsdale, and had a good view of the harbour, bristling with masts, from the outskirts of the town. The road rose gradually for six miles, then undulated gently for thirteen more, the surface being rather bumpy, with a thin coating of sticky mud. Beyond Janestown, the soil was more porous and the running excellent. At Latheron, the monotonous contour of the country was relieved by two peaks, called the Pass of Caithness; the only two hills of any height in this county.

There was an inn at Dunbeath, but the day was young, and being innocent of the work in store for me, I pushed on. A nasty dip at the west end of that village, and a change from partial cultivation to moor and heather, gave me a hint to prepare for collar work. This commenced with a rise of three miles, the first part being steep; three more of level brought me to Berrydale, where the eye rested with pleasure on the pine woods and broom which thrive in that secluded dale. The road wound down to the village, but the ascent on the south side of the ravine was very severe; in fact, the approach on both sides may be termed dangerous. After riding two miles of incline beyond Berrydale, I ran round a dell of farmed land among bleak hills, on a rougher surface, then rode and walked two miles to the culminating point of the Ord. From thence the road serpentined, and gradually descended until the last mile was reached, then it dipped abruptly to Hemsdale, where I arrived at 2 p.m.

The whole stage from Dunbeath is occupied by the Ord of Caithness, which is a promontory formed by the abrupt termination of the range of hills which divide that county from Sutherland. The road, which runs at about 1,200 feet above the sea, was at one time very dangerous, but is now safe enough, having been well engineered. The scenery was melancholy in the extreme, and contrasted unfavourably with that of the west coast.

There having been no inn between Dunbeath and Hemsdale, I arrived at the latter place in a most famished condition, and on requesting them to place some refreshment before me with all dispatch, was much disconcerted by the cool information that I could not have anything until the three o'clock dinner, and it required a good deal of persuasion to induce them to alter the dictum.

After a short rest I strolled down to the wharf, and being much interested in watching the process of cleaning and packing herrings, my curiosity was sufficiently excited to make me wish to learn further details of a trade which furnishes employment to so many thousands annually, and which, I understand, adds a million sterling to the national income.

I here dot down a few gleanings on the subject.

The Dutch first turned their attention to the importance of herring fishery. Britain took it up in 1749, and a Fishery Board was established in 1808. The different classes employed in the trade are: Fishermen, fish-curers, gutters, packers, coopers. The nets are 50 yards long and 14 deep, with an inch mesh. It is usual to join twenty-six of these together, thus making the net 1,300 yards in length; to this is attached a rope of 120 yards, causing the total length to be about four-fifths of a mile. In the evening the boats proceed to the fishing ground (at Wick a tug is hired for this purpose) pay out their nets, and drift all night. The fish run their heads into the mesh, and the gills, acting like the barb of a hook, prevent their retreat. At daylight, the crew—four men and a boy—begin to haul in; an exciting time, for the silvery prize is almost as uncertain as that of a lottery. Great care is taken to shake the fish clear of the net into the boat, or they would become bruised and worthless.

On landing, the herrings are measured by the cran—four baskets or thirty-six gallons—gutted, sorted, and placed in separate tubs.

Matties have the roe and milts moderately developed, and are the best eating.

Full fish are large, but not so well-flavoured.

Spent fish are lean and unpalatable, having just performed the function of spawning.

After the process of gutting, they are worked to and fro in salt until a proper quantity has adhered to each; this is done as soon as possible, to preserve the scales and appearance. They are then carefully packed in barrels with salt, being stowed on their backs for the Continent, and on their sides for the Irish market. After a few days the casks are opened, and most of the pickle which has been formed is poured off, and the barrels filled up by adding more fish of the same date. In about a fortnight they are finally headed up and shipped off to Stettin, Ireland, or other Roman Catholic countries.

Smoked or Red Herrings.—The fish are at once salted into barrels for two or three days, then put on spits and repeatedly plunged in cold water, and after having been dried in the open air, they are suspended in rows in the smoking house and exposed to the smoke of oak billets for ten or twelve days. The bright yellow colour is given by burning sawdust, and those intended for exportation are smoked from fourteen to twenty-one days.

Bloaters are cured by a more rapid process, being first put in a strong pickle for six or eight hours, then spitted, washed, and smoked from six to ten hours; when cooled and packed they are ready for sale.

Kippered Herrings are partially salted in pickle, then cut open and slightly smoked.

The success of the Hemsdale fisheries of late years has induced numbers of families to migrate from the west coast, and the side of the hill is sprinkled with their dwellings, the small amount of level space being already covered by the village.

4.15 p.m. Started tor Golspie. The road undulated along the foot of the hills which soon began to recede from the coast. From Brora* the condition of the road and scenery began to improve; cultivation appeared on all sides, and the nearer slopes were clothed with the hardy pine tree.

A monument, conspicuously placed on an eminence, told me that the celebrated seat of the Duke of Sutherland was near at hand. At six o'clock, I stopped at Dunrobin Castle, but was rather glad than otherwise to find that there was no admittance, so I went on to the pretty rural village of Golspie,† and had some tea at the Sutherland Arms.

Having noticed a heavy bank of clouds gathering in the northwest, I thought it advisable to take advantage of the lovely evening to make as much southing as possible; therefore, 7.45 p.m. found me *en route* for Dornoch. My directions were to avoid the little ferry, and to leave the station on the left, and then I could not go wrong. The road was level and good, and, having passed round the head of a picturesque cliff, I was running merrily down through a wood when I came to a point where there was a branch road to the station, which lay close to on the left with water immediately beyond it.

"This is the road which I am to avoid," thought I, and paddled on. My suspicions were presently aroused by the road becoming narrower, but as the water was still on my port hand I concluded that I was going right. Just as I exclaimed, "Ah! there's the bridge at last," a man appeared, who told me that I was running away from Dornoch and making for Lairg. On referring to

---
*There is some pretty scenery about Loch Brora.

†Besides the Castle and grounds, there is an interesting museum to see. A mile-and-a-half above the inn, there is a fine cascade in a pretty glen.

my map I found that, sure enough, I was well into Strath Sleet, so I had to retrace my steps for two miles to the rejected turning, and having passed by the station door I found that the road crossed Loch Sleet by an embankment, which had been concealed from my view by the foliage.*

The road on the opposite side, which was in splendid condition, led me at first for a short distance by the sea-side, then it turned to the right up a slope—most of which was rideable—for three miles, through fine woods; at the top of the hill I turned off the main road to the left, and ran quietly down in the dark to Dornoch, where I astonished the good people at the old-fashioned inn by arriving at 10.30 p.m.

DISTANCE.

Wick to Lyboter	13½ miles.
Lyboter to Dunbeath	7½ "
Dunbeath to Berrydale	6 "
Berrydale to Hemsdale	0 "
Hemsdale to Golspie	18 "
Golspie to Dornoch	12 "
In Strath Sleet	4 "
Total	71 "

Very fine.

FIFTIETH DAY.
DORNOCH, BONAR BRIDGE, TAIN, BLACK ROCK, DINGWALL.

9.45 a.m. Left the ancient capital of Sutherland, a mere village with a large church. The varying opinions concerning the advisability of taking the Meikle Ferry had caused me to leave the point to be decided by the weather, and as it was a calm fine day, I made up my mind to run round the Firth.

The first two miles were rather rough, but on joining the highway again the surface was splendid, and I had a most enjoyable run of fourteen miles to Bonar Bridge. The road undulated on the wooded side of the hill at about half-a-mile from the sea, and every now and then I had charming peeps of the blue water and mountains in the distance. I preferred walking up some of the rises, but a good bicyclist could fly them all with ease.

Bonar is situated on both sides of the Firth, and has an attractive looking inn, which I passed after crossing the bridge. The

* I had passed the turning to the little ferry without noticing it.

road on the south side was nearly level, with a magnificent surface; this compensated for the scenery which became bleak towards the east end.

1 p.m. Arrived at Tain and lunched at the "Royal" hotel, where I heard what the landlord had to say about the ferry, and make the case to stand as follows.

For the Ferry.	Against the Ferry.
A saving of 19 miles of road.	Delay in waiting for boat (housed on north side).
	Time occupied and discomfort experienced, owing to the small boat.
	Bad roads leading to the Ferry on both sides.

2.30 p.m. Left Tain, a small agricultural town. I saved three miles by taking the direct road to Alness, and can recommend this way, which lies through a level and highly farmed district, with several fine parks and family seats.

Two miles from Tain I took the right road at the fork, and again after crossing the bridge at Park Hill. At Evantown I left my tricycle at the primitive inn, and walked up the road on the north side of Aultgrast water for half a-mile, then followed its course by a foot path through a wood for about the same distance, when I came to the spot where the stream issues from what is locally called the Black Rock.

This is an extraordinary chasm or rent in the earth, two miles in length, and 100 feet in depth; its width, which is only fifteen feet at the surface, narrows to about three at the bottom. Here and there the shrubs and bushes which conceal the opening have been cleared away and the space railed in, to enable the spectator to view the gulf in safety. It is a moot question as to whether the channel is waterworn, and having been asked for my opinion I took particular notice of its features. Stopping at several of the view points, I observed that the foaming torrent, in forcing its way between the conglomerate cliffs, had carved them into a series of points, so that if the sides had been pressed together they would have fitted in like the teeth in a crocodile's jaw. Between the clearings, both chasm and stream were hidden from view, and the roaring of the latter, as though from the bowels of the earth, had a curious effect. The upper end of the chasm was a little wider, and while standing on a bridge which had been thrown across it,

I noticed that the stream at every bend was scooping out the soft sides of the cliff until the excavation reached an angle which shot the water over to the other side. As these cheese-shaped cavities could be traced all the way up the cliff, no further proof was needed that the channel was waterworn.

The cyclist should on no account miss the Black Rock, which for a sight of its kind is unique. If in haste, he can leave his machine at the entrance of the wood, and get an idea of it in half an hour; but it takes more than an hour to see it thoroughly.

Having had tea at Evantown I ran on to Dingwall, under the shade of trees, and through a delightful country, giving undeniable evidence of agricultural prosperity, the air being sweetened by the scent of fresh hay from the meadows on either side of the road. The prettiest bit was by the waters of Cromarty Firth, where clouds, trees, and rocks lay mirrored on the calm, peaceful surface.

At the entrance of the town I spied a curious old obelisk, strengthened by bands of iron. On enquiring its history, I was informed that it had been erected at the desire of one of the earls of Cromarty, in order to prevent his loving spouse from carrying out her threat of dancing on his grave. It was late when I put my vehicle into the coach house at the "Caledonian."

DISTANCE.

Dornoch to Bonar Bridge	14 miles.
Bonar Bridge to Tain	15 „
Tain to Dingwall	22 „
Total	51 „

Very fine.

FIFTY-FIRST DAY.
DINGWALL, STRATH PEFFER, BEAULLY, KILMORACH FALLS, INVERNESS.

FROM an early hour the town began to fill with excursionists bound for Strath Peffer, to witness the opening of the Town Hall by the Duchess of Sutherland. Having heard a great deal about the beauties of that Strath, I considered it a duty to deviate from my course in order to see it with my own eyes.

10.15 a.m. Left Dingwall, and after travelling two miles of level and three of rise, the latter being rather steep, I found myself in a street of hotels and villas. Banners and flags were flying, and crowds of well-dressed and orderly holiday folk were promenading about. On expressing my disappointment at the tameness of the scenery, I was sent up to the top of the hill for a view of the dale beyond, but I still held to my opinion.

I now returned to Dingwall and took my way through the town on to the Beauly road, which lay chiefly through park lands to the Muir of Ord, a flat sandy plain, where I entered the county of Inverness. At Beauly, I saw the ruins of the Priory, and lunched at the hotel, where I was detained two hours by the heavy rain. The town is encircled by low hills partially clothed with pine trees, but owing to the nature of the soil, there is a lack of richness in the colour of the foliage and grass.

4 p.m. Started for Kilmorach Falls, and after proceeding a mile on the Inverness road, I turned to the right and went on for another mile to a farmhouse, where I left my tricycle. After passing the manse I crossed the bridge and took a foot-path close by the river, which led me through some pretty grounds to a summer-house; then descending some steps to the water's edge, I had a good view of the Falls. The cliffs are curiously waterworn, and although the height of the Falls is inconsiderable, they are set off by a series of cascades and the picturesque surroundings. "I should like to make one of a pleasant pic-nic party here some day," thought I while rambling back to my tricycle.

I regained the highway, and felt my spirits rising higher and higher while speeding along through soft pastoral vales, with gleams of sunshine falling on my path through the dark green shade of the oak, beech, and other trees, whose stately proportions formed a pleasing contrast to the stunted specimens further north. On either side the smiling meadows were adorned with floral beauties of every description, and the notes of the song-birds echoed sweetly through the woods. My happiness was rendered complete by having a road like asphalte, with just a sufficient rise and fall to vary the motion, and I frequently exclaimed in an ecstasy, " Verily, this is a cyclist's Paradise." The latter part of the way to Inverness ran by the side of Loch Beauly, the sky and water scenery adding to the charm of the evening.

Passing the entrance to the great Caledonian Canal, I piloted myself through the town to the "Royal" hotel, where I had an insight into what the ordinary tourist has to undergo in the height of the season. All the officials, from the polite manager to the junior Boots, were rushing about in a distracted manner in their vain efforts to attend to everyone at the same time, while from different quarters came exclamations of, " Waiter, isn't my dinner ready ? " " Waiter, I ordered tea an hour ago, and there's no sign of it yet ! " " Waiter, will you bring the champagne, for the third time of asking ? " However, I suppose that, like myself, they got what they wanted, in course of time.

While conversing during the evening I ascertained that one of my companions was a native of Skye, and was invited by him to relate my experiences in that island. I spoke of the force of the wind, and asked him if it were really true that the mail car had ever been blown over. He replied: " Not only has that happened to my knowledge, but I can tell you of something still more extraordinary. One morning, during a gale, I was looking out of the window of my house in the direction of two good-sized boats belonging to me, which were lying bottom upwards on the beach, when suddenly I saw one rising in the air, and the next moment it was resting on the top of the other, as though it had been placed by hand."

DISTANCE.

Dingwall to Strath Peffer and back	11 miles.
Dingwall to Beaully	9 ,,
To Kilmorach Falls and back	3 ,,
Beaully to Inverness	12½ ,,
Total	35½ ,,

Very fine.

FIFTY-SECOND DAY.

INVERNESS, FALLS OF FOYERS, FORT AUGUSTUS.

My intention had been to run round Loch Ness, but on hearing that the road beyond Foyers was very bad, I decided to cut off the lower part by crossing the Ferry there. It rained all night and up to 10.15 a.m., when I started for Foyers, and turning to the left at Inverness Bridge, I followed the lower route.

Beyond the town the road at first undulated by parks and mansions, then ascended on to a moor. The saturated surface was very heavy, and obliged me to walk up some of the slopes. From the highest point I had an extensive view of Loch Ness, but was disappointed with the monotonous appearance of the hills in which it is cradled. After a run down of two miles I came to the lake (6 miles from Inverness), and enjoyed a lovely ride for some distance through the sylvan woods by which it is bordered. Emerging from these I had to follow the road along the bare side of the hill, which now rose abruptly from the water. About five miles from Foyers the high land receded, and the slope again became clothed with wood, but the road began to rise and fall at distressing angles, each gradient being sharper than the last. Two miles further on I came to a fork, and seeing a milestone on the lower road I naturally took it to be the highway, but very shortly found myself near Inverfarikaig, and as I was just getting into the hot and tired stage, I did not bless the clever individual who had placed the milestone in such a misleading position. However, I reached Foyers in time for luncheon.

The commodious, but apparently unfrequented hotel, occupies a commanding position overlooking the broad waters of the lake.

I made my way by a path through the wood to the Falls, having the roar of the water for a guide, and in about ten minutes' time a column of spray, ascending from a rocky ravine, brought to my mind the day when, at the distance of several miles, I saw the spray arising from Niagara. I hurried down to the ledge of rock which projects in front of the Falls, in order that I might see the whole effect at once.

The stream issues from a narrow opening, but being at the time very full, it shot out in a grand brown and white mass, in shape exactly resembling a mare's tail. It fell sixty feet into a linn surrounded by grim rocks, with a shock which caused the point on which I was standing to vibrate sensibly. There were some pretty rainbows, but the blinding showers of spray quickly drove me to higher ground, from whence I surveyed the course of the stream, as it wound through the rugged gorge. It was a grand sight, and quite up to my expectations.

"How about the ferry?" said I to the hotel people on my return; "can the man be relied upon, for it is too late to waste time?"

"Oh yes, if you make a smoke he is sure to come over," was the reply.

I took a box of matches, and amused the ostlers by going off on my tricycle with my arms full of straw. On my way down I passed a score of yelling tourists who had just landed from the steamer, and I felt thankful that I had been beforehand with them at the

Falls. I took my machine across a field to the beach, the ferry house being opposite at the distance of half a mile.

After collecting some wood, wet and dry, large and small, I laid my fire on the most scientific principles, and, having applied the match, soon had the satisfaction of seeing a dense column of smoke arise from it. As there appeared to be no signs of a move on the other side of the water I sounded my whistle, shouted, piled on wet wood, whistled again, waved frantically, executed a war dance, hailed loudly, in strictly Parliamentary language, all to no purpose.

"I won't have my trouble for nothing, I *will* make him hear," cried I in a rage; but I didn't, although it was perfectly calm at the time.

On prying about I discovered a flat bottomed boat moored in the creek, and felt strongly tempted to "cut it out," but fortunately I was saved from committing this rash action, for the owner had carefully removed the paddles.

"Five o'clock, what is to be done now?" thought I.

"Return by the same road," prompted common sense, but obeying the natural instinct of all cyclists, I determined to go on whatever might happen.

To commence with, I had a long weary hill to climb. Up and up I went, pushing, struggling, perspiring; near the top, just as I was beginning to look forward to the run down which must come sooner or later, I met two sportsmen, who, on hearing that I was bound to Fort Augustus, strongly advised me to give up the idea, as the hills were "frightful." However, the die was cast. While walking down the abrupt descent I passed close by the upper falls, but had not time to see them. I came down to a vale in the bosom of the mountains, extending for seven or eight miles, most of which I rode on a fair surface. The beautiful tints of the evening sky, the exhilarating mountain air, with the variety and wild grandeur of the scenery, soon put me into a good humour again.

I was both surprised and relieved to find an inn in this remote locality (Whitebridge). It was a poor place, but they did their best, and a cup of hot tea was very refreshing. Anglers occasionally stop here for the fishing in the adjacent tarns.

I continued my journey at 7.30 p.m., and rode for about two miles, then the hills began in earnest. There was one tremendously steep pitch leading into a charmingly picturesque glen, about four miles from Fort Augustus, and I am sure that anyone would have gone into fits of laughter had they seen the comical figure I cut, as, with set teeth and bent back, I held on to my tricycle with one hand, and to the brake with the other, while vigorously digging my heels into the ground in my endeavours to prevent the machine from taking charge. On reaching the crest of the hill overlooking Fort Augustus, there was just sufficient light for me to have a magnificent panoramic view of the Great Glen, and of the mighty peaks of Ben Nevis, which were sketched faintly on the pale western sky, and the deepening twilight gave the scene a solemn grandeur which would have probably been dissipated by the searching rays of a noonday sun. I now had another remarkably precipitous descent to make, a mile in length. I mounted at the foot of the hill, and while approaching the town in the dark, the full deep tones of the convent bell tolled forth Nine! the whole effect being very impressive.

On arriving at the inn, I asked if I could have a bed.

"No, sir," replied the maid, looking suspiciously at my poor innocent steed, "we're full."

She was about to shut the door, when I stopped her and requested to see the landlord. This had the desired effect, for a room was discovered, and I afterwards ascertained that the hotel was nearly empty. I ought to have had the matter investigated, but the fact was that I was too thankful to get rest and peace to care about stirring up the mind.

Later on I noted in my journal that, in spite of the hard work, the trip from Foyers had been very enjoyable, and that cyclists who want a little wild mountain scenery without going far for it should take this route.

Distance.

Inverness to Foyers	18 miles.
Foyers to Fort Augustus	14 „
Total	32 „

Showery forenoon; very fine the rest of the day.

FIFTY-THIRD DAY.
Fort Augustus, Drumnadrochet, Inverness.

Fort Augustus is situated on a flat green sward at the S.W. corner of Loch Ness, and although I cannot go quite so far as an elderly lady, who declared that it was the most lovely spot in Scotland, it is no doubt a pretty place and worth a visit.

After taking a look at part of the canal and the fine convent which has been erected on the site of the old Castle, I started for Inverness at 10.15. The running was very good for thirteen or fourteen miles, but the last seven or eight to Drumnadrochet consisted of rather troublesome ups and downs on a stiff clay surface, which caused the machine to work heavily. I was charmed with the trip, for the northern bank, which appeared so monotonous from the opposite shore, was luxuriantly clad with birch, hazel, ash, and a thick underwood of pretty shrubs, brightened by purple heather and the verdant bracken.

Passing the sequestered and attractive looking inn at Invermoreston, I presently stopped at the Ferry House to try and find out the meaning of the man's inattention on the previous evening. After rapping once or twice, I stepped in. No one at home, and a neighbour explained that the missing Charon had gone to work at a distance! While pursuing my way, I heard a rustling in the wood above me, and glancing up I saw a pretty little deer looking askance at me, not ten yards off. On catching my eye, he bounded off a few paces, then stopped again to scrutinize the strange object below; and so we parted.

I ran close above the ruins of Castle Urquhart, which are picturesquely situated on a promontory jutting into the lake, no doubt a strong position in the age of chivalry. The road now turned to the left and ascended, and from the summit of the rise I had a lovely view of Glen Urquhart. A gleam of sunshine lighted up the emerald park-land of the vale, while deep gloom rested upon the semi-circle of hills by which it is closely hemmed in, cast by the heavy clouds which rested upon them. A nearer approach did not dispel the pleasing impression, for the contrast between the precipitous hills with their mantle of dark pine, and the smiling luxuriance of the vale with its rustic cottages and running streams was delightful. I was surprised to find only two people at the inn, for I should have thought that this charming spot, so near Inverness, would have been much sought after, and I can strongly recommend the lover of nature to pay it a visit. The inn was certainly in rather a rough condition, but the landlady informed me that they were going to build a new one.

2.30 p.m. Left for Inverness. The scenery began to lose its attractions, but the surface improved. The road undulated rather steeply as far as the 6½ milestone, when it ran at a dead level for two miles by the canal side, then went over a stiffish hill, the last two miles into Inverness being on a decline. It rained during the latter part of my journey, and on my arrival I heard that it had been wet nearly all the time that I had been away.

Having consigned my tricycle to a competent man for a thorough cleaning and a few minor repairs, I put up at the " Royal " hotel.

DISTANCE.

Fort Augustus to Drumnadrochet .. .. .. 21 miles.
Drumnadrochet to Inverness .. .. 14¼ „

Total .. .. 35¼ „

Half-an-hour's rain in the saddle; wet night.

FIFTY-FOURTH DAY.
INVERNESS, CULLODEN FIELD, CAWDOR CAS, FORRES.

IN the afternoon I went to see the Clach-na-Cuddew,* which is attached to the drinking fountain in front of the new Town Hall. After walking round the Castle Hill, I tramped off to Tom-na-Heurich (the hill of fairies), the shape of which really does, as the guide books say, resemble a boat, keel uppermost. This hill has been turned into a cemetery of rather a novel description, for graves border the paths which wind round the wooded sides, and the summit is laid out in the style of a botanical garden, interspersed with obelisks. From thence I had a capital view of the town and the charming vale to the westward; in fact, the cemetery is *the* sight of Inverness. On returning I got into my cycling suit, and having sent off my portmanteau to Edinburgh, I, at 1.30, started for Cawdor.

I paddled along the Perth road for three miles, then turned off to the left and gradually ascended to a windmill, from whence I enjoyed a magnificent panoramic view of Inverness, basking in the

*The Palladium of the burgh.

sunshine at the head of the Firth. The summits of the mountains which formed the background were enveloped in rain clouds, through which the sun occasionally shot a golden gleam.

Two miles further on level ground, through an open heath partially converted into arable land, brought me to the celebrated battle field of Culloden (8 miles from Inverness). A fir plantation now covers the ground on which the hottest part of the fight occurred, and a few unenclosed mounds show the last resting place of many brave hearts. On the opposite side of the road is a cairn, bearing the following inscription :—

"The battle of Culloden was fought on this moor, 16th April, 1746. The graves of the gallant Highlanders, who fought for Scotland and Prince Charlie, are marked by the names of their clans."

A local guide informed me that the rough head stones to the different clans had been erected quite recently by the present owner of the property (Mr. Duncan Forbes), who had been instructed where to place them by old people, to whom the word had been passed on from generation to generation.

My cicerone pointed out the dyke across which the English cavalry had charged with such fatal effect; the big stone from whence the Duke of Cumberland had directed the battle, and the two cottages which had been left standing, one having been used by the Duke for stabling his horses.

After spending some time in examining the features of the field, I proceeded onwards through the moor and down by a gradual descent into a wooded and well cultivated district.

I had just passed through a village (Cantray, I think), and was about to enter a wood, when, seeing a shower ahead, I stopped to put on my mackintosh. While doing so, a weasel popped out his head from between the furze bushes on a wall, then withdrew it and appeared again a few yards further on. I was quite interested in watching his movements, for he was evidently actuated alternately by fear and curiosity, a tricycle being no doubt a novelty to him. Presently a man came up, and I thought it my duty to inform him of the whereabouts of this destructive animal. Bang! but when he shouted gleefully "I've killed it," a pang of remorse shot through me for having betrayed a creature which had honoured me with so much attention.

The cyclist, travelling by this route, should frequently enquire the way, for I had to take many turns both to the right and left before arriving at Cawdor, a truly rural hamlet, watered by a murmuring stream overshadowed by an avenue of noble trees.

I put my tricycle away at the inn,* and ascertained that when the family is in residence, the castle is only open to the public between the hours of 3 and 5 p.m. Fortunately it was then just four o'clock, so having obtained an order from the landlord (1s.) I trudged off to that romantic building, and crossed the moat by a real drawbridge, the pattern of the chain by which it was suspended being a proof of its antiquity.

I was received and shown round with the greatest courtesy by the housekeeper. The rooms are hung with tapestry, and, like Glammis, everything is kept up in the old style. The chimney-piece in the dining-room is quaintly carved, and amongst other devices is that of a fox with a pipe in his mouth. This is regarded as a great curiosity, for the date of the chimney-piece is prior to that of the introduction of tobacco into England by Sir Walter Raleigh.

I had always looked upon the hawthorn story† as an idle tale, but there was the tree sure enough, rooted in the dungeon of the tower, with its head piercing the ceiling above. It has long been dead, but does not show any signs of decay. The coffer (an antique iron chest) rested by its side.

King Duncan's room is still shown, although it has no pretension to being the original one, for that, with other parts of the castle, was destroyed by fire some years ago.

After an excellent tea at the inn, I ran across a pastoral plain, on a dead level of eight miles. Half-a-mile from Nairn was the turning to Forres, and as I knew that there was nothing particular to be seen in the former town, I contented myself with a passing view, and headed eastward. My singular good luck in dodging the rain had been remarkable all through the tour, and lately more so than ever. All the way down the east coast I had seen it raining on the hills to the westward. During my run round Loch Ness I escaped it again, and to-day, although it threatened all about me, I only had one slight shower, and I rode to Forres in brilliant sunshine with a clear sky to the north, while about two miles to the southward it

---

* The cyclist is recommended to ride from Cawdor to the Streens on the Findhorn, then to follow the river down to Forres.

† The tradition is that the founder was led, either by a dream or the advice of a wizard, to build the castle round the third hawthorn tree where an ass laden with a chest of gold should stop. A small recess in the roof is shown as being the hiding place of Lord Lovat after Culloden.

was coming down in torrents. The highway on which I was travelling was well macadamized, with a firm surface; whereas the road from Inverness to Cawdor had been sodden and heavy, and the plain between that and Nairn was positively flooded.

It was dark when I put my machine into the stables opposite the "Waverley Temperance," where I put up, having resolved to give this class of hotel another trial for strictly economical reasons.

DISTANCE.

Inverness to Cawdor	15 miles.
Cawdor to Forres	15¼ „
Total	30¼ „

One shower.

FIFTY-FIFTH DAY.
THE FINDHORN RIVER.

On enquiry I learned that the "blasted heath" is near Brodie, so that I must have passed it unnoticed last night, and I decided to devote my energies to-day to visiting the Findhorn, which my friends at Crieff had told me in nowise to miss.

The ostler exhibited great consideration for my comfort and welfare, or more probably a strong desire that I should hire his horses.

"You can't go along there, sir, the road is awful bad."

"I don't mind that," replied I.

"There are frightful precipices," rejoined he, trying another tack.

"All right:" said I, for the more he tried to put me off, the more excited my curiosity became, and the more determined I was to go.

11 a.m. Mounted my tricycle and ran on the Grantown road to the first Altyre Lodge, where I turned into the grounds on the right, and soon came to the river banks, which are thickly wooded on both sides. I was disappointed at first, but about half a mile further up stream splendid pink cliffs, from 100 to 200 ft. sheer, presented themselves. Beyond this the banks became broken and diversified, and the narrowed river twisted, tumbled, and roared over and between huge boulders of rock which had been shed from above.

About two miles further I came to the second lodge, where I found myself in a dilemma, for the gate was locked, I could not make anyone hear, and the pedestrian exit was apparently too narrow for my tricycle to pass through. However, on noticing that the posts were not quite parallel, I pushed the small wheel through first, then, by raising the machine on end, I had just managed to squeeze it through when the lodge-keeper appeared, and wanted to know how I had spirited my tricycle over the gate. Taking his advice I left my vehicle and walked to the spot on which the German princes had picnicked, and then by the banks for about three-quarters of a mile. The river became more grand and wildly beautiful as I advanced, for every bend brought a change of scene, and I compared it in my own mind to the Nitto, on a much more magnificent scale; the only disappointment being that the herons had deserted their old haunts near the mouth of the river.

On regaining my "Cheylesmore" I hied up to the road again, and continued to the sixth milestone; then turned off to the right and ran down for a mile to the keeper's house. His son conducted me to the junction of the Dervie and Findhorn, and to " Randolph's Leap;" here the river contracts to twenty feet, and the beauty and grandeur of the scenery reaches its culminating point; an immense volume of jet black water was being hurried through this narrow channel.

I understand that the Findhorn is more subject to sudden freshes, or spates, than any other river in Scotland. This is illustrated by the torn and ruined state of the rocky banks. I was shewn the peg which marks the limit of the great flood* in 1829, and roughly calculated that it was 150 yards up a slope from the bank, and 50 feet above the present level of the water. My guide informed me that a sudden rise of 20 or 30 feet is not an unusual circumstance even now.

Tourists usually drive to the second lodge, walk by the banks to Randolph's Leap, and meet their vehicles there; a bicycle might be taken that way, but I doubt if the path is wide enough for a tricycle.

Mounting again, I rode on for about a mile; then struck across by a rough district road to Dava Bridge, and on by Dumphail and the Grantown road, back to Forres. The town looked very pretty as I neared it. Cluney Hill, richly wooded, and surmounted by a lofty monument to the memory of Nelson, forms a very conspicuous object, and is the fashionable promenade of the place.

In the evening I walked to Sweno's Stone, which stands by itself in a meadow about half a mile eastward. It is about 20 feet high,

* See Sir R. Lander's account of this wonderful flood.

and both sides are covered with carved figures of warriors and animals. The history of this stone is somewhat obscure, but it is supposed to have been erected by Malcolm II. or Macbeth, to celebrate the expulsion of the Danes. Between Sweno and Forres is another stone marking the spot where witches used to be burnt.*

I was told that, had I gone higher up the Findhorn, I should have come to some wonderful cliffs, called "The Screens," but I had seen enough to satisfy me that no tourist should leave Scotland without visiting what I considered the finest river scenery in North Britain.

DISTANCE.

On wheels .. .. 23 miles.
Very fine.

FIFTY-SIXTH DAY.
FORRES, ELGIN, BANFF, PETERHEAD.

THE "Waverley Temperance" was a decided success, as far as economy and comfort were concerned; but there was a lack of society and I only had one meal in company.

8 a.m., got under way. The morning was calm and fine, and there being a good road and nothing particular to see *en route*, I decided to push on to Peterhead. I experienced gentle undulations to Elgin, where I arrived at 9.15, and lost no time in visiting the Cathedral,† at the north end of the neat looking town. With the assistance of the guide I soon got a general idea of the ruins which, although not extensive, are very symmetrical, and the stones are highly finished, in the way of filagree and carved work.

9.40 a.m. Proceeded on my journey, and shortly crossed a fine bridge over the Spey, a broad river, whose scoured banks and dry patches of shingle showed traces of freshes. While passing through Fochabers I had a glimpse of Gordon Castle, surrounded by splendid trees, the last I saw for many a long mile, for the country now became open and only partially cultivated. I struck the coast at Cullen, a clean fishing village, or perhaps it calls itself a town—if so, I apologize. There was a smart dip into and rise out of it; while

---

*The castle mentioned by Shakespeare was on an eminence at the western extremity of the town.

†Founded in 1224. Burnt by the Wolf of Badenoch, in 1390. It was rebuilt in the form of a Jerusalem cross, with a lofty spire; was dilapidated by Regent Moray in 1568. The two western towers are of massive but elegant proportions, and form the most entire part of the ruin. Length, 289ft.; breadth, 144ft.

walking up the latter I was overtaken by a young bicyclist, who accompanied me for some miles, when he turned back, saying that he must not be late for dinner. "Afraid of having your pudding stopped," thought I.

Ran through Potsoy at 12.35, arrived at the Banff hotel at 1.30, 44¼ miles between breakfast and luncheon, being the quickest run that I had yet made. The road was magnificent all the way, and the only compulsory dismounts were at Cullen and at the promontory into Banff.

After a sumptuous meal with strawberries and cream, and other luxuries unattainable on the West Coast, I started again at 3.0 p.m., not caring to see the Castle. After descending the steep side on which Banff is situated, I skirted the shore to Macduff, at the east of the bay. I walked up a stiff bit out of that, then rode up a gradual ascent for about three miles to the summit of the range of hills. I then parted with the telegraph wires on the main road, and turned to the left on to a loose and stony surface. The contour of the land between this and Peterhead consisted of ridges of hills running from N. N.E. to S. S.W., with valleys between; so that I was, as it were, heading against the grain of the country; something like travelling in a boat against the long, heavy swell of the ocean. The road became gradually worse and worse, and the scenery more and more bleak as I advanced, for there was not a shrub to vary the monotony of the endless and rounded hills. I passed by sombre peat moss tracts, and as the turf was being cut and carried, the traffic of the heavily laden carts rendered the road in some places almost impassable.

By-and-by I came to New Pitsligo, the village, people, and surroundings being of the most melancholy description. From thence the gradients were not so tiresome, but the road was very rough and bad to Mintlaw, where things began to take a more cheerful aspect, and after a short rest I finished my journey more rapidly.

As the "Temperance" hotel, at Forres had answered so well, I enquired for one at Peterhead, and was directed to Mrs. Cruikshanks. It was badly situated amongst a number of sheds and out-houses, but the interior and the management left nothing to be desired, and I was glad to find plenty of good company. Great astonishment was expressed at the length of my day's run and the little fatigue that I had apparently experienced. I explained that distance is always a minor consideration, the state of the road and the direction of the wind being of the first importance to a 'cyclist; and that I had had heavier work between Altnaharra and Betty Hill, a distance of 26 miles, than during the 80½ of to-day.

DISTANCE.

Forres to Elgin	12 miles.
Elgin to Fochabers	9 ,,
Fochabers to Cullen	10½ ,,
Cullen to Potsoy	5 ,,
Potsoy to Banff	8 ,,
Banff to Pitsligo	18 ,,
Pitsligo to Mintlaw	9 ,,
Mintlaw to Peterhead	9 ,,
Total	80½ ,,

Very fine.

FIFTY-SEVENTH DAY.

PETERHEAD, BULLERS OF BUCHAW, ABERDEEN.

PETERHEAD, the most eastern town in Great Britain, is situated on a low point of land, and has a secure harbour and fine docks. It is the principal whaling port in the Kingdom, and is the nursery of some of our finest seamen.

After breakfast I went down to the docks, and found them crammed with herring boats, just arrived. It was a very exciting scene. In the lucky boats, the men, with beaming faces, were standing up to their middle in silvery fish, and shovelling away cheerily O! In others, they were disconsolately turning over their nets and picking out a stray fish here and there.

I went on board the celebrated whaler, "Eclipse," which had just returned from a most successful cruise. She was barque-rigged, with auxiliary steam power, but a smaller vessel than I had expected to see. I was allowed to go below and examine the manner in which she had been strengthened with wood and iron beams, in order to resist the fatal embrace of the ice floes.

In the hold were a number of large iron tanks, used in the first place for storing coal, but their contents were now infinitely more valuable than "black diamonds," viz., seal oil. The men were at work whipping it up in buckets and pouring it into casks, and I was struck by its clear and colourless appearance. One of the crew informed me that the fresh skins of the seals are thrown into the tanks and left there until the end of the voyage, when they are found to be floating in the oil which has exuded from the fleshy parts. On this occasion they had brought home a prize of three thousand skins, and I visited the shed where they were being sorted, salted, and stowed in different parts of the building ready for sale. The shades of colour varied from nearly black to light brown; the latter, being from the young animals, were the most valuable, and now fetch from eight to nine shillings each, in their raw state; but their market value was far higher in former days.

The characteristic of Peterhead is oil. The long-booted sailors were covered with oil, the faces of the women and children shone with oil; everything one touched was covered with it, and the lower town reeked with it. Fortunately, my hotel was free from this nuisance.

11 a.m. Left Peterhead for Aberdeen. The road ascended for two or three miles to the flesh-coloured granite quarries; this valuable stone is here so abundant that not only are the houses and walls built of it, but the very roads are mended with it, which made me feel as though I were crushing gold under my wheels.

When about five miles from Peterhead I turned to the left, and after walking for three-quarters of a mile on a narrow, bad track, I came to the "Bullers of Buchaw." I had read and heard so much about this natural curiosity that I expected to see something very wonderful. The oval basin, commonly called "The Pot," has been excavated in the cliff by the action of the sea, to a distance of two hundred feet inland, its breadth being about one hundred feet, and depth fifty feet. The entrance is bridged over by a natural arch of rock. As it was a calm day "The Pot" was not boiling, which is *the* thing to see; and as to the cliffs, after the magnificent specimens on the West Coast these seemed insignificant, and altogether I left with feelings of disappointment. On regaining the high road I pursued my way on a loose surface through which the heads of large stones protruded themselves, making the riding jolty. The bleak district through which I was passing, with its occasional patches of wretched looking crops, was a melancholy sight. Moreover, I was still going against the grain of the country; in fact I might have been compared to a certain animal with long ears, for I was "braeing" all day.

I lunched at Ellon, a village with one or two good houses and clump of scraggy trees. The inn was desolate in the extreme. The

A TEMPTING SUGGESTION.

landlord handed me some slices of beef and a fid of bread, which I ate from a bare deal table, with a form for a seat, the only furnished room having been let to some sportsmen. Being hungry I felt inclined to growl at the short commons, but as the bill was only sixpence I could not complain.

From Ellon the surface improved somewhat, but the undulations were still troublesome, and the country devoid of trees all the way to Aberdeen, where I arrived at 5.30 p.m.

While walking along the cobbled streets at the entrance of the city, I was accosted by a gentleman who astonished me by saying:

"Why don't you ride on the pavement, you would get on much better?"

"Quite so," replied I, "but is it not against the rules?"

"Oh no, I can give you leave," said he, "come along, I will see that no one interferes with you."

The offer was tempting, but I did not like to run the risk of injuring anyone. I put up at Forsyth's "Temperance," which is quite a first-class hotel, in Union-street.

The number of wheelmen whom I had met during my tour could be counted on my fingers, viz.: four bicyclists at Galston in Ayrshire, one at John o' Groat's, and one at Cullen. I fully expected to see them flying about Aberdeen in all directions, but not even a bicycle met my eye; and as to tricycles, I was told by Boots that mine was the first he had seen in the town.

There is an excellent Public Reading Room near the hotel, where I had the privilege of perusing all the English papers and periodicals for the sum of one penny.

DISTANCE.

Peterhead to Ellon	18 miles.
Ellon to Aberdeen	16 "
Bullers and back	1½ "
Total	35½ "

Foggy afternoon; no rain.

FIFTY-EIGHTH DAY.
Aberdeen, Ballater, Invercauldy Arms.

LOOKED round the docks. There had been an enormous haul of herrings the night before, and I was told that one boat had actually taken 100 crans! This may have been a sailor's yarn to a greenhorn, but I noted it down at the time, and also the fact that they were hawking the fish about six for a penny. The granite buildings and the fine broad streets of Aberdeen are magnificent, but rather too prim and formal to be pleasing to the eye.

9.15 a.m. Started for Ballater, and followed the tram out of the city. The road on the north side of the Dee was rather bumpy, but I made a very rapid run to Banchory, a pretty village by the river, though fast being spoiled by the new buildings which are rising on either hand to accommodate the ever-increasing rush of visitors. Trees, which I had not seen since leaving Fochaber, now threw their shadows across my path. From Banchory the road led me by the water side through picturesque wood and rock scenery, varied by meadows and cultivated patches, but my enjoyment was marred by the heavy state of the surface. Moreover, I came in for a heavy shower of rain, so that I was glad to find myself before the kitchen fire of the inn at Kincardine O'Neill, where the cheery welcome of the landlady warmed my heart, as did the glowing embers my body. As the inn appears to be little frequented, I have much pleasure in recommending it to the tourist. It struck me as being quiet, comfortable, and well managed, and my luncheon will be a specimen of the moderate charge: cold beef, cabbage, potatoes, omelette, butter, cheese, strawberries and cream—1s. 9d., including attendance.

It rained until 3 p.m., when I resumed my journey, the country becoming more tame and the road softer and worse in every way as I advanced. Aboyne, seated on a haugh, is reputed to be lovely, but I had not time to search out the charms which were not apparent from the road. Leaving the woods behind, I now ascended a rough hill through a wild heath (Muir of Dinnet) to Ballater, which is pleasantly situated on a plain of emerald green closely encompassed by roundish hills, with Lochnagar in the distance. I had the privilege of seeing all the beauty and fashion of the place, who were witnessing the manœuvres of a company of volunteers on the sward.

I had tea at the wee "Temperance" inn, and was making arrangements for staying the night, when the last train brought in a crowd of second-class tourists; and hearing that there was a humble inn near Balmoral, I decided to take refuge there.

6.30. p.m. Left Ballater and commenced my travels by pushing my " Cheylesmore " for a mile up a hill, ankle deep in clayey mud. I then tried riding, or rather ploughing, for two miles, when I was rewarded for my discomfort by a magnificent vista of the Dee Vale. The slopes of the hills were clothed with dusky pine down to the banks of the broad and rapid river, which swept majestically through the glen. In the background the mountain tops cut in and out of one another in a manner which added a novel attraction to the scene. The rest of the way was nearly level, but its slushy condition was most unpleasant, and I felt it all the more from having a vivid remembrance of the splendid roads on the West Coasts, where mud or ruts are unknown; in fact, I had escaped them almost everywhere. I had a good view of Balmoral Castle on the opposite side of the river while riding by, and reached Invercauldy Arms at 8.30 p.m. I felt curious to know what kind of quarters I was going to have. The woman said that the tourist apartment was engaged, but if I didn't mind she could let me have a cupboard bed in the other part of the house. There was a dash of novelty about this that pleased me, and after looking at it I closed with her offer, and thought myself uncommonly fortunate in being so well provided for.

During the evening I conversed with three young men who were on a pedestrian tour; they said that the road when dry was very good, its present deplorable condition being due to continuous rain.

DISTANCE.

Aberdeen to Banchory	18 miles.
Banchory to Kincardine O'Neill	8 ,,
Kincardine O'Neill to Ballater	16 ,,
Ballater to Invercauldy Arms	10 ,,
Total	52 ,,

Two hours' rain.

FIFTY-NINTH DAY.
Braemar, Spittal of Glenh Shee, Blairgowrie.

My cupboard bed with its chaff mattress was very comfortable, and I should no doubt have slept like a top, had not my slumbers been disturbed, first by a fellow who played the bag-pipes until one or two a.m., and afterwards by the mail-car man who came thundering at the door at four. However, I scored my halt here as being a good stroke of business, for the charge was exceedingly moderate, and it turned out that, had I gone on to Braemar, I should not have had a bed at all.

9 a.m. Got under way. The sylvan scenery between the fourth and first milestone was delightful; the variety of crags and wooded hills, the devious windings of the river through sunny glades and by an occasional country seat, being charmingly picturesque.

Unfortunately, I did not get a good view of the peaks of Lochnagar, and I was much disappointed with the monotonous outline of Ben Muich-dhui; a patch of snow on its summit being the sole guide to its height (4,390 ft.), which, from my point of view, seemed inconsiderable.

While paddling leisurely along, I saw three deer emerge from the wood, but they took no more notice of me than sheep would have done. A few minutes afterwards I heard the report of a gun. "Ah! the poor creatures have been stalked and shot," thought I. The last mile to Braemar[*] was an ascent, and the road passed close by the castle. It has four storeys with turrets at the angles, and I admired its antique appearance very much. The village is on an eminence overlooking the haugh land and low hills, these being formed by the junction of three glens.

I was obeying my programme by passing through this hot-bed of tourists, when some gentlemen, who were watching the start of the heavily laden coach, accosted me and requested an inspection of my "Cheylesmore." After I had explained its principles and given some account of my tour, I gleaned from them that both hotels were overflowing, numbers having to rough it on sofas, &c.; and that the villagers, having let their cottages for £25 a month, were themselves living in shanties knocked up for the time being. This lack of house room is owing to the fact that the laird will not allow the village to be extended.

[*] A good centre from which to ascend Ben Muich-dhui, Lochnagar, or to visit the Linn of Dee and the falls in the neighbourhood.

From the top of the rise beyond Braemar I rode down a gentle decline for two miles, on a better surface; the road then ascended for a mile or so, till the gradient compelled a dismount. While walking up this I was overtaken by a bicyclist, one of my late audience, who had good-naturedly come to escort me for a while At the watershed he pointed out the scene of a sad accident, where a lady had been thrown from the coach, and killed by falling down the precipice. I here parted from my brother wheelman, and cautiously commenced the steep descent of Glen Shee, dismounting to an awkward corner commonly called "The Devil's Elbow." I rode down the remaining mile or two, but it was rough work, the surface being loose and bad. I passed a clergyman and his wife, who were picnicing on the side of the hill, and evidently enjoying the view; for my part, although some features of the glen were rather grand, I failed to see the sublime beauty which one reads about.

From the foot of the hill the road ran in a series of bothering ups and downs to Invercauld at the Spittal, where I arrived at two o'clock. I waited and dined with the Dunkeld coach passengers, several of whom eagerly asked me about the chance of getting beds at Braemar and Oban, and I am afraid that my replies did not tend to improve their tempers. I was rather amused than otherwise during my tour, to notice that, although nearly all Scotch tourists run on the same track at the same time, yet each seems to think that while others may be put to discomfort, yet it is hard that he cannot have exactly what he requires.

My bill for luncheon was 2s. 9d., and I felt sufficiently curious to ask why so peculiar a sum was demanded. "Well, sir," said the waiter with a smirk, "the odd threepence is for me." I paid without a murmur, feeling glad that I had had so little to do with tourists' head-quarters. A heavy shower having just ceased, I started at 4 p.m. for Blairgowrie. The road was simply execrable, a series of short, but stiff undulations covered with deep mud, so that what with this and the monotonous scenery, my trip would have been far from enjoyable had it not been for the lovely evening; for the pure air and the magnificent tints of the western sky made up for the discomforts of the way. I stopped and had tea at the "Percy Arms" with the clerical picnic party, who hailed from Dundee, and were in raptures over their day's outing. While chatting I did not notice the flight of time, and it was 8 p.m. before I was again on wheels.

The glen improved as I advanced, but the road was nearly as bad as ever to Catley Bridge, a small village prettily situated at the junction of the rivers Airdle and Shee, having a large " Temperance " inn. I now got on to a broad, muddy, but well macadamized road, which rose through park lands. The last four miles were all down hill, and I glided along through the deep gloom of a magnificent wood, having the roar of a mighty torrent on my left, echoing from the depths of the ravine. Half-way down I emerged from the trees on to a bridge, and saw a house (Craighall) perched on a splendid cliff high above my head. I halted to admire the rocks, the foaming stream, the rustic bridge, and the dense woods; there just being sufficient light to throw a halo of romance upon the scene.

I soon came to the outskirts of Blairgowrie, and after crossing another bridge over the same river (Ericht), I found my way to the " Royal " hotel at 9.45 p.m.

DISTANCE.

Invercauldy Arms to Braemar	6½ miles.
Braemar to Spittal of Glen Shee	15 ,,
Spittal to Blairgowrie	20 ,,
Total	41½ ,,

A shower during luncheon.

SIXTIETH DAY.
BLAIRGOWRIE, PERTH.

BLAIRGOWRIE is a busy town, the jute manufacture forming the principal industry. It is situated amid an undulating agricultural country, and the attractions of Craighall, and other places in the neighbourhood, draw a good proportion of tourists in the season.

11 a.m. Started for Perth in a Scotch mist; the road, after declining for a mile or two and then rising again, ran level for three miles through a wood, the surface being soft and heavy. From the Bridge of Isla a fine broad road led me through a highly farmed district interspersed with parks and mansions, and I caught an occasional glimpse of the picturesque banks of the river. After spinning gaily on level ground for some distance, I enjoyed four miles of decline to Perth, passing Scone and other beautiful places on the way.

The crops looked in splendid condition, but I was told that, although the stalks were yellow, there had not been sufficient sun to ripen the ear. The mist having merged into rain, I reached the " George " hotel in a drenched condition, and, as the weather seemed hopeless, I decided to go no further that day.

The cam arrangement of my tricycle had annoyed me lately by jamming and then suddenly slipping; thus nearly causing me to overbalance myself on several occasions. This afternoon I took the crank to a skilled blacksmith, who, after listening to the revolutions, said that they wanted a good oiling, and after he had applied some they appeared to work correctly; I did not like to have the covers taken off, as I doubted the man's ability to re-secure them properly. I may as well anticipate my story by mentioning that the jamming continued, and when I took the machine to the makers at Coventry, they proved to my satisfaction that this was owing to the cams being clogged with thick oil. The proper thing to do under the circumstances is to apply paraffin oil until all the greasy matter has been removed; this can be effected through the lubricating holes on the crank axle, without removing the covers.

Later in the day I walked about the interesting old town, and amongst other things saw Curfew Row and Glover's Yard, the scene of the chief incident in " The Fair Maid of Perth."

DISTANCE.

Blairgowrie to Perth .. .. 15 miles.
Moist and unpleasant.

SIXTY-FIRST DAY.
PERTH, AUCHTERARDER, DUNBLANE, STIRLING.

10.30 A.M. Left Perth[*] in bright sunshine. The road crossed a low range of hills, and from the highest point, about three miles from Perth, I had an extensive view of bonnie Strath Earn as far as the eye could reach in the direction of Crieff. I then ran for about two miles to the south side of the range, from whence I looked down on the river flowing through a pastoral vale, the different colours cast by the light and shade having a very pleasing effect. The road, which had been muddy, now became firm, and I had a capital spin down the hill and for several miles on the level beyond.

When approaching Auchterarder, a pelting shower drove me under some trees; this was followed by two others in quick suc-

[*]The seat of Government was moved from Perth to Edinburgh in 1482 by James III. There is a good road with fine scenery through the Carse of Gowrie to Dundee.

cession, which detained me for some time and converted the road into a river. Auchterarder is on the side of a steep hill, a place not often patronised by visitors, I should imagine; for my humble luncheon order at the "Crown" inn appeared to create as much excitement in the commissariat department, as my "Cheylesmore" did among a crowd of bystanders.

The country beyond Auchterarder was open and undulating, with a narrow but very fair road. Two miles on the other side of Blackpool I struck into the highway, and, turning to the left, proceeded rapidly to Dunblane. That ancient town had been in a chrysalis condition during my visit in June, but now it was gay with lawn tennis parties, and enlivened by the constant roll of vehicles and with crowds of tourists of all kinds and denominations.

The lovely evening (it had not rained here) induced me to halt at the "Stirling Arms," and to stroll about while tea was being prepared. Again I regretted my folly in having anything to do with fashionable resorts, for I was charged 2s. 3d. for plain tea, two eggs, and a wash.

I had a charming ride to Stirling, and enjoyed another glorious view of the Carse from the hill above Bridge of Allan; the tints of the setting sun were gorgeous. The tourist is strongly recommended to take the view from this standpoint on a fine evening.

I put up at the "Queen's" again, and amused myself with promenading the crowded streets.

DISTANCE.

Perth to Auchterarder	14 miles.
Auchterarder to Dunblane	14 ,,
Dunblane to Stirling	6 ,,
Total	34 ,,

An hour's heavy rain (local).

SIXTY-SECOND DAY.
STIRLING, BANNOCKBURN, FALKIRK, LINLITHGOW.

IN the afternoon I crossed the ferry and walked to Cambuskenneth Abbey; only the tower and part of the wall remain of this interesting ruin. After seeing the grave of James III., which has been restored by the order of Queen Victoria, I returned to the town and paid the Cemetery and Castle a second visit. It was a beautiful day, and I could clearly distinguish the highest peak of Ben Lomond, on which

I had stood two months ago; it was quite like seeing an old friend, in fact I was more in love with Stirling and the neighbourhood than ever.

In the afternoon I ran out to Bannockburn (3 miles). The "bore stone," protected from the rapacious tourist by an iron grating, is situated on the summit of an eminence, and shows the position of the centre of the Scottish army on that eventful day. A flagstaff, the base of which is carved round with thistles, stands near the stone. A man, who acted as cicerone, showed in what manner the ground had been occupied by the Scotch forces, and pointed out the line they had formed from the burn to St. Ninan's village, also the spot where the fight between Bruce and Sir Henry de Bonne took place, and the site of the cavalry pitfalls. The features of the country, however, have materially altered since those warlike days, owing to building and cultivation. "Gillies Hill" must still be there, but I was surprised to find that none could tell me for certain which of the two hills in the background it was.

Having returned to St. Ninan's I took the highway on the right for Falkirk, and found it to be in a rutty and pitty condition; the land southward seemed to be very poor, and the scenery nothing to speak of. I asked for Torwood Forest, it was not to be seen. I enquired for the sites of the great battles* which had been fought near Falkirk; no one that I asked knew anything at all about them; in fact I was rather amused to find that I was giving instead of receiving information. The Carron Iron Works must be very extensive, for I noticed that the grass, foliage, and even the sheep were blackened for some distance on each side of them.

Falkirk is an antiquated narrow-streeted town. I wished to see Sir John Graham's tomb, but as the gate of the churchyard was locked I passed on to Linlithgow, traversing on the way a series of undulations, some of them being rather stiff work for my "Cheylesmore" to master.

After my evening meal at the "Star and Garter" I walked to the Palace,† a massive quadrangular pile, on a green knoll overlooking

---

* Edward I. defeated Wallace; Sir John Graham was killed and interred in the parish churchyard. In 1746 Prince Charlie defeated General Hawley.

† The site was formerly occupied by the Castle, so cleverly captured by a party of Bruce's men concealed in a cart of hay. The driver stopped the cart under the portcullis, cut the horses adrift, and gave the preconcerted signal, "Call all," upon which the men leapt out from under the hay, and being joined by others lying in ambush, rushed in and took and destroyed the Castle, as related in "Tales of a Grandfather." It was rebuilt by the English, and converted into a Palace by James IV. In 1542 Queen Mary was born there ; the apartment is still shown. The building was reduced to its present state by Hawley's dragoons, who set fire to it in 1746.

a lochan. While viewing the ruin of this once magnificent and favourite residence of the Scottish kings, which has figured so conspicuously in the history of the nation, the melancholy feelings, which involuntarily stole over me, were heightened by observing the neglected state of the grounds. The once beautiful lake, also, was covered with green slime, through which grimy swans were forcing their way.

From the interesting old church* I went to see the house from which the Regent Murray was shot; it has been pulled down, but a medallion on the new building marks the position. There are several quaint old houses in the town, and the grotesque figures round the fountain—a copy of the ancient one—are worth inspection.

DISTANCE.

Stirling to Falkirk	11 miles.
Falkirk to Linlithgow	8 ,,
Total	19 ,,

Very fine.

SIXTY-THIRD DAY.
LINLITHGOW, EDINBURGH, HADDINGTON.

ALTHOUGH the road was rather bumpy I made a rapid run to Edinburgh, and rode with comfort along its well-paved streets to the "London" hotel, where I arrived at 11 a.m., with the faint hope of securing a bed. This was soon dispelled, for I was told that as it only wanted two days to the Review, I should be fortunate to get a night's lodging anywhere for 25s. I thanked my stars that I possessed a steed which would quickly and economically convey me clear of this range of charges, and, when required, would in the same manner place me on the scene of action.

I went to the Clarendon goods station for my portmanteau, but it was not there. Having obtained permission to leave my tricycle, I proceeded to the Leith Walk station, where I found my missing luggage and made myself presentable, preparatory to enjoying myself.

When a small boy I had seen Edinburgh, and had always retained a most pleasing impression of it; but having since travelled nearly all over the world, I feared that a second visit would dispel the

---

* James IV. received the supernatural warning before the battle of Culloden in the aisle of this church, as related in "Lord of the Isles."

charm. It happened to be just the contrary. The day was lovely, calm and bright, and, while passing along Prince's street, with all the picturesque beauty of the town before me, I rapturously exclaimed: "This is indeed the fairest city in the world."

I went over the Castle and all the old places with unfeigned pleasure, and after calling on a friend, got into cycling costume, sent off my portmanteau to England, and trotted out my steed at 6 p.m. With the exception of a rise out of Musselburgh the road was level nearly all the way to Haddington, and although the surface was rather irregular, I made good progress and arrived at the quaint old inn ("George") at 8.15, glad to find myself clear of the Review excitement.

DISTANCE.

Linlithgow to Edinburgh	16 miles.
Edinburgh to Haddington	17 „
Total	33 „

Beautiful day.

SIXTY-FOURTH DAY.
HADDINGTON, DUNBAR, DUNSE.

A TRIBUTE to the memory of John Knox has been paid by the natives of Haddington, who have lately, with much ceremony, planted a tree on the site of his birthplace.

10.30 a.m. Started for Dunbar, and having gained the top of the rise leading out of the town, I found myself on a tolerably even road, which, between the fifth and first milestone, was a dead level. I put my machine away at the "Red Lion" and walked to the ruins of the Castle.* The sole remains of this once celebrated stronghold are a few detached masses on the rocky points, and some fragments of walls, scattered here and there about the green, now used as a promenade.

The landlord of the inn recommended me to see the Earl of Dunbar's monument in the kirk, which he declared to be the finest

* This once important fortress was the key of that part of Scotland. The most noted incident in its history was its successful defence by "Black Agnes." When the battering rams of the besiegers discharged massive stones against the battlements, she caused her maidens, as if in scorn, to wipe away the dust with their handkerchiefs, and when the Earl of Salisbury commanded a huge military engine called the "Sow" to be advanced to the foot of the walls, she, in a scoffing rhyme, advised him to take good care of his sow, for she would make him farrow her pigs.

in Scotland. Perhaps it is, but I did not think so. I had intended to visit Tantallon Castle, but hearing that the road was bad, I, at 2.45, proceeded on my journey to Dunse.

The road was undulating and rather rough for three miles, then the surface became splendid, and I ran through an agricultural country to Cockburnspath. From thence I encountered small braes, and on presently coming to a B.U. danger board, I prepared for emergencies ; the slope on both sides of the ravine was moderate, the element of danger being a sharp turn on to a narrow bridge at the bottom. The B.U. have acted wisely in erecting the board, for otherwise the reckless cyclist would surely ignore the gradient, and thus run the risk of injuring either himself or others.

I now ran down through a glen to "Grant's House" (a public), where I turned to the right on to a narrow bad road which led me over a hill, across a wild and dismal moor, and so down to Preston, which was deep in mud ; and, to make matters worse, a Scotch mist came on.

From Preston the road was hilly but pretty good, with more civilised surroundings. I overtook a number of girls returning from work in the fields, and, the condition of the road rendering our speed about equal, we passed and re-passed each other several times, interchanging a few words on each occasion. During my tour I had noticed the superior physique of the Scotch women, but I was particularly struck with the appearance of these strapping girls, who were the picture of health, with cheeks like rosy apples. I had to pay for lingering to admire them by getting a ducking, for just before I got in a tremendous downpour came on, and I appeared at the door of the "Swan" looking more like a drowned rat than an enamoured cyclist.

DISTANCE.

Haddington to Dunbar	11 miles.
Durban to Grant's House	13 ,,
Grant's House to Dunse	9 ,,
Total	33 ,,

Half an hour's heavy rain. Very wet night.

SIXTY-FIFTH DAY.
Dunse, Lauder, Path-head.

THE coffee room at the "Swan" was small, but the company was agreeable, and I learned that the land about Dunbar and Lauder is remarkable for its fertility, the speciality of the latter being potatoes.

As torrents of rain were still falling, I gave up the idea of visiting the battlefield of Dunse Law,* and the question which occupied my mind was: "How am I to get to Edinburgh for the Review to-morrow?" Ascertaining that it would take me two hours by rail, with a change on the way, I decided to face the weather and get as near the city as possible that night, by road.

1 p.m. Left Dunse, a small country town surrounded by low hills, and headed for Lauder. After three miles of gradual ascent on a good road, I turned to the right at a fork, and, after traversing a wooded ravine, crossed a lonely moor, and then jogged through a lane on to the highway near "Whitehouse" inn. The features of the country and the weather now began to improve, and an undulating road, with a good surface, conducted me to Lauder, a one-streeted village, where I pulled up at the "Black Bull" and enjoyed a cup of hot tea. I was not able to see the bridge† which had been converted into a gallows for the favourites of James IV., as it stands on private property.

Learning that there was a kind of drover's inn ("Crathie Arms"), near Path-head, I resolved to run on there and take my chance of getting a bed.

6 p.m. Rode on level highway for four miles, and half way up the "Big Hill" (part of the Lammermuirs), walking the remainder of the three miles ascent. I now found myself on a bleak moor, and while riding along the top of the range I observed a dense cloud of mist rolling up from the valley ahead, which, after wreathing and swirling itself into a thousand fantastic shapes, enveloped me in its folds and blotted the outer world from my gaze. What with the fog and the dusk of the evening, it was all I could do to distinguish the line of the road, and I soon found myself whirling down to the valley on the north side of the hill.

---

* Vestiges of General Leslie's camp are to be seen on the summit of Dunse Law at the back of the town.
† The Scotch nobility hanged the minions of James IV. from this bridge, in 1482.

The road was level and good to Path-head, and I paddled cautiously through this extensive village in the dark, arriving at the "Crathie Arms" at 8.30. My venture turned up trumps, for instead of having to prick for a soft plank to lie on, I had a nice clean bed ; and the parlour, only used on great occasions, was placed at my disposal. The people were civil and attentive; in short I had fallen on my legs.

DISTANCE.

Dunse to Lander	18 miles.
Lander to "Crathie Arms"	18 ,,
Total	36 ,,

Rained until 3 p.m; dull and foggy.

SIXTY-SIXTH DAY.
EDINBURGH REVIEW, ROSSLYN.

I WAS awakened by a brilliant sun, and, on looking out of my window, saw that the road was already crowded with holiday folk, who were streaming northward in every description of vehicle; but there was a watery appearance in the clouds that I did not like the look of.

9.30 a.m. Started for Edinburgh. The road was level to the brow of the hill overlooking Dalkeith. The spires and red tiles of the town peeping through green foliage, the river winding through the vale, with Edinburgh in the distance, formed a most pleasing picture.

I made a rapid run from the glen in which Dalkeith lies, and pushed on through the suburbs of the city, leaving to fortune to decide what was to become of my tricycle. By-and-by my further progress was stopped by a policeman, and I consulted him as to the housing of my steed.

"Why not leave it with the fruit-seller over there?" suggested he.

"Brilliant idea," thought I. Yes; he would put it in a corner inside the railings, and see that no one interfered with it. I was now free to stroll through the principal thoroughfares, and to admire the decorations in Prince's and other gaily dressed streets.

A gentleman, of whom I asked the way, volunteered to pilot me to Arthur's Seat, and I had the pleasure of his company during the day.

At 12.30 p.m. we settled ourselves down in a snug billet under the lee of the crags on the summit, and while discussing some sandwiches with which I had provided myself before leaving the inn, he pointed out the principal buildings and other notable objects.

We afterwards watched with great interest the movements of the troops, and saw the single volunteer taking his place in the company, the company joining the battalion, and the battalion reinforcing the brigade. Then, after a time, we could see long lines of colour winding, like rivulets, from the different rendezvous towards the one great mass in front of the grand stand, while the strains of martial music broke at fitful intervals on the ear.

This, no doubt, was by far the prettiest part of the Review, and from no place could it have been seen to greater advantage than from our exalted standpoint. It was very amusing also to watch the crowds of people pouring from all quarters, in all kinds of costumes, and, for the most part, hurrying to one common centre, Salisbury Crags, where they perched themselves in myriads like a cluster of bees.

About 2 p.m. a forest of umbrellas opened out, and, sad to relate the rain which then commenced gradually increased; pools of water appeared on the parade ground, and the uniforms of the patient citizen soldiers began to wear a faded appearance.

"Will the Queen venture out in such dreadful weather?" was now the anxious question heard on all sides. Presently there was a stir about the Palace, and a closed carriage drove up to the door. We looked again—an open carriage had taken the place of the closed one, then a bugle sounded, guns fired, and huzzas rent the air as Her Most Gracious Majesty drove through a heavy rain-squall to inspect her loyal troops. We saw the royal procession pass slowly along the front of the line, and the commencement of the march past; then, as the thickening rain rendered everything indistinct, we descended, deeply regretting that this display of patriotism should have been so deplorably marred by the weather.

I found my tricycle all right, and having paid the man, rode off, chuckling at the thought that I had probably seen the review more conveniently and economically than any one of the thousands of visitors who had assembled there that day.

I paddled for five miles up a steady rise on the highway to Peebles, then turned to the left; having reached Rosslyn, after a mile of district road, I enquired if there were room at the hotel. Right glad was I to hear the answer, " Yes, sir, we have one room; a gentleman left this morning."

A good-natured female insisted on showing me the stables, and when I begged her not to trouble, as she would get wet, she laughed and said that she was quite accustomed to it, and I afterwards noticed that the men were lounging about and smoking their pipes, just as ordinary folks would do on a sunny day.

I had a pleasant evening with a married couple, who were congratulating themselves on not having ventured out; the Review party arrived late, wet through, and complaining bitterly of the various delays to which they had been subjected.

DISTANCES.

"Crathie Arms" to Edinburgh	9½ miles.
Edinburgh to Rosslyn	6 ,,
Total	15½ ,,

Very wet after 2 p.m.

SIXTY-SEVENTH DAY.
ROSSLYN, PEEBLES.

RAIN! rain!! How miserable everything looked to be sure. "Ah well, I can't grumble, after having been so fortunate all along," thought I.

After breakfast I sallied forth to the chapel,* where I was especially delighted with the exquisite stone carving, the edges being as clean as though cut on wood. I was highly amused with the boy guide. He asked me in a very soft tone if I would like to have the objects in the interior explained, and, on my replying in the affirmative, he immediately assumed his professional voice, and bawled, " Turn to the right and you will observe "—as though he were addressing a multitude in St. Paul's Cathedral, instead of one humble individual in a wee chapel. After a time, I asked him a question; he answered in a natural tone, then continued his description as before, rattling it off in the usual sing-song manner which always makes me think of a barrel organ.

* " This chapel may be pronounced unique, and I am confident it will be found curious, elaborate, and singularly interesting. The style of arhitecture combines the solidity of the Norman, with the minute decorations of the latest specimens of the Tudor age."—*Britton.*

After a look at the Castle and the romantic glen, which I regretted seeing under circumstances so unfavourable, I returned to the hotel, and awaited my bill with some anxiety, for my friends of last night had had to pay Review prices, viz., bed, 10s., and other things in proportion; but I was relieved to find that I was charged the ordinary tariff.

Noon. The rain ceased and I started for Peebles. Having regained the highway, I ran on a splendid undulating road to Penicuick, the Pentland Hills forming the principal feature in the landscape. After crossing the North Esk, the road was principally against the collar, with one or two short and rather steep hills, to the highest point, which is about a quarter of a mile beyond Leadburn inn. All the rest of the way was on a gentle decline, first across a moor with the Moorfoot Hills on the left, then through a glen which became more picturesque as I advanced. The view of Peebles, lying in the bosom of graceful hills, surrounded on all sides with wood and water, formed one of the most captivating bits of scenery that I had come across in my tour. It seemed, however, as if I were running into a trap, and how to escape without having to climb a big hill was a puzzle to me. The crops had been sadly battered down by the late storm, and I was surprised to see how much they were behind those I had lately seen in the north, which were being reaped, whereas these had not commenced to turn colour; but I supposed that this was due to the difference of elevation.

The only bad bit of road was that over the moor, but of course it was all very muddy.

Just as I entered the yard of the "Cross Keys" at 3.30 p.m., down came the rain, so I made " all snug for the night."

DISTANCE.
Rosslyn to Peebles .. .. 16 miles.
Very wet except from 12 to 3.30.

SIXTY-EIGHTH DAY.
Peebles, Moffat, Locherby.

WHEN P. and I first crossed the border we could hardly understand a word that was said, but as I got on very well in the Highlands, I thought that my ear had become accustomed to the brogue. The dialect in Aberdeenshire, however, was rather puzzling, and here at Peebles I was as much adrift as ever.

I had the choice of several roads to Carlisle, and selected that by Moffat and Gretna Green. The ostler, whom I consulted about my route, directed me to turn to the left when eight miles out, in order to cut off the angle at that point.

8 a.m. Started in glad sunshine. At the west end of this quaint town the road rose rather steeply for a mile to Nidpath Castle,* a gaunt edifice situated between the road and the Tweed. The view from this point, of the river winding through the glen, the beautiful larch woods, with a glimpse of Peebles in the vale below, was as charming a picture as one could wish for.

I now mounted and made fair progress up the road, which worked its way cleverly among what had appeared to me yesterday to be a barrier of hills. When about eight miles out, I saw a muddy track leading steeply up a moorland hill on the left. " I prefer going round a mile or so to taking a short cut of that kind," thought I, and passing it, I rode through a fine park by Stobo Castle without seeing any other turning. When about 10½ miles from Peebles I came on to the highway, and, turning to the left, saw a milestone marked " Edinburgh, 22." I now had a capital run for some miles to a fork, where, to my surprise, the best road turned off to the right, while mine became green and disused, and so continued to the village of Broughton, which is prettily situated, somewhat like Peebles on a smaller scale.

On arriving at "Crook" inn I asked the distance to Peebles. "Sixteen miles," replied a man in the stable. "Only sixteen miles!" cried I, "why, it is 35½ to Edinburgh from here, is it not?" "Yes." "Well, I have travelled 13½ along that road, and 10½, before I got on to it, which makes the total 25, how do you account for that?" "Why, you've come the wrong road, that's all," and away he went. An inspection of my map showed me that I had gone half-way to Carstairs, and that I had passed Castle Craig instead of Stobo. This may seem to have been a very stupid mistake, but it must be remembered that the roads which appear straight on the map really twist and turn about, so that, on the whole, I think that I was lucky in having made so few bungles. "Crook" inn stands in a treeless glen near the Tweed, and was a place of some importance in the coaching days; now, it is only patronized by the sportsman or the chance visitor who desires a change of air with quietude and economy.

*A highly romantic incident in connection with this building is related by Sir Walter Scott.

I TRACE THE SOURCE OF THE TWEED.

1.10 p.m. Started for Moffat. After I had travelled two or three miles, a black cloud appeared above the precipitous side of the glen. Happening to be abreast of a house on the slope of the hill, I left my tricycle, scrambled up to it, and obtained shelter in the kitchen; there I chatted with the cook, who was making some tempting-looking scones for the shooting party who were out with their guns. Presently I noticed that the squall was crossing just behind me, so I mounted and proceeded, and by-and-by escaped another downpour by a few yards.

As I ascended, the Tweed rapidly diminished in volume, and I reached a point where several little rills met. I traced these with my eye until they were lost in the bog on the side of the hill, and I noted in my journal that I had had the honour of seeing the source of the river of song.

From "Crook" inn, the road had risen steadily for nine-and-a-half miles; it was stony and disused, but I rode the whole way excepting the last steep bit. At the summit I had a remarkable view of the rounded tops of the southern uplands, rolling in and out of one another for miles, exactly as I had seen them pourtrayed in a sketch in "Geikie's Scenery of Scotland." While riding along the top I was greatly surprised to meet a lady and gentleman, for I had been so accustomed to travel for miles among mountains without meeting anybody, that it did not occur to me at the moment that I was approaching a great touring centre. They were looking hot and tired, and eagerly asked me the distance to the nearest inn; their faces fell considerably when I said ten miles, but hearing that there were two shielings a little further on, they trudged off with renewed spirit.

I now came to the "Devil's Beeftub," a deep precipitous dell, the source of the river Annan. Here I had a vista of the green vale to Moffat, nestling prettily among the trees; beyond that, a mighty plain stretched away into hazy distance. An L.O.H. run of seven miles took me right into the town, but the stony state of the road was unpleasant, and the gradient in some places rather steep.

On approaching the town, a change came o'er the spirit of the scene. My path no longer led me over the bleak and lonely mountain, but ran by shady trees, where ladies were seated here and there with novels in their hands. By-and-by I passed gay groups of tennis players, actively endeavouring to keep the ball going over the net, while scattered couples were apparently very pleasantly engaged in the more secluded corners of the ground.

At 3.15 p.m. I was cordially greeted by my hostess of the "Star," who was much interested in hearing of my adventures since last we met.

I saw the rain pouring into the "Beeftub," but on being assured that it would cling to the hills, I, at 5.15, started for Locherby, and paddled on a level but rather bumpy road, through tame scenery, to the "King's Arms," where I rested for the night.

DISTANCE.

Peebles to "Crook" inn (my way)	23 miles.
"Crook" inn to Moffat	16 ,,
Moffat to Locherby	16 ,,
Total	55 ,,

Escaped a few showers.

SIXTY-NINTH DAY.
LOCHERBY, GRETNA GREEN, CARLISLE, PENRITH.

9.30 A.M. Started for Carlisle. Pleasant undulations. When nearing Gretna Green I made enquiries of two respectable young men, who said that it was a mistake to imagine that people had ever been married there by a blacksmith. In their opinion the idea must have originated from the saying "that a couple could be joined together at Gretna Green, as easily as a blacksmith could weld two pieces of iron." They pointed out Gretna Hall (once an hotel), where the Gordian knot of the Upper Ten used to be tied, and also said that if I were curious on the subject, there was a man in Springfield who still carried on the business. Curious, decidedly, I was, and besides, I thought it just as well to sift the matter to the bottom, for who could tell but what it might come in handy some day? Springfield consists of two rows of wretched dwellings, and when I enquired for the house of the "marrying man" I was directed to one of the cottages. The door was opened by a female, who, on learning my business, asked me to sit down while she called her husband. Presently an elderly working man came in, and, in reply to my questions, said that he still married people occasionally, but that the trade was falling off. I asked if a law had not lately been passed to put a stop to this kind of thing; he replied that several cases had been tried, but that nothing had come of it. He showed me his register, and I particularly noticed that one marriage had taken place only two months before. The following is a copy of the printed certificate.

KINGDOM OF SCOTLAND,
COUNTY OF DUMFRIES,
PARISH OF GRETNA.

THESE ARE TO CERTIFY, TO ALL WHOM THEY MAY CONCERN:
That   from the Parish of
                  in the County of
and
from the Parish of
in the County of
being now both here present, and having declared to me that they are Single Persons, have now been Married after the manner of the Laws of Scotland: As witness our hands at Gretna this
Day of   18

WITNESSES,

I rose to leave, and was about to offer sixpence, but as the man had given me a printed form, I thought I would be liberal and tendered a shilling. For a moment I innocently imagined that he was going to decline it as being too much, but instead of that he announced in a decided tone "Half-a-crown is *my fee*." I checked a remonstrance and paid the money, saying to myself, "Serves me right, meddling with matrimony is sure to burn the fingers."

I stopped at the toll house on the borders, and peeped into the room where many a happy pair have been "turned off," and also saw the large red brick house next to it, which has been built from the proceeds of the same. A few yards beyond the gate I crossed the Lark, and entered old England again, and felt more than ever convinced that,

"Mid pleasures and palaces, though we may roam,
Be it ever so humble, there's no place like home."

I arrived at Carlisle at 1.15, and while dining with some gentlemen, I related my experiences at Gretna Green, with the view of getting further information. They laughed heartily at the way in which I had been taken in, but I maintained that there must be something in it, because the "marrying man" seemed to be a well-known individual, moreover there was his register. To this one of the party replied that he had lived in the neighbourhood of Gretna Green all his life, and was sure that those sort of marriages could not take place now, and that the register was a forgery. Another kindly offered to make full enquiries, and to let me know the result of his investigation. In about a fortnight I received the following letter from him:—

"I have ascertained from one of the oldest residents near Gretna Green, that it is illegal to contract a marriage there, unless one or both of the parties have been residing twenty-one days in Scotland previous to the same. James Beattie, the only blacksmith who was ever known to have married parties, is still living, although advanced in years, and keeps an inn at Springfield. I understand several parties did get married at the place where you saw the register, but at the same time they are not legal."

Carlisle was the end of my programme, and I had made sure that by the time I got there I should be quite sick of tricycling, but, when it came to the point, the bright sunshine, the exhilarating exercise, together with a feeling of "Don't give in, old fellow," made me determine to run right through to Coventry, weather permitting.

After seeing the places of interest in the town, I resumed my journey southwards, the road consisting of a series of tiresome undulations with a good surface. I had an excellent view of the Cumberland hills, but I am bound to confess that they appeared very tame compared to those in bonnie Scotland.

5.45 p.m. Arrived at Penrith, which lies in a dell, and as the weather bore an unsettled appearance, I hung my hat up for the night at the "White Hart." This was my first experience of a B.T.C. hotel, and it left a most favourable impression, for the table was both excellent and abundant, and the accommodation all that could be desired.

DISTANCE.

Locherby to Carlisle..	25 miles.
Carlisle to Penrith ..	18 ,,
Total ..	43 ,,

AUGUST 29TH.

WHEN called in the morning I saw torrents of rain beating against the windows. Later on, there being no signs of improvement, I reluctantly came to the conclusion that, under the circumstances, to go on by road would be folly, so I took the next train to Coventry.

On handing over my " Cheylesmore " for renovation, I remarked to the makers that it was, no doubt, owing to the admirable construction of the machine, that it had not been smashed to pieces at Strome Ferry. Moreover, that although the accident had thrown the right wheel slightly out of the parallel, yet the vehicle had carried me splendidly, and that I should have much pleasure in recommending it

---

IN conclusion, I strongly advise, from my own experience, a tour in the " Land of the Mountain and of the Flood." In this country, where historical, poetical, and romantic associations meet one on every side, the cyclist, instead of being tied down to certain lines of route and halting places, is like the bee, free to settle where he pleases, and having taken the essence out of one place, can flit on to the next. He may thus see all the objects of interest, and at the same time avoid the expensive hotels in their immediate neighbourhood.

One of the charms of riding in Scotland is the diversified scenery. The bleak moor quickly gives place to the lovely lake, cradled amid woodland hills, and from a gloomy pass one may emerge on to a quiet strath, watered by its softly-flowing stream. All this, with the pure, bracing air, and the exhilarating exercise, combine to give both mind and body healthy recreation.

Moreover, whilst the railway traveller is being whirled along the line, and perhaps losing a choice bit of scenery in a tunnel, the independent wheelman can select his pace, and thus take in the beauties of nature according to his own individual taste.

In Scotland he has the further satisfaction of traversing excellent roads. Even those in Skye and on the west coast, although hilly, are remarkable for their splendid surface, devoid of mud or ruts.

I am glad to say that I found nearly all the Scotch inns comfortable and moderate. My daily expenses, as before stated, amounted to twelve shillings, including tips, postage, and minor repairs to the machine; but I met a bicyclist who was averaging ten shillings a day, and I have no doubt that anyone with care could manage on that sum.

For a short tour let me advise the cyclist to take the train to Berwick, and thence spin through Tweeddale, see Edinburgh, Glasgow, the Falls of the Clyde, and return by Carlisle.

With regard to guide books, I carried a Paterson, which was useful in the lowlands, but the intending tourist will do well to read up Black, Murray, and Anderson's " Highlands." The angler will find " Sportsman's Guide " and Young's " Sutherland " full of useful information.

HINTS.

The following are a few hints for beginners :—(1) Choice of machine. (2) How to propel. (3) To keep in order. (4) Equipment. (5) On the road.

Choice of Machine.

Anyone who beheld the bewildering maze of spokes and the great variety of machines at the Stanley Show this year, might have been puzzled to decide upon the best kind of tricycle. For my part I did not see one which I preferred to my own, but I will not presume to express an opinion on the subject. I merely advise the intending purchaser to procure the assistance of an experienced rider, and to select the vehicle which most nearly combines the following points : Safety, simplicity, moderate hill-climbing power.

I would also caution him not to buy or hire a second-hand article, unless he is quite sure that it is in perfect order.

Safety.—Look for strength of construction, sufficient breadth for stability, and a powerful brake.

The position of the steering-wheel is a much-disputed question. I have found an open front very convenient for mounting and dismounting quickly, and when I went over the brae at Strome Ferry I should certainly have sustained very serious injury, to say the least, had I been boxed up among the wheels.

It is important, however, to see that the rear wheel bears well, otherwise, when descending steep gradients it is liable to be lifted off the ground. My " Cheylesmore " has never shown any tendency to play me this trick, but I always take the precaution to lean well back when going down hill.

There is no advantage in having a very sensitive steering arrangement. On the contrary, it becomes a constant source of anxiety and danger to the rider, whose whole time is occupied in trying to keep the machine from sheering about.

Simplicity is of the utmost importance. Complication of any kind means friction, and only too frequently a " break-down," which cannot be repaired by an ordinary blacksmith. I think that the best way of transmitting the power is by means of chains. If short and strong they stretch very little, can be easily tightened, and give and take on rough roads. I have never had any trouble with mine, and if blacklead is used as a lubricator they keep clean and in good order.

Hill-Climbing.—Too much stress is laid upon this point. Can you drive it over all the hills? How do you manage when you come to a steep incline? are questions that one is invariably asked by non-riders; their tone implying that to dismount at any time would be discreditable and tedious. For my part I quite enjoy a walk occasionally, for by bringing other muscles into play, it rests and relieves those used for propulsion. Therefore content yourself with a tricycle which will carry you over the generality of slopes, and do not have a machine with larger wheels than forty-eight inches. I find the forty-four inch speedy, and an excellent hill-climber.

Note.—The seat should be cut away to allow the free use of the legs. Sit high, for by so doing you are brought over your work, and can apply your weight with greater advantage. Having selected your machine, master all its details, and learn how to take it to pieces and to put it together again.

To Propel.

Press on the front treadle, and allow the rear one to rise until it has passed the perpendicular, then push, and not before. This latter is the difficulty with beginners, who are prone to apply pressure on the rising treadle, thus working one against the other. The feet should not leave the pedals, for the crank revolves inside them. After a little practice the learner will get into the stroke, and thrust mechanically at the right moment. When you can make fair way on level ground, select a moderate slope and see how far you can work up it. Your daily progress can thus be marked, but do not attempt too much at a time.

To Keep the Machine in Order.

In these days of ball bearings and plated spokes, half the labour of cleaning and "oiling up" has been done away with. Nevertheless, the owner should frequently examine everything minutely, for a small bit of grit or a little rust may not only interfere with the harmony of the working parts, and render pleasure a toil, but the

FURTHER ADVICE.

machine may be permanently injured as well. The bearings should be cleansed every now and then with paraffin oil, care being taken to lubricate immediately afterwards.

A good motto for the cyclist is, *Trust no one.*

EQUIPMENT.

Always carry a spanner, can of oil, bell, and lamp. If about to take a journey, besides the above take a screwdriver, small pair of pliers, a few spare nuts, a piece of rag or cotton waste, some tyre composition, a knife, and some stout string. The best oil is pure sperm, with a few drops of paraffin to prevent it from clogging.

Wear either flannel or woollen clothing, with a muffler to put on when standing about. Do not overload the machine.

During my late tour I carried three shirts, one pair of trousers, one waistcoat, three pairs of socks, six handkerchiefs, collars, slippers, washing-gear, note and guide books. These stowed very well in one of Anderson and Abbott's waterproof tricycling bags, which I strapped to the backbone of my "Cheylesmore," with another strap to the spindle of the seat, to keep the bag from slipping back when going up hill. Total weight, 18lbs.

The trousers should be strongly seated; boots without nails; a close-fitting soft hat (well ventilated), with a brim or peak to protect the face from the sun and the eyes from insects; a light waterproof (which should be kept in a case when not in use) and a pair of gloves will complete the outfit.

ON THE ROAD.

I extract the following from "Nauticus on his Hobby-Horse":—

1. "Study the map and note down the principal towns and villages on the route.

2. "Before starting, carefully examine and oil every part of the machine that requires it, tighten up all the nuts, and test them occasionally during the day.

3. "Go easy for the first mile or so until the muscles are fairly in tune.

4. "On approaching a hill gauge it, and decide whether to 'spring' it or to dismount and walk up.

5. "Directly you begin to feel distressed, either in mounting a hill or on heavy ground, at once get off and walk.

6. "Avoid stiffness by being careful never to strain the muscles through undue exertion in spurting, etc.

7. "Fatigue may be reduced to a minimum by adding the weight of the body to the thrust of the leg in a steady pressure."

To these I will add:

Before starting, spin all the wheels to make sure that they revolve freely.

Slacken the speed and keep a good look-out when turning a corner.

Never fly down a hill at top speed, for nearly all cycling accidents are due to recklessness. Keep the brake touching, and dismount if there is any doubt about the gradient.

When travelling rapidly, the rider will find it a good plan to fix his eye upon the road a few yards in front, he will then detect the slightest deviation from his course, and correct it before the angle becomes dangerous.

Remember that the spoon-brake is not so effective when the tyres are wet.

If the brake is put on hard suddenly, a somersault will be the result.

Travel slowly on a bad surface, for if one of the wheels gets into a rut, the machine is liable to be suddenly shot across the road.

When working up hill, grasp the handles firmly, and use them as a fulcrum against the thrust of the leg. A good way of getting a rear-wheeler up a long steep incline is to turn it round and push it up backwards.

When encountering horses that are being exercised, avoid passing on the side of the led horse. A judicious "Woa" will generally reassure a restive horse, but if the animal exhibits excitability the cyclist should dismount.

During my late tour, I was frequently accosted with, "How far have you come to-day?" as if the cyclist's sole object was merely to "reel off" so many miles. I strongly advise the youthful wheelman not to be tempted to over-exertion for the sake of scoring distances, because true comparison of such can only be obtained on the racing-path. For instance, with a strong, fair wind, on a good road, a hundred miles can be done with comparative ease; but turn the rider the other way, and even on the same description of track he will barely cover half the distance in the time.

'On looking over my notes I observe that, as a rule, my runs were in the inverse ratio of the work performed. As an example, I take the following :—Forres to Peterhead, 80¼ miles, and Altnaharra to Betty Hill, 26 miles. Now the latter gave me nearly twice the labour of the former. Therefore, when touring, let your object be to enjoy yourself, and to see the country intelligently.

REFRESHMENT.

The diet should be of the plainest and most wholesome description. The beginner will at first be possessed with an overpowering thirst; this he should endeavour to control. During the latter part of my trip I seldom drank anything between meals.

Alcoholic beverages give a fillip for the moment, only to be succeeded by a greater prostration of the system. I usually take pure milk, milk and soda-water, milk with an egg beaten up in it, cold tea, Zoedone, or some other drink of the kind. Milk, when drunk in large quantities, curdles in the stomach, therefore it should be sipped, and a biscuit eaten at the same time.

In taking leave of my readers, let me advocate this economical and delightful recreation, which is similar to that of walking, with the following advantages :—

(*a*) It is better exercise, because it brings more muscles into play.

(*b*) Instead of plodding along at the same uniform pace, the cyclist is now slowly walking up a hill, then, with his legs at rest, running swiftly down on the other side, or, with but little effort, bowling along at the rate of eight or nine miles an hour on a level road; thus enjoying an endless variety of motion, while the mind is pleasantly occupied in contemplating the different scenes which pass before him.

(*c*) Last, but not least, for the same exertion *three times* the distance can be covered.

ADDENDA.

P.'S CONTRIBUTION.

Crianlarich to Loch Earnhead. Undulating and good by the river Dochart for about twelve miles, then to right, uphill, rough and unrideable, to Killin Station. Downhill and good from thence to Loch Earnhead, 6 miles.

Loch Earnhead to Crieff, 19. Level and good, with pretty scenery.

Invergarry to Fort Augustus, 7. Rideable undulations, good.

Drumnadrochet to Beauly, 15. Walked two miles up a stiff brae, then fair riding with roads gradually improving; the last three or four miles splendid, with pretty country.

Novar to Bonar Bridge, 27. Good road, rises I should think 800 feet above the sea; very dreary for some miles along the top; moorlands, no habitations. The road descends to the sea level about four miles from Bonar Bridge.

Bonar Bridge to Laing, 10½. There are two roads. I was advised to take the right, although it was more hilly than the other. Having a fair wind I rode all the way; the character of the road is pretty good.

Tongue to Betty Hill, 12. Rough and precipitous.

Golspie to Little Ferry. Bad; awkward small boat.

Little Ferry to Dornoch. Mostly bad; route not recommended.

Brora to Meikle Ferry, 17. Mostly bad; good-sized boat.

Tain to Invergordon, 12. Very good road.

Invergordon to Inverness, 19. There is no village on the opposite side of ferry. There are some large ferry boats, but I crossed in a small one. I did not get much riding for about three miles on account of bad roads, but after that the road was generally good. On first landing the track is difficult to find, and there are no guide posts. Good ferry from Kessoch to Inverness.

Inverness to Nairn, 15. Splendid road.

Fochabers to Kéith, 9.
Keith to Huntley, 11. } Roads good, except a mile or two about Huntley.
Huntley to Insch, 16.

Do not lose sight of the railway between Huntley and Insch, and pass by Leith Hall. By leaving the railway, I found myself at the village Rhynie, and had to return.

Insch to Aberdeen, 27. First four miles rough, then very good.

Queensferry to Edinburgh. Splendid road.

Lauder to Langholm, 57. Through Earlstone, Jedburgh, Hawick. Rough to Earlstone, the remainder good, except on leaving Jedburgh over a steep rough hill (unrideable). The best way to Hawick from Jedburgh is to run back two miles and turn to the left near Anerlim.

Langholm to Carlisle, 20. Firm and pretty road by the Esk.

HOTELS.

HAVING always heard that the great drawback to a tour in Scotland was the expense of the hotels, P. and I determined, by making careful enquiries beforehand, to see if we could not find cheap, good quarters; as a result, we recommend the hotels below. The cooking and attendance was excellent, and we found everything scrupulously clean. Our bills for substantial tea, bed, and breakfast ranged from 3s. to 8s. 6d., averaging about 6s. 6d.; in short, our experience of Scotch hotels has been most favourable.

Aberfeldy, "Temperance."
Aberdeen, Forsyth's "Temperance."
Alnwick, "Star."
Altnaharra Hotel.
Arrochar Hotel.
Auchnasheen Hotel.
Auchterarder, "Crown."
Ayr, "King's Arms."

Balmacarra Hotel.
Banchory, "Berry House."
Banff, "Fife Arms."
Belford, "Blue Bells."
Betty Hill Inn.
Berwick, "Red Lion."
Blair Athole, "Bridge of Tilt."
Blairgowrie, "Royal."
„ "Station."
Bonar Bridge, "Commercial."
Brechin, "Crown."
Broadford Inn (Skye).

Cairndow Inn, Loch Fyne.
Cawdor Inn.
Comrie, "Temperance."
Crook Inn, Dumfries-shire.
Crieff.
Cumnoch (Old), "Dumfries Arms."
Cupar Fife, "Royal."
Cupar Angus, "Royal."
Crianlarich Inn.

Dalmally Inn.
Dalwhinnie Inn.
Dingwall, "Caledonian."
Dornoch, "Sutherland Arms."
Durness Hotel.
Drumnadrochet Inn.
Dumfries, "Commercial."
Dunbar, "Red Lion."
Dundee, Lamb's "Temperance."
Dunfermline, "Imperial."
Dunkeld, "Royal."
Dunse, "Swan."
Dunvegan Inn (Skye).

Foyers Hotel.
Forres, "Waverley Temperance."
Fort Augustus Hotel.
Fort William, "Macdonald Arms."

Gairloch Hotel.
Garve, Mrs. Fraser's Cottage.
Glasgow, "St. Enoch."
Galston, "Black Bull."
„ "Portland Arms."
Golspie, Hill's.
Glengarry Inn.

Haddington, "George."
Hemsdale, "Commercial."

Insch Inn, Aberdeenshire.
Invergordon, "Commercial."

LIST OF HOTELS.

Invermoriston Inn.
Inverary, "Argyll Arms."
Inverness, "Royal."
   „   Gellion's.
Inveruglas, Loch Lomond.
Inchnadamph.

John-o'-Groat's House.

Killin, "Bridge of Lochy."
Kincardine, "O'Neill Inn," Deeside.
Keswick, "Royal."
Kinlochewe Inn, L. Maree.
Kinross, "Salutation."

Lauder, "Black Bull."
Langholm, "Crown."
Linlithgow, "Star and Garter."
Locherby, "King's Arms."

Melrose, "King's Arms."
Moffat, "Star."
Montrose, "Queen's."
Moy Inn, Loch Laggan.

Newcastle-on-Tyne, "Royal Turf."

Oban, "King's Arms."
Oversaig Inn, Loch Shin.

Peebles, "Cross Keys."
Penrith, "White Hart."

Perth, "George."
Peterhead, Mrs. Cruikshank's "Temperance."
Persey Inn, between Spittal and Cally Bridge.
Poolewe Inn, Loch Maree.
Portree, Skye, "Royal."

Roslin Hotel.
Rhiconich Inn.

Sanquhar, "Queensberry Arms."
Shiel Inn.
Sligachan Inn (Skye).
Spean Bridge.
Strome Ferry Hotel.
Scourie Inn.
Stirling, "Queen's."
Staffin Bay (Skye).
Stonehaven Hotel.

Tain, "Royal."
Taynuilt Inn.
Thurso, "Royal."
   „   "Commercial."
Tongue Hotel.
Trossachs Hotel.
Tomdoun Inn.

Ullapool, "Royal."
Uig Inn (Skye).

THE END.

ADVERTISEMENTS.

BOOKS & PERIODICALS
PRINTED & PUBLISHED BY
ILIFFE & SON, "The Cyclist" Office, Coventry.

THE TRICYCLISTS' "INDISPENSABLE" ANNUAL AND HANDBOOK. A Guide to the Pastime and Complete Cyclopædia on the subject. By Henry Sturmey, Editor of *The Cyclist*, &c., &c. This is the only complete work on the subject, and contains fully illustrated descriptions of 200 varieties of the Tricycle, with explanatory notes on their construction and methods of driving, based on a series of practical trials. Also exhaustive chapters on the management and care of Tricycles, with hints about riding and selecting them; as well as a full view of the pastime and sport for the past year, besides much other information. Demy 8vo., 250 pages, 175 Illustrations. Price, post free, ONE SHILLING AND SIXPENCE.

"THE CYCLIST" AND BICYCLING AND TRICYCLING TRADES' REVIEW. The Leading Journal devoted to the kindred Sport and Trade of the Wheel. Published every Wednesday Morning, in Town and Country. Fullest and Earliest Information on all points. Edited by Henry Sturmey and C. W. Nairn. Price 1d. Annual Subscription, 6/6.

"THE TRICYCLIST." WEEKLY ON FRIDAY MORNING—Edited by LACY HILLIER—deals fully, soundly, and pleasantly, with the Sport, the Pastime, and the Trade. Price 2d. Annual Subscription, per post 12 months, 10s. 6d.; 6 months, 5s. 4d.; 3 months, 2s. 8d.; Single copy, 2½d.

THE "WHEEL WORLD," Companion Monthly to *The Cyclist*. The Leading Magazine. Good Articles and humorous Cartoons and Illustrations. Well sent out. Edited by Henry Sturmey and C. W. Nairn. 25th of each month. 3d. Monthly; Annual Subscription, 4s.

THE "INDISPENSABLE" BICYCLISTS' HANDBOOK. A complete cyclopædia on the subject. By Henry Sturmey. Fully Illustrated Descriptions and Dissertations on the Machines and Novelties of the Year. Published Annually in July. 300 pages. 100 Illustrations. By post, 1s. 6d.

THE COMPLETE "GUIDE TO BICYCLING"; OR, HOW TO BECOME A BICYCLIST. By Henry Sturmey. No possessor of a Bicycle should be without this Work. Price, 1s.; by post, 1s. 2d. Second Edition now in the Press.

"PRINCIPLES OF TRAINING" for Amateur Athletes, ITS ADVANTAGES AND EVILS. WITH SPECIAL REGARD TO BICYCLISTS. By H. L. Cortis (Amateur Champion at all Distances, 1880, and present holder of nearly all the records). Price, 1s.; by Post, 1s. 2d.

"THE CYCLIST" XMAS NUMBER (1881). Humorous Articles, Poems, Ballads, Adventurous Rides, Puzzles, &c. &c. Over 80 Original and Humorous Illustrations, and Illuminated Cover. Edited by Henry Sturmey. Price, 1s.; by Post, 1s. 2d.

ILIFFE & SON, PRINTERS AND ENGRAVERS, COVENTRY, Printers of all the above works, are prepared to estimate for, and execute in the best style, printing of all descriptions; Bookwork, Magazines, Pamphlets, Trade Catalogues, Price Lists, &c., &c. Estimates on application.

CPSIA information can be obtained at www.ICGtesting.com
Printed in the USA
LVOW08*1223071013

355778LV00007B/352/P